Windows 98

from

A to Z

201 West 103rd Street, Indianapolis,
Indiana 46290

Keith Powell

Windows 98 from A to Z

Keith Powell

Copyright © 1998 by Que Corporation

FIRST EDITION

International Standard Book Number: 0-7897-1625-9

Library of Congress Catalog Card Number: 97-81383

01   00   99   98   4   3   2   1

Printed in the United States of America

First Printing: June 1998

Trademarks

Executive Editor
Christopher Will

Development Editor
Kate Shoup Welsh

Managing Editor:
Sarah Kearns

Project Editor
Tom Lamoureux

Copy Editors
Daryl Kessler
Audra McFarland
Kate Givens

Indexer
Craig Small

Technical Editor
John Purdum

Production
Cyndi Davis-Hubler
Terri Edwards
Donna Martin

Contents

To my friends, who have each helped me through life thus far:
to Frank and Genevieve Snow, who helped me to believe in myself when it mattered most;

to Kim Feicke, who makes me think of others;

to Cari Skaggs, who helped me get started writing again;

and to Vannessa Tomlinson, who makes me feel.

Acknowledgments

Writing this book was a very enjoyable—but hard (at times)—experience that I will hold close as a good memory. Luckily, I was fortunate enough to have plenty of assistance from several others.

First, I want to thank Kate Welsh at Macmillan for all of her timely guidance, support, patience, guidance, and hard work.

I also want to thank John Purdum, the technical editor, without whose guidance I am sure quite a few not-so-correct items would have slipped through.

Thanks to Dean Miller and Chris Will for giving me the chance to write the book, and for having the faith in me to get it done on time.

Thanks also to Joe Westermeyer and Rich Nardi, both of whom indirectly gave me the idea for this book, and to Robert Smudde who encouraged me to continue consulting full-time while attempting to write a book part-time.

Finally, thanks to my family, especially my parents, and friends for all their motivation.

About the Author

Keith Powell has over nine years of professional computing experience and is presently a Senior Consultant for KPMG Consulting in Chicago, as part of KPMG's Electronic Commerce practice. Keith has an MBA from Keller Graduate School, an M.S. in History and a B.S. in History/Political Science from Illinois State University, and an Associates degree from the College of Lake County.

As a Microsoft Certified Product Specialist completing the final requirements for the Microsoft Certified Systems Engineer certification, he devotes much of his time in the Microsoft Windows and BackOffice arena for clients. Keith is also a co-author of the recently released *Sams Teach Yourself MCSE Microsoft Exchange Server 5.5 in 14 Days.*

A native of Chicago who spends much of his free time either in Chicago's great museums or rollerblading along Lake Shore Drive, Keith can be reached via email at either kpowell@kpmg.com or WorldMir@inil.com.

Tell Us What You Think!

As a reader, you are the most important critic of and commentator on our books. We value your opinion and want to know what we're doing right, what we could do better, what areas you'd like to see us publish in, and any other words of wisdom you're willing to pass our way. You can help us make strong books that meet your needs and give you the computer guidance you require.

Do you have access to the World Wide Web? Then check out our site at http://www.mcp.com.

note... If you have a technical question about this book, call the technical support line at 317-581-3833 or send email to **support@mcp.com**.

As the executive editor of the group that created this book, I welcome your comments. You can fax, email, or write me directly to let me know what you did or didn't like about this book—as well as what we can do to make our books stronger. Here's the information:

Fax: 317-581-4669

Email: cwill@mcp.com

Mail: Christopher Will

Comments Department

Que Corporation

201 W. 103rd Street

Indianapolis, IN 46290

Introduction

Windows 98 is the most recent edition of the Microsoft desktop operating system known as Windows. Windows 98 is considered the next generation of desktop computing. It builds directly on the general user interface design of Windows 95, while raising the complexity and inner workings another notch. Windows 98 is more graphical than Windows 95 in many ways, and makes upgrading directly from either plain old DOS and/or a DOS/Windows 3.1 operating environment a snap.

Like most people, you probably do not want to know everything about the inner workings of your computer and its operating system. You just want to be up and running as quickly as possible with Windows 98. This book gets you to that point. Windows 98 From A to Z provides numerous screen shots that walk you step-by-step through all the listed tasks and references.

You can accomplish the necessary tasks and improve your desktop productivity as quickly as possible by using this book's alphabetically arranged, thumb-tab organization. This definitive resource provides the answers as you need them! It is alphabetically organized to familiarize you with

- The Active Desktop
- The Add/Remove Programs feature
- The Add New Hardware wizard
- Desktop themes
- Dial-Up Networking
- Favorites
- File management
- Finding Files
- Getting Started
- Internet Explorer 4.0
- Help with Windows 98
- Installing Windows 98
- The Maintenance wizard
- Microsoft Chat 2.0
- Microsoft NetMeeting
- Microsoft Outlook Express
- Open Database Connectivity

- The Resource Kit
- Shortcuts
- The taskbar and toolbars
- View Channels
- Windows Update
- x86

and many, many more!

There are dozens of revolutionary new features in Windows 98, most of which involve Microsoft's integration of Internet technologies directly into the Windows 98 operating system. This includes the complete revision of Windows Explorer into an Internet browser in its own right. For example, using this technology, you can open the **My Computer** window, type a Web address (URL) in the address box, and be taken directly to that location on the Internet! Additionally, there are updated versions of Microsoft NetMeeting, Microsoft Chat, Internet Explorer, Outlook Express, Personal Web Server, and FrontPage Express built into Windows 98.

Windows 98 goes a long way toward making your computer much easier to manipulate. The online help files are expanded with greater detail, and several talking videos aid in making Windows 98 that much easier to use.

Who Should Read This Book

This book is designed for all users of Windows 98, with a specific focus on beginning users. This book is organized such that anyone can quickly jump to the topic about which they need information. All you need to know is the first letter of the Windows 98 feature, utility, or option that you want help with, and then go to that letter in the book. If you don't find what you're looking for right off the bat, check the comprehensive index—you're sure to find what you're looking for!

How to Contact the Author

You can find more information about me at my Web site (http://www.inil.com/users/worldmir). In addition, feel free to contact me via email at either kpowell@kpmg.com or WorldMir@inil.com. I may, at times, have trouble finding the time to quickly answer every query, but I do appreciate your feedback.

A

A
B
C
D
E
F
G
H
I
J
K
L
M
N
O
P
Q
R
S
T
U
V
W
X
Y
Z

Accessibility Options

The accessibility options of Windows 98 are enhancements of those available for Windows 95. These features enable individuals with mobility, hearing, and/or visual impairments to use a personal computer without the hassle of installing special equipment. Available options include the following:

- **StickyKeys**—When this feature is enabled, Windows users can use the Shift, Ctrl, or Alt keys in combination with another key (but only pressing one key at a time).

- **FilterKeys**—When this feature is enabled, Windows ignores brief or repeated keystrokes, and slows the repeat rate if need be.

- **ToggleKeys**—When this feature is enabled, Windows generates tones when a user presses the Caps Lock, Num Lock, or Scroll Lock keys.

- **SoundSentry**—When this feature is enabled, Windows generates visual indications when your system makes a sound.

- **ShowSounds**—When this feature is enabled, your programs display captions for words they speak and sounds they make.

- **High Contrast**—When this option is enabled, Windows uses colors and fonts designed for easy reading.

- **MouseKeys**—When this option is enabled, you can use your keyboard to control your mouse pointer.

To determine whether any of these options are available on your PC, follow these steps:

1. Click the **Start** button, choose **Settings**, **Control Panel** (see Figure A.1). This opens the Control Panel window, shown in Figure A.2.

2. The Accessibility Options icon will probably appear in the Control Panel window, which means that at least one of the accessibility options has been installed on your PC. Move the mouse pointer to the Accessibility Options icon and then double-click the primary mouse button. This opens the Accessibility Properties dialog box, shown in Figure A.3. As shown in the figure, this dialog box has five tabs, each of which provides options for configuring various accessibility settings.

Figure **A.1**

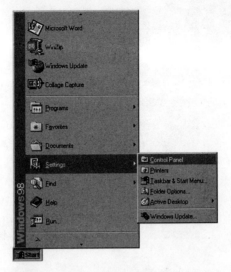

Figure **A.2**

3. Experiment with the accessibility settings. For example, to enable the
    StickyKeys feature—which enables you to use a single finger to perform
    a key-combination command—click the Keyboard tab, and then place a
    check mark in the **Use StickyKeys** check box by clicking it once.

A
B
C
D
E
F
G
H
I
J
K
L
M
N
O
P
Q
R
S
T
U
V
W
X
Y
Z

Figure **A.3**

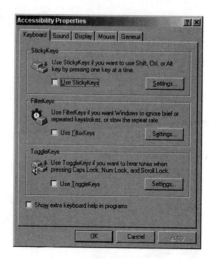

4. Click the **Settings** button to open the dialog box shown in Figure A.4.

Figure **A.4**

5. Click the **Use Shortcut** check box to select it, and then click the **OK** button (or press the **Enter** key). You have now correctly set up the StickyKeys accessibility option.

If you don't see the Accessibility Options icon in the Control Panel window, but you want to experiment with these options, you will need to add them. For instructions on adding a Windows 98 optional feature, see the section titled "Add/Remove Programs" later in this chapter.

Windows 98 users have two sets of options available to them:

- **Accessibility Options**—This set of options requires about 600,000 bytes of hard drive storage space. It includes the tools necessary for changing

the keyboard, sound, display monitor, and mouse in a manner that
makes them easier to use by persons with disabilities.

 Enhanced Accessibility—This set of options requires about 3.5 million
bytes of hard drive storage space. It includes a screen-magnification tool
and more choices for altering the mannerisms of the mouse device.

If you are not sure which level to install, select both so that Windows 98 will
install all the available options. Then shut down and restart your computer to
make these options available for use.

Accessibility Wizard

After the accessibility options are installed on your PC, a quick way to get
them up and running is to use the Accessibility Wizard. To run the
Accessibility Wizard, follow these steps:

1. To open this wizard, click the **Start** button, choose **Programs**,
   Accessories, **Accessibility**, **Accessibility Wizard**, as shown in
   Figure A.5.

Figure **A.5**

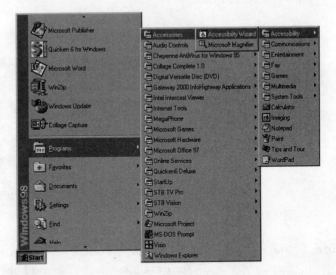

2. In the first screen of the wizard, shown in Figure A.6, select the smallest
   text you can read, and then click the **Next** button.

A
B
C
D
E
F
G
H
I
J
K
L
M
N
O
P
Q
R
S
T
U
V
W
X
Y
Z

Figure **A.6**

3. The Text Size screen, shown in Figure A.7, enables you to change the size of text and other items on your screen. This is helpful for persons with visual impairments. After you have selected the options you want, click the **Next** button.

Figure **A.7**

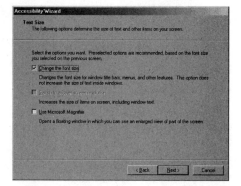

note... The options available on the Text Size screen are aimed at the visually impaired. Notice, for example, that the second check box in the Text Size screen is grayed-out (indicating that this option is not a valid selection). This is because the screen resolution of this monitor is at a standard SVGA resolution of 640×480 (in pixels). In short, a single pixel represents a dot of color on your screen—640 horizontally and 480 vertically—changing according to your computer's screen resolution. A discussion on how to change the screen resolution is covered under the "Display Options" entry later in this book. The rule of thumb is that the higher the screen resolution, the smaller the characters appear onscreen to the user.

4. The Set Wizard Options screen, shown in Figure A.8, is fairly straightforward. Just click any check boxes that apply to your situation, and then click on the **Next** button.

Figure **A.8**

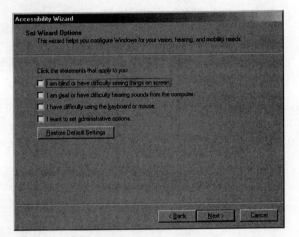

note... The Restore Default Settings button will immediately apply the original, standard Windows 98 colors, fonts, and window sizes to your computer. That is, clicking this button will enable you to go back to the way your computer was probably configured the day you first received it. This is a nice feature, in case you have chosen some wacky font or too dark (or bright) a color scheme. One button fixes everything, instead of having to go back and redo each item separately.

5. Use the Set Automatic Timeouts screen, shown in Figure A.9, to specify whether accessibility features should remain on after the computer has been idle for a specified period of time. Make your selection by clicking one of the radio buttons. If you select the first radio button, the time limit must also be set. In this example, StickyKeys, FilterKeys, ToggleKeys, and High Contrast features will automatically turn off after the computer is idle (that is, no keys have been pressed and the mouse

A

B

C

D

E

has not moved) for five minutes. After you have made your selections, click the **Next** button to continue.

Figure **A.9**

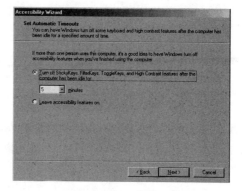

6. Click the **Yes** button in the Default Accessibility Settings screen, shown in Figure A.10, if you want your accessibility selections to be available to you whenever you log on to your PC, and then click **Next**.

Figure **A.10**

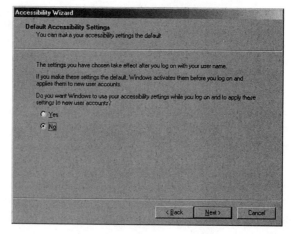

7. Click the **Save Settings** button in the Save Settings to File screen, shown in Figure A.11, to make a copy of all the accessibility options you have selected in the wizard. This file can then be transported to another computer, which is useful if you use multiple PCs (such as a laptop or another desktop at work).

F

G

H

I

J

K

L

M

N

O

P

Q

R

S

T

U

V

W

X

Y

Z

Figure **A.11**

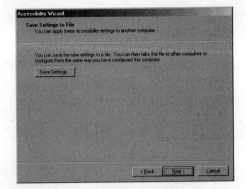

8. As shown in the Save As dialog box in Figure A.12, the default filename
   for your accessibility settings is **MySettings.acw**. You can easily change
   this filename to make it more descriptive, personalized, or memorable.
   (For information about properly naming a Windows 98 computer file, see
   the "Explorer" entry later in this book). Click the **Save** button to continue
   to the final screen of the Accessibility Wizard.

Figure **A.12**

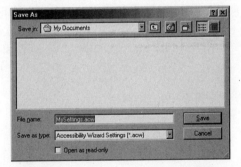

9. Completing the Accessibility Wizard screen, shown in Figure A.13, lists
   all the changes you have made to your accessibility configuration. To
   accept all the changes, click the **Finish** button. To cancel all the
   changes, click the **Cancel** button. If you are undecided about a specific
   change, click the **Back** button to review the previous screens.

A
B
C
D
E
F
G
H
I
J
K
L
M
N
O
P
Q
R
S
T
U
V
W
X
Y
Z

Figure **A.13**

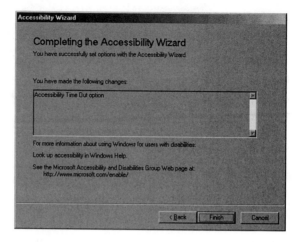

Accessories

Microsoft tosses around two terms: *accessories* and *components*. To the average person, these might seem to be similar terms. In Windows 98 terminology, however, they are not. Accessories refers only to those features listed in the Accessories area in the Windows Setup tab of the Add/Remove Programs Properties dialog box, shown in Figure A.14; *components* refers to everything else. The following Windows 98 features are accessories:

- Calculator
- Desktop Wallpaper
- Document Templates
- Games
- Imaging
- Mouse Pointers
- Paint
- Quick View
- Screen Savers
- Windows Scripting Host
- WordPad

Figure **A.14**

The rest of the Windows 98 features found in the Accessories menu (to reach this menu, click the **Start** button, and then choose **Programs, Accessories**) should be considered Windows 98 *components*.

note... For more information about these accessories, see their respective entries in this book.

Installing all the Windows 98 accessories requires 18 MB of disk space; the installation of all the Windows 98 components on your hard disk drive will consume 145.3 MB of storage space. These are important facts to remember, especially if you are using Windows 98 on an older computer that might have a limited amount of hard drive space. To install one or all of these Windows 98 accessories, use the Add/Remove Programs feature of the Windows 98 Control Panel (a discussion of this feature is available in the section of this chapter titled "Add/Remove Programs").

Active Desktop Environment

The Active Desktop environment, which is built into Windows 98, was first introduced by Microsoft in Internet Explorer 4.0 (a Web browser) in the fall of 1997. Having the Active Desktop feature quite simply means that the Windows 98 desktop can display Web content saved in HTML (Hypertext Markup Language) format, and can update it each time you connect to the Internet. For example, suppose you place on your Active Desktop a news site that is updated daily. Each time you connect to the Internet, that news site will be automatically updated on your PC's desktop. Additionally, favorite *channels* can be placed on the Windows 98 Active Desktop (for more information about channels, see the entry titled "Channels" later in this book).

To initiate the Active Desktop feature, follow these steps:

1. Right-click a blank spot on the Windows 98 desktop to open a shortcut menu, and then click the **Active Desktop** entry to view your Active Desktop options, shown in Figure A.15.

Figure **A.15**

2. A check mark next to the **View as Web Page** option indicates that the Active Desktop feature has been initiated; web content can be saved and activated directly from the Windows 98 desktop. If no check mark is present, click the **View as Web Page** option to initiate it. That's all it takes!

To customize the Active Desktop to suit your needs, follow these steps:

1. Click the **Customize My Desktop** option.
2. Select the Web tab of the Display Properties dialog box, shown in Figure A.16.

Figure **A.16**

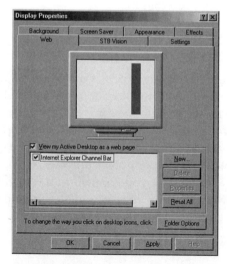

note... The Display Properties dialog box shown here might have more tabs than the one you see on your screen. One of the tabs in this figure is for configuring my computer's display monitor, which has its own custom software drivers.

note... The other tabbed items in the Display Properties dialog box are discussed in the section titled "Display Properties."

3. Click the **View My Active Desktop as a Web Page** check box to activate or deactivate this feature.

note... Viewing your Active Desktop as a Web page permits the use of active content directly on the Windows 98 desktop area. This content can come in the form of HTML (or web) pages, animated GIF graphics (such as the popular dancing 7-Up guys found on many web pages), and so forth. These items appear to float on your desktop, meaning that the normal Windows 98 background graphic appears on the bottom layer, with the active content appearing on the middle layer, and the normal icons that sit on the desktop (such as the Recycle Bin or My Computer) on the top layer. To try this, add a background, then place some active content (such as the Channel Bar) on top of it , and then drag your Recycle Bin on top of that. See how they stack?

Take this one step further, and you can begin to see the Microsoft vision for the desktop. It becomes an extension of the Internet Explorer web browser—or vice-versa, meaning that your Internet web browser is now your desktop folder and file manager. Everything is done in the same way, making Windows 98 that much easier to use, while increasing your productivity capabilities.

4. Click the **New** button if you want to add an Active Desktop file (HTML, GIF, JPEG, BMP, and so on) to your Windows 98 desktop. The dialog box shown in Figure A.17 appears.

5. If your PC is already connected to the Internet—via a *local area network* (LAN) connection or a *Dial-Up Networking* (DUN) connection—you can choose **Yes** to download additional Windows 98 graphics and web items directly from the Active Desktop Gallery at Microsoft's web site. If your PC is not connected to the Internet (or if you do not want to visit the Active Desktop Gallery), click **No** to proceed.

A
B
C
D
E
F
G
H
I
J
K
L
M
N
O
P
Q
R
S
T
U
V
W
X
Y
Z

A   Figure **A.17**

B

C

D

E

F

G   **note...** Clicking the **In the Future, Do Not Show Me This Dialog Box** check

H   box instructs Windows 98 to discontinue the automatic display of this

              dialog box at startup, meaning that you will no longer be prompted to

I   go to the Microsoft web site for free Active Desktop content. Instead,

              you will be prompted with the next window in the process, shown in

J   Figure A.18.

K

L   6. If you know the exact location of the Active Desktop item you want, type

              it in the Location text box, shown in Figure A.18. If you do not know the

M   exact location, click the **Browse** button to scan the hard drive for the

N   desired item.

O   Figure **A.18**

P

Q

R

S

T

U

V

W   7. Find the file you seek by selecting its parent drive and folder from the

              Look In drop-down list of the Browse dialog box, shown in Figure A.19.

X   When you find the file, click it to select it (in this case, the file

Y   **WULOGO.GIF** from the Windows subdirectory has been selected), and then

              click the **Open** button to return to the preceding screen.

Z

Figure **A.19**

8. As shown in Figure A.20, the file's pathname automatically appears in the Location text box. Click the **OK** button to continue.

Figure **A.20**

9. As shown in Figure A.21, `WULOGO.GIF` is highlighted and displayed in the Web tab of the Display Properties dialog box. To accept this change to the Active Desktop, click either the **Apply** button or the **OK** button. Choosing the **Apply** button enables you to stay in the Display Properties dialog box and customize the Active Desktop in other ways; clicking the **OK** button applies the change and returns you to the Windows 98 desktop.

10. The file `WULOGO.GIF`, shown along the bottom half of the screen, is the Windows Update graphic (see Figure A.22).

note... Instead of using the logo shown in Figure A.22 to update any web content on your desktop, you can right-click a blank part of the desktop, select **Active Desktop** from the shortcut menu, and then click the **Update Now** menu option.

A
B
C
D
E
F
G
H
I
J
K
L
M
N
O
P
Q
R
S
T
U
V
W
X
Y
Z

A
B
C
D
E
F
G
H
I
J
K
L
M
N
O
P
Q
R
S
T
U
V
W
X
Y
Z

Figure **A.21**

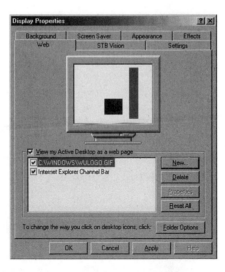

Figure **A.22**

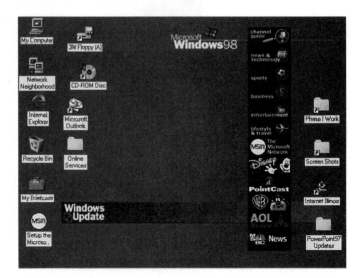

Active Movie Control

The Active Movie Control is useful for playing various multimedia files on Windows 98. These multimedia files can be in the form of movies, sounds, songs, and so on, and can originate from your PC, the Internet, or perhaps even a corporate intranet. To use the Active Movie Control, follow these steps:

1. Click the **Start** button, choose **Programs**, **Accessories**, **Multimedia**, **Active Movie Control** (see Figure A.23).

Figure **A.23**

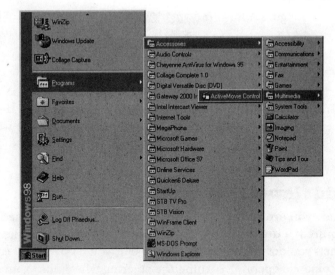

2. In the **Open** dialog box, shown in Figure A.24, search for the parent drive and folder of the file you want to view by opening the **Look In** drop-down list (click the down-arrow button next to the **Look In** text field). When you find the file you seek, click it to select it.

Figure **A.24**

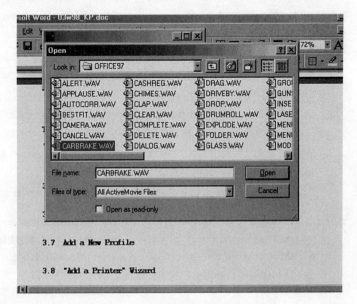

A
B
C
D
E
F
G
H
I
J
K
L
M
N
O
P
Q
R
S
T
U
V
W
X
Y
Z

3. Click the **Open** button to confirm your selection; this opens the window shown in Figure A.25.

Figure **A.25**

4. To start playing the selected multimedia file, click the **Play** button (the right-arrow button in the bottom-left corner of the window). After the file begins playing, the **Play** button changes to a **Pause** button.

Add New Hardware

When you are adding new hardware to a computer, a piece of software is required: a *driver*. Think of a software driver as being like the driver of a car. When you act as the driver of your car, you control how certain aspects of the automobile operate. Turning the steering wheel, for example, causes the car to move in a particular direction; pressing the gas or brake pedal results in the automobile moving faster or slowing down; turning the ignition key causes the car's engine to start (well, usually). Likewise, a software driver controls how a particular piece of hardware reacts to commands being processed by the computer's brain, or *CPU*.

To add the software drivers necessary for adding hardware—such as a new modem, DVD-ROM drive, or network interface card—use the Windows 98 **Add New Hardware Wizard**:

1. Click the **Start** button, choose **Settings**, **Control Panel** (as shown in Figure A.26).
2. Double-click the **Add New Hardware** icon in the Control Panel (see Figure A.27) to start the Add New Hardware Wizard.
3. Before continuing with the wizard, be sure to close any running applications.
4. Click **Next** in the wizard's opening window, shown in Figure A.28.

note... It is possible that this wizard will start automatically when you boot your system, especially if the hardware you want to add goes inside the Windows 98 computer (such as a new hard drive, CD-ROM device, or internal modem).

Figure **A.26**

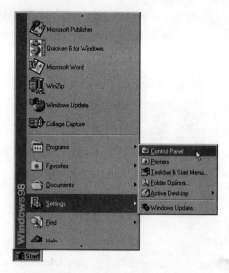

Figure **A.27**

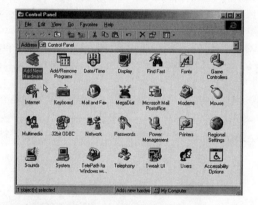

Figure **A.28**

A
B
C
D
E
F
G
H
I
J
K
L
M
N
O
P
Q
R
S
T
U
V
W
X
Y
Z

A
B
C
D
E
F
G
H
I
J
K
L
M
N
O
P
Q
R
S
T
U
V
W
X
Y
Z

5. As shown in Figure A.29, Windows 98 searches first for Plug and Play devices, and then for non–Plug and Play devices. Click **Next** to instruct Windows 98 to conduct the search.

Figure **A.29**

note... A *Plug and Play* device is just a hardware component automatically recognized by the Windows 98 operating system. For more information about Plug and Play devices, see the section titled "Plug and Play."

6. In this example, you are not trying to install a Plug and Play device. After it fails to find Plug and Play hardware, Windows 98 asks whether you want it to search for non–Plug and Play hardware, as shown in Figure A.30.

Figure **A.30**

7. The **Yes** button is selected by default, instructing Windows 98 to search for non–Plug and Play devices. In this example, however, you know exactly what you are attempting to install (software drivers), so it's much faster to click the **No, I Want to Select the Hardware from a List** radio button, and then click **Next**.

8. Use the scrollbar along the right-hand side of the screen to view all the Hardware Types menu choices (see Figure A.31). The device you want to

install does not appear to be listed; click the **Other Devices** option, and then click **Next** to select your device's manufacturer and model.

Figure **A.31**

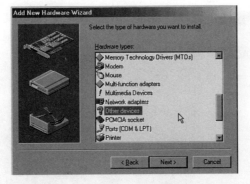

9. Use the scrollbars to view the devices available for installation. For this example, select the **Legacy Serial Infrared Devices** entry to see all the available models, select **AIRport APA-9230 External Infrared Adapter** (a wireless communications device) from the Models list (as shown in Figure A.32), and then click **Next**.

Figure **A.32**

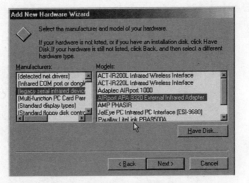

note...   This is a good way to determine whether that new, snazzy piece of telephonic equipment that you have your eye on is compatible with Windows 98. (If it is, chances are it will show up somewhere in these lists.)

A
B
C
D
E
F
G
H
I
J
K
L
M
N
O
P
Q
R
S
T
U
V
W
X
Y
Z

A
B
C
D
E
F
G
H
I
J
K
L
M
N
O
P
Q
R
S
T
U
V
W
X
Y
Z

note... If you have the floppy disk(s) or CD-ROM containing the Windows 98 software drivers, click the **Have Disk** button to continue the process.

10. Click the **Finish** button, shown in Figure A.33, to complete the process.

Figure **A.33**

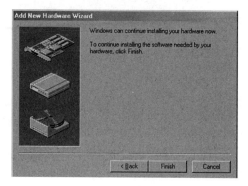

11. To determine whether the hardware device was correctly installed, double-click the **System** icon in the **Control Panel** (shown in Figure A.34).

12. Click the **Device Manager** tab in the System Properties dialog box, shown in Figure A.35.

Figure **A.34**

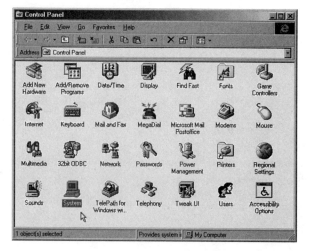

Figure **A.35**

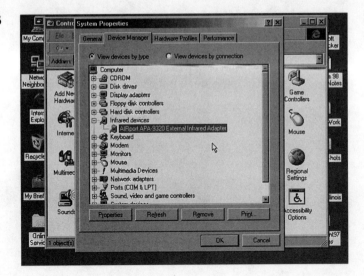

13. Click the plus symbol (**+**) next to the Infrared Devices entry; note that your new hardware is installed.

note... Had there been a problem with your installation, either a red *X* or a yellow exclamation point (**!**) would appear next to the device name.

Add Printer Wizard

Adding a new printer to a computer used to be rather complex, especially when you had to get all the applications installed on that PC to work correctly with the new printer. Under Windows 95, that changed because of the Add Printer Wizard. In Windows 98, this wizard still exists. To run this wizard, follow these steps:

1. Click the **Start** button, choose **Settings**, and then choose **Printers**, as shown in Figure A.36.

2. Double-click the **Add Printer** icon, shown in Figure A.37, to start the wizard.

3. In the first screen of the Add Printer Wizard, shown in Figure A.38, click **Next**.

A
B
C
D
E
F
G
H
I
J
K
L
M
N
O
P
Q
R
S
T
U
V
W
X
Y
Z

Figure **A.36**

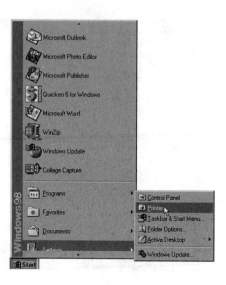

Figure **A.37**

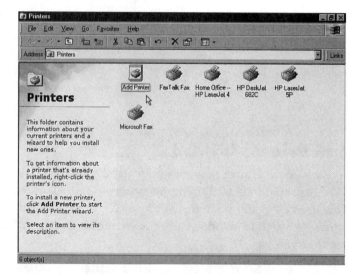

4. In the dialog box shown in Figure A.39, you must specify how the printer is attached to your PC. A *local printer* is physically attached to the computer via a parallel printer cable (also known as a *Centronix* cable). In the case of a network connection, both the *network printer* and your PC are physically attached to a network device (usually known as a *hub, concentrator,* or *MAU*). Make your selection, and then click **Next.**

Figure **A.38**

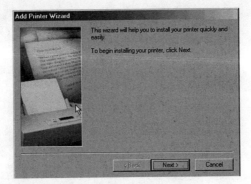

Figure **A.39**

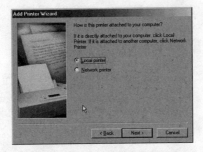

note... If the computer is a home computer or a laptop (and you are not at the office), there is a 99.999% chance that it uses a local printer, not a network printer.

5. To determine the make and model of the printer you are installing, look on the cover of the instruction manuals that came with the printer or on the print device itself. (Hewlett-Packard, for example, marks its printers very clearly.)

6. Select your printer's manufacturer from the Manufacturers list, and then select your printer's model from the Printers list, as shown in Figure A.40. Click the **Next** button to continue.

7. If you have not yet done so, plug in the printer, turn it on, and connect the parallel print cable into the parallel port (also know as *LPT1*) on the back of your PC.

8. Unless your printer is a serial print device, make sure the **LPT1** option is selected in the Available Ports list, as shown in Figure A.41. Click **Next** to continue.

A
B
C
D
E
F
G
H
I
J
K
L
M
N
O
P
Q
R
S
T
U
V
W
X
Y
Z

A

B

C

D

E

F

G

H

I

J

K

L

M

N

O

P

Q

R

S

T

U

V

W

X

Y

Z

Figure **A.40**

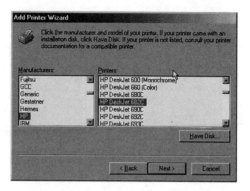

Figure **A.41**

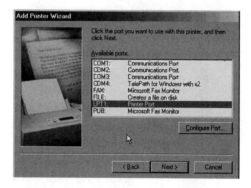

note...   If you are attempting to connect a serial print device, such as an older dot-matrix printer, select the exact serial communications port to which the printer cable is connected. If you have connected the serial printer cable to your computer's COM*x* port (where *x* is the serial port number, such as 1 or 2), for example, the option you select in the Available Ports list should correspond to this port number. If the back of your PC uses letters rather than numbers to describe the COM ports, COMa is the same thing as COM1, and so on.

9. Type a descriptive name for the printer in the Printer Name text box (see Figure A.42). If you want Windows 98 to always use this printer by default, click the **Yes** button. Click **Next** to continue.

Figure **A.42**

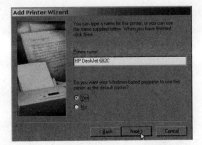

note... If you already have at least one printer installed on your PC, the screen shown in Figure A.42 will default to the **No** button.

10. If you want to print a test page to ensure that the printer has been installed correctly, make sure the **Yes** button is selected (as shown in Figure A.43), and then click the **Finish** button.

Figure **A.43**

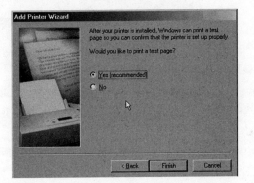

note... After you click the **Finish** button, Windows 98 will probably want to install some new software printer drivers before placing the new print device inside the Printers window. Windows 98 might prompt you to insert your Windows 98 CD-ROM disc in the computer's CD-ROM disk drive should it require additional files that do not already exist on your computer's hard drive.

11. If you can read the printout, the printer has been installed correctly. If not, it is possible that you installed the wrong driver. If this is the case, you should carefully repeat steps 1–10.

A
B
C
D
E
F
G
H
I
J
K
L
M
N
O
P
Q
R
S
T
U
V
W
X
Y
Z

12. Return to the Printers window by clicking the **Start** button, then choosing **Settings**, **Printers**. The newly installed print device should be present, as shown in Figure A.44.

Figure **A.44**

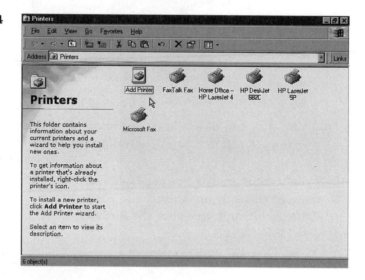

Add/Remove Programs

The Add/Remove Programs feature of Windows 98 enables you to easily add and remove programs and Windows 98 components. You access this feature from the Control Panel, as follows:

1. Click the **Start** button, and choose **Settings**, **Control Panel**, as shown in Figure A.45.

2. Double-click the **Add/Remove Programs** icon in the Control Panel (see Figure A.46).

3. You have a few options in the Install/Uninstall tab of the Add/Remove Programs Properties dialog box (shown in Figure A.47):

   ▪ You can install new applications or components.

   ▪ You can remove installed software from your hard drive.

Figure **A.45**

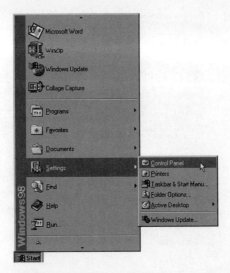

Figure **A.46**

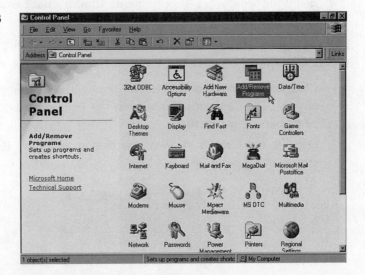

Adding New Programs or Windows 98 Components

When it comes to adding new programs or components, you have the following two options:

- Installing a non–Windows 98 application such as Microsoft Office by clicking the **Install** button (see Figure A.47).

A
B
C
D
E
F
G
H
I
J
K
L
M
N
O
P
Q
R
S
T
U
V
W
X
Y
Z

Figure **A.47**

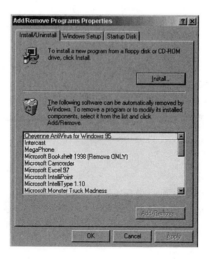

▓ Installing Windows 98 components that are not installed in your version of Windows 98.

For this example, install a Windows 98 feature (the Web TV for Windows) that was not preloaded on your PC. To do so, follow these steps:

1. Click the **Windows Setup** tab to display the full list of Windows 98 add-on components (components need not be installed on your computer to be displayed in this list).

2. Scroll to the Web TV for Windows option, and click its check box, as shown in Figure A.48.

Figure **A.48**

note... Next to each component, a check box appears. If a box containing a check mark is shaded, it means that only some of that component's options have been installed. If the checked box has a white background, it means that all of that component's options have been installed. To change a box from gray to white, just click a gray box to deselect it, and then click it again. It should appear as white, indicating that all the component's options are installed.

3. Click the **OK** button to continue the installation process.

4. As shown in Figure A.49, Windows 98 prompts you to insert the Windows 98 CD-ROM if the appropriate files do not exist on your hard drive.

Figure **A.49**

5. Insert the CD-ROM, and then click the **OK** button to continue. As shown in Figure A.50, Windows 98 displays a progress dialog box that indicates which files are being installed in the hard drive and that shows how far along the installation process is.

Figure **A.50**

6. In the event that a Version Conflict dialog box appears, as shown in Figure A.51, it is usually best to keep the file in question.

A
B
C
D
E
F
G
H
I
J
K
L
M
N
O
P
Q
R
S
T
U
V
W
X
Y
Z

Figure **A.51**

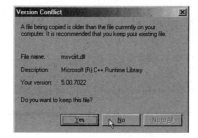

note... Unfortunately, in the event of a version conflict, there is no perfect way of knowing which version is the best one to keep. When in doubt, stay with the original file. You can always go back and reinstall the program should this be an improper choice. Windows 98 will try to advise you of the best course of action by providing its recommendation within the text of this dialog box (look closely at the last line of the top paragraph).

7. When Windows 98 finishes copying the required files, it might request that you restart your computer to complete the process (see Figure A.52). If you want your new settings to take effect immediately, close all active programs, and then click the **Yes** button to reboot your PC.

Figure **A.52**

Removing Applications and Windows 98 Components

To remove a built-in Windows 98 accessory, utility, or component, just use the same process that you used to install the application, only in reverse. To remove the Web TV for Windows component that you added earlier, for example, just uncheck the **Web TV for Windows** check box in the Windows Setup tab of the Add/Remove Programs Properties dialog box, and then click **OK**. Windows 98 will automatically uninstall this component, and delete any of the necessary files.

note... A Windows 98 *component, utility,* or *accessory* is a piece of software that comes with the Windows 98 operating system at the time of purchase. A Windows 98 *application* is a non–Windows 98 piece of software that does not come in the same box as Windows 98 did. Microsoft Money 98, for example, is a home-finance software application that can be both installed and deleted from your PC by using the Add/Remove Programs dialog box, but it is a distinctly separate piece of software from anything found inside Windows 98. Applications are installed and deleted via the Install/Uninstall tab of the Add/Remove Programs dialog box; all Windows 98 components, utilities, and accessories are installed and removed via the Windows Setup tab.

To remove a Windows application from Windows 98, follow these steps:

1. Click the **Install/Uninstall** tab of the Add/Remove Programs Properties dialog box. As shown in Figure A.53, this tab lists all the 32-bit Windows programs that are installed on your machine. To uninstall any of these programs, select the one you want to delete (in this example, **Windows 98 Uninstall Information** is selected), and then click **OK**.

Figure **A.53**

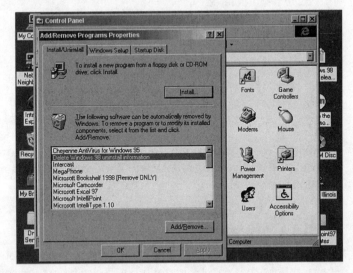

A
B
C
D
E
F
G
H
I
J
K
L
M
N
O
P
Q
R
S
T
U
V
W
X
Y
Z

note... The Windows 98 Uninstall Information option permits you to uninstall Windows 98 if it is an upgrade to a previously existing version of Windows (3.1 or 95). After you have decided that you do not want to remove Windows 98 now or in the future, it is wise to uninstall this program to save space. Another reason for removing the Windows 98 Uninstall Information is that it will prevent you from accidentally deleting the Windows 98 operating system.

2. Click the **Yes** button in the dialog box shown in Figure A.54 to confirm that you want to remove this program.

Figure **A.54**
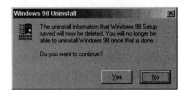

3. As shown in Figure A.55, Windows 98 confirms that the appropriate files have been deleted.

Figure **A.55**
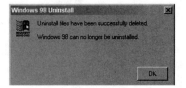

4. Windows 98 returns you to the Add/Remove Programs Properties dialog box; as you can see, the Delete Windows 98 Uninstall Information option is no longer present.

Audio Compression

Windows 98 has a series of audio compression codecs built in to it, as well as several others that can be installed. A *codec* (short for *compressor/decompressor)* is essentially a series of software programs that permits the Windows 98 operating system to better manage any installed audio (as well as visual) devices. To put it another way, a codec is either an audio or a video compression methodology that both compresses and decompresses an audio or visual stream of data that is being processed by your computer. This can be very helpful now that PCs have become more multimedia focused, especially when processing huge amounts of this type of data for audio/visual presentations. A very popular type of video codec in use today is known as MPEG.

A

B

C

D

E

F

G

H

I

J

K

L

M

N

O

P

Q

R

S

T

U

V

W

X

Y

Z

B

A
B
C
D
E
F
G
H
I
J
K
L
M
N
O
P
Q
R
S
T
U
V
W
X
Y
Z

A
B
C
D
E
F
G
H
I
J
K
L
M
N
O
P
Q
R
S
T
U
V
W
X
Y
Z

Backup

The backup option that is built into the Windows 98 operating system is very powerful. It permits you to save your computer data files, applications, graphics, and so on, to a variety of media devices such as tape, removable disks, hard drives, and the like. The biggest improvement of this software as compared to the Windows 95 version is that it enables users to back up to a SCSI (Small Computer Systems Interface)-connected device such as a tape drive. The purpose of the Windows 98 backup software is to help protect you from data loss in case your PC breaks down.

Before starting Backup, make sure that the backup hardware device has already been correctly installed and is operational (refer to the "Add New Hardware" entry for assistance). If you are backing up your data to either a floppy disk or the hard drive, it is okay to start the Backup software now.

1. To start the Windows 98 Backup process, click the **Start** button, and then choose **Programs**, **Accessories**, **System Tools**, **Backup**, as shown in Figure B.1.

Figure **B.1**

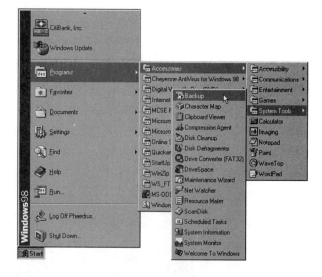

2. As Figure B.2 shows, you are prompted with three choices:
   - To create a new backup job
   - To open one that you created previously
   - To restore files from a previous backup session

Because this is the first time you are running Backup, the default choice of creating a new backup job will be your selection. To continue, click the **OK** button.

Figure **B.2**

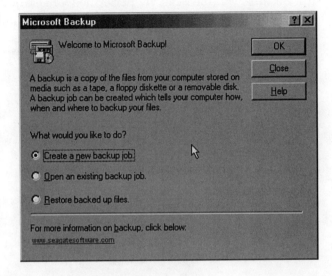

3. Next you are prompted for the size of the backup job (see Figure B.3). In other words, you must specify whether you want to back up your entire computer or specific preselected files. Choose the default setting **Back Up My Computer** and then click the **Next** button.

Figure **B.3**

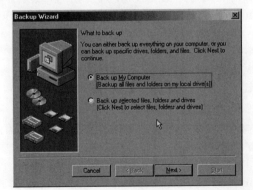

A
B
C
D
E
F
G
H
I
J
K
L
M
N
O
P
Q
R
S
T
U
V
W
X
Y
Z

4. The next dialog box, shown in Figure B.4, asks whether you want to back up all the files on your computer, or whether you just want to back up any files that have been created or changed since the previous backup. Because you have not yet performed a backup, the default, **All Selected Files**, is appropriate. Click **Next** to continue.

Figure **B.4**

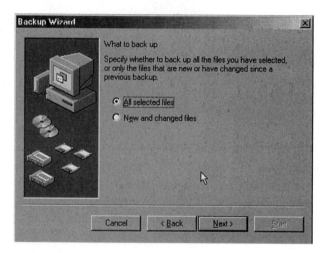

5. As Figure B.5 shows, you are asked to specify where these files should be backed up. For this example, back up your files to the local hard drive. The default is to save all files to the root directory of **C:**; however, this is a bad idea because things get messy when you use the root directory for nonessential files. Instead, save your backup job, called **MyBackup.qic** (this name is automatically assigned by the Windows 98 Backup software, but it can be changed) in a specially created directory called **C:\MyData**. Click **Next** to continue.

6. When you're prompted to specify how to back up (see Figure B.6), choose one of the following options:

   - **Compare original and backup files to verify data was successfully backed up.**   It's wise to select this option because it just verifies that the job was successful.

   - **Compress the backup data to save space.**   This option is useful because it alters the manner in which data is stored so that files require less space than normal.

Figure **B.5**

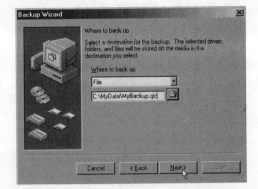

Figure **B.6**

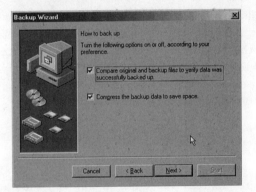

tip...   Both of these options will slow the backup process; if you are in a hurry, you might want to skip either or both of them.

7. After you have set these parameters, click **Next**. The ensuing screen, shown in Figure B.7, enables you to give your backup job a name (**Untitled** is the default). When you are satisfied with the name, click **Start**.

tip...   I suggest using a date-naming scheme so that you can quickly and easily sort through backups. Just put today's date in a *YYMMDD* format, (where *YY* = the last two digits of the current year, *MM* = the two digits for the current month, and *DD* = the two digits for the current day). As I write this chapter, for example, the date is February 5, 1998, which translates to **980205**.

A
B
C
D
E
F
G
H
I
J
K
L
M
N
O
P
Q
R
S
T
U
V
W
X
Y
Z

A

B

C

D

E

F

G

H

I

J

K

L

M

N

O

P

Q

R

S

T

U

V

W

X

Y

Z

Figure **B.7**

8. Backup displays a running total of the number and size of files being copied, as shown in Figure B.8. This screen is present only for the time it takes for the backup software to estimate the number of files and total size of all those files that are to be included in the backup process.

Figure **B.8**

9. The Backup Progress dialog box (it will bear the name of the backup job) shown in Figure B.9 will appear automatically as soon as the file and size estimates are complete. Unfortunately, there is no chance for you to save this information on the screen to review at your leisure. (If you are working on a fast PC, or if it is a small backup process, this screen will appear and disappear quickly. Do not let that scare you.) The Backup Progress dialog box contains a wealth of information concerning the backup process, including the following:

- The total number of files backed up
- The total amount of space used
- How long the backup process took (this is helpful for planning future backup jobs)
- Whether any errors occurred

Figure **B.9**

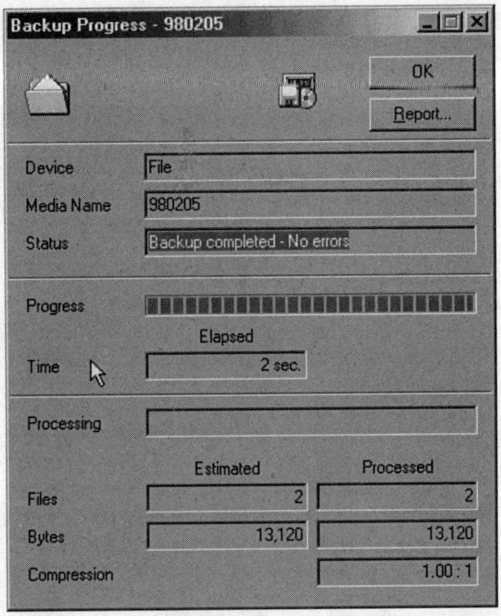

Backup Progress - 980205	
	OK
	Report...

Device	File
Media Name	980205
Status	Backup completed - No errors

| Progress | |

	Elapsed
Time	2 sec.

| Processing | |

	Estimated	Processed
Files	2	2
Bytes	13,120	13,120
Compression		1.00 : 1

A
B
C
D
E
F
G
H
I
J
K
L
M
N
O
P
Q
R
S
T
U
V
W
X
Y
Z

10. Although this screen contains a lot of useful information, you should wait until the backup process completes before clicking on the **Report** button. You will know the process is done when the Microsoft Backup dialog box appears, as shown in Figure B.10.

Figure **B.10**

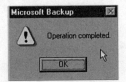

Click the **OK** button to return to the **Backup Progress** dialog box you were just looking at.

11. Click the **Report** button to view and print a summary of the Backup Progress dialog box, shown in Figure B.11.

Figure **B.11**

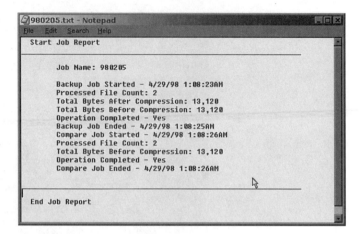

12. Click the **OK** button to end this backup process and return to the
Microsoft Backup window, shown in Figure B.12.

Figure **B.12**

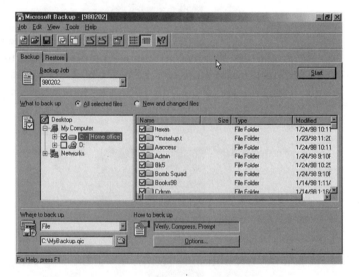

note...   All the checked boxes in the Backup tab indicate that those drives and
folders are set to be backed up the next time the backup job is execut-
ed. You can select any combination of hard drives, folders, and files.

13. Click the **Options** button to view the Backup Job Options dialog box, shown in Figure B.13. Each of the tabs in this dialog box boasts a series of options for configuring the Microsoft Backup software. As you click each of these tabs, you will realize that these options are, for the most part, quite straightforward.

Figure **B.13**

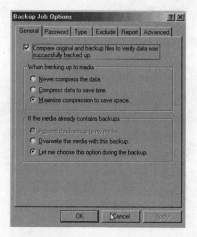

note... I suggest that you experiment with these options to determine which ones work best for you.

14. Click the **OK** button to return to the Backup screen. To exit, click the **Close** button (x) located in the upper-right corner of the screen.

Broadcast Data Services

The Broadcast Data Services component of Windows 98 is a brand new feature. It contains numerous other features and functions within it, including the Windows 98 Announcement Manager, which is how Windows 98 handles the practice of receiving Internet channel broadcasts across a network. The Announcement Manager prepares your PC for receiving the various Internet TV programs that are broadcast across the Internet by applying your specially configured broadcast filters to these programs.

If you have installed the Broadcast Data Services on your computer, the Announcement Manager will run automatically in the background whenever the PC is operational. To install the Broadcast Data Services, follow these steps:

A
B
C
D
E
F
G
H
I
J
K
L
M
N
O
P
Q
R
S
T
U
V
W
X
Y
Z

1. Open the Control Panel by clicking **Start**, selecting **Settings**, and then choosing **Control Panel**, as shown in Figure B.14.

Figure **B.14**

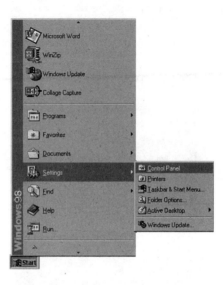

2. Double-click the **Add/Remove Programs** icon in the Control Panel, shown in Figure B.15.

Figure **B.15**

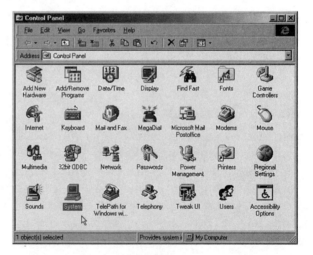

3. In the Add/Remove Programs Properties dialog box, click the **Windows Setup** tab. Scroll to the bottom of the Components list and click the **Web TV for Windows** check box to select it, as shown in Figure B.16.

A
B
C
D
E
F
G
H
I
J
K
L
M
N
O
P
Q
R
S
T
U
V
W
X
Y
Z

Figure **B.16**

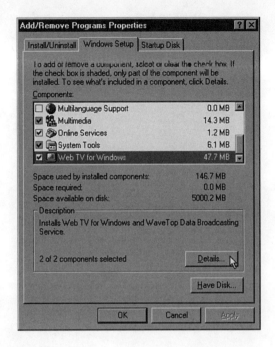

4. Click the **OK** button. Web TV for Windows, 47.7 MB of program files, will be installed on your computer.

5. After you restart your PC, the installation process is complete. You will now be able to watch TV programs being broadcast across the Internet— provided of course, that you have a TV Tuner card installed in your PC (if not, you can buy one for approximately $150).

Bus Mouse

A bus mouse is a mouse that has a round connector on the end of its wire and connects directly to a port on the back of the PC. It does not, however, plug into any of the serial or COMx ports (where x is the port number).

A
B
C
D
E
F
G
H
I
J
K
L
M
N
O
P
Q
R
S
T
U
V
W
X
Y
Z

C

A
B
C
D
E
F
G
H
I
J
K
L
M
N
O
P
Q
R
S
T
U
V
W
X
Y
Z

A
B
C
D
E
F
G
H
I
J
K
L
M
N
O
P
Q
R
S
T
U
V
W
X
Y
Z

Calculator

Microsoft provides a calculator within Windows 98. The Calculator program offers two types of calculators:

- **Standard** This is probably the type of calculator you're used to and have used for years; it is most useful for calculations using the decimal number system.

- **Scientific** This type of calculator supports a variety of numbering systems such as hexadecimal, decimal, octal, and binary.

To use Calculator, follow these steps:

1. Click the **Start** button, choose **Programs**, **Accessories**, **Calculator**, as shown in Figure C.1.

Figure **C.1**

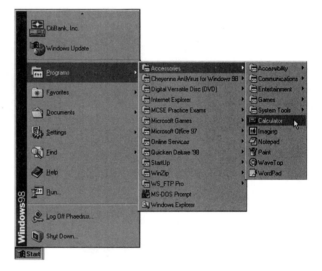

2. The standard calculator, shown in Figure C.2, opens. This calculator works just like the one you have at home, except that you use the mouse pointer rather than your fingers to click its keys. The standard calculator contains all the basic arithmetic and memory functions, along with a few extras—such as the capability to calculate square roots, percents, and the reciprocal of a number.

Figure **C.2**

note...   In addition to being able to use your mouse to click numbers on the calculator, you can type numbers by using your numeric keypad.

3. To switch to the scientific calculator, click the **View** menu option and then click **Scientific**.

4. The scientific calculator offers a host of features and functions that are probably better explained in a math book than here. To switch back to the standard calculator, just click the **View** menu option and then choose **Standard**, as shown in Figure C.3.

5. To close Calculator, click the **Close button** (×) in the upper-right corner of the program's window.

A
B
C
D
E
F
G
H
I
J
K
L
M
N
O
P
Q
R
S
T
U
V
W
X
Y
Z

Figure **C.3**

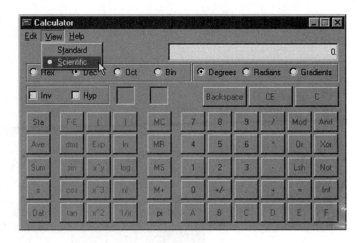

CD Player

To use the CD Player feature of Windows 98, you must have the following four things:

- A CD-ROM drive in your PC
- A usable sound speaker
- A sound card
- A music compact disc

If you have not yet installed your CD-ROM drive and speakers, refer to the "Add New Hardware" entry along with any documentation accompanying your CD-ROM drive and speakers. To operate the CD Player, follow these steps:

1. Put your music CD into your CD-ROM drive.
2. Start the CD Player software by clicking the **Start** button, and choosing **Programs**, **Accessories**, **Entertainment**, **CD Player**, as shown in Figure C.4.
3. The Windows 98 CD Player window opens (see Figure C.5).

note... The total length (in minutes and seconds) of the music CD is displayed in the lower-left corner of the CD Player window.

4. Display the toolbar by clicking the **View** menu and selecting **Toolbar**. The toolbar appears along the top of the CD Player window, as shown in Figure C.6.

Figure **C.4**

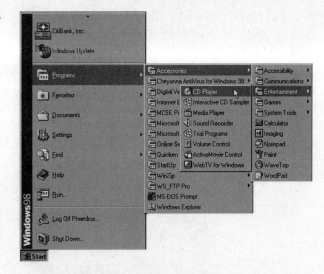

Figure **C.5**

Figure **C.6**

5. To begin playing the CD, click the **Play** button. (This button resembles the Play button on a VCR; it resembles an arrowhead pointing to the right.)

6. To change the volume, click on the **View** menu option and then select **Volume Control**. This opens the Volume Control window, shown in Figure C.7.

Figure **C.7**

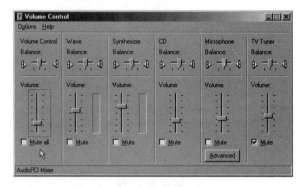

7. Click the **Options** menu option and select **Properties** to open the **Properties** dialog box, shown in Figure C.8. This window shows you the available types of audio options:

- Playback
- Recording
- Other (such as voice commands)

Figure **C.8**

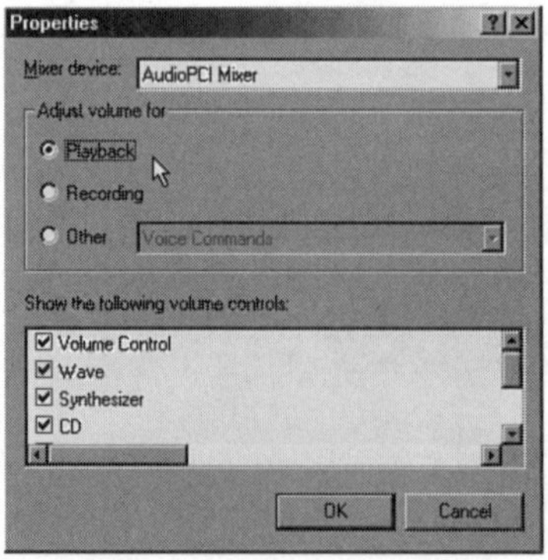

8. Select your options and return to the Volume Control window by clicking the **OK** button.

9. To close the Volume Control window, click the **Close button** (×) in the upper-right corner of the screen.

10. To close CD Player, click the **Close button** (×) in the upper-right corner of the screen.

Channels

In Windows 98 terminology, a channel is a web site designed to push its content to your PC according to the schedule you set. Channels enable you to regularly receive updates to certain Web sites without having to navigate around the Internet to find them.

The Channel bar should already be present on the Active Desktop, as shown in Figure C.9. If it is not, refer to the section titled "Active Desktop Environment" to learn how to display it.

Figure **C.9**

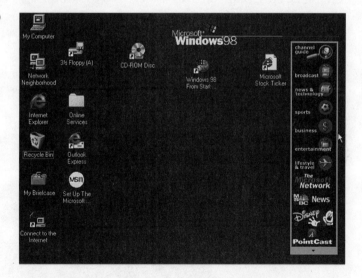

Hover your mouse pointer over a button in the Channel bar, such as the Channel Guide button. As shown in Figure C.10, Windows 98 automatically displays information about the feature you are pointing to.

A
B
C
D
E
F
G
H
I
J
K
L
M
N
O
P
Q
R
S
T
U
V
W
X
Y
Z

Figure **C.10**

To use the Channel bar, follow these steps:

1. Make sure that you are connected to the Internet (see the section titled "Dial-Up Networking" for information about creating a dial-up connection to the Internet), and then click the **Channel Guide** button in the Channel bar.

2. This opens the default browser (usually Microsoft's Internet Explorer 4) and displays the Microsoft Active Channel Guide as the default site (see Figure C.11).

Figure **C.11**

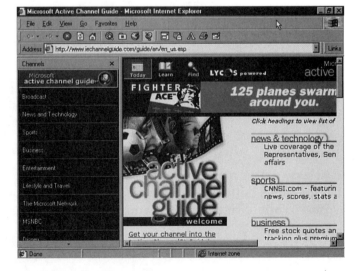

3. Click any channel category that appears along the left side of the window. (I have selected the **Lifestyle and Travel** category, as shown in Figure C.12.)

Figure **C.12**

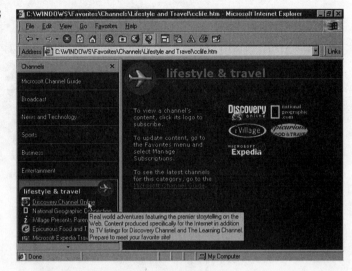

tip... Hover over a channel to view information about it, as shown in Figure C.12.

4. Right-click a channel from within the channel category you selected in step 3 (I selected **Discovery Channel Online**) to view the menu shown in Figure C.13. Click the **Subscribe** command to start the channel subscription process.

5. As a result, various files will be copied to your PC. The progress of this operation is shown in Figure C.14.

6. In the Modify Channel Usage dialog box, shown in Figure C.15, you are asked whether you want to subscribe to this Internet channel and, if so, at what level. To subscribe to the channel and to customize how often downloads occur, select the third radio button, and then click the **Customize** button.

A
B
C
D
E
F
G
H
I
J
K
L
M
N
O
P
Q
R
S
T
U
V
W
X
Y
Z

A
B
C
D
E
F
G
H
I
J
K
L
M
N
O
P
Q
R
S
T
U
V
W
X
Y
Z

Figure **C.13**

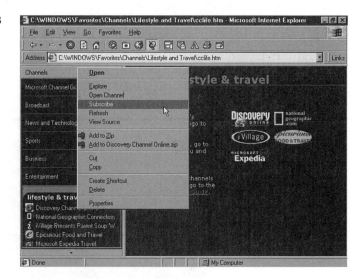

Figure **C.14**

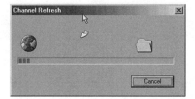

Figure **C.15**

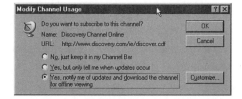

note...   Keep in mind that the technology on which these channels are designed tends to stuff a lot of useless files onto your hard-disk drive in short periods of time. You might quickly find yourself running out of disk space unless you keep your number of subscriptions low and their options minimized.

7. The first screen of the Windows 98 Subscription Wizard, shown in Figure C.16, opens. Specify whether you want to download only the channel's home page or all of the channel's content, and then click the **Next** button.

Figure **C.16**

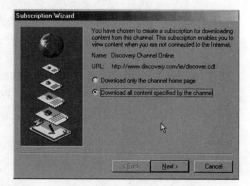

8. If you want to be notified via email when the page has changed, click the **Yes** option. If you do not want to be notified, choose **No**, as shown in Figure C.17. Click **Next** after you have made your selection.

Figure **C.17**

tip...   To change the default email address, click the **Change Address** button. You will be prompted to enter another email address along with the SMTP email server name, which you must obtain from either your ISP or your company's system administrator. Click the **OK** button to return to the Subscription Wizard screen shown in Figure C.17.

9. In the screen shown in Figure C.18, click the **Scheduled** button and select an automated schedule from the adjacent drop-down list.

A
B
C
D
E
F
G
H
I
J
K
L
M
N
O
P
Q
R
S
T
U
V
W
X
Y
Z

A
B
C
D
E
F
G
H
I
J
K
L
M
N
O
P
Q
R
S
T
U
V
W
X
Y
Z

Alternatively, click the **Manually** button to set your own pace. Click the **Finish** button to complete the wizard and return to the Web browser screen.

Figure **C.18**

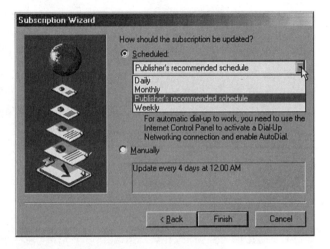

10. Right-click the channel you just subscribed to in order to view the short-cut menu, as shown in Figure C.19.

Figure **C.19**

11. Click the **Open Channel** option. The channel you chose appears within your web browser window, as shown in Figure C.20. When you are finished, close the browser by clicking the **Close button** (×) in the upper-right corner of the browser window.

Figure **C.20**

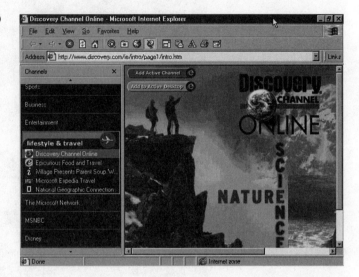

Character Map

The Windows 98 Character Map offers an easy way to quickly add special characters to whatever application you might be using, such as a word processor, spreadsheet, or graphics tool. To use the Character Map, follow these steps:

1. Click the **Start** button, choose **Programs**, **Accessories**, **System Tools**, **Character Map**, as shown in Figure C.21.

2. Click a symbol in the Character Map window to make it larger and easier to view. To place a character in the Characters to Copy text box, either double-click the character, or single-click to select it and then click the **Select** button. Figure C.22 shows the heart character enlarged for view and in the Characters to Copy text box.

3. Click the **Copy** button to copy the character in the Characters to Copy box onto the Windows 98 clipboard (see the section titled "Clipboard" for further details).

A
B
C
D
E
F
G
H
I
J
K
L
M
N
O
P
Q
R
S
T
U
V
W
X
Y
Z

A
B
C
D
E
F
G
H
I
J
K
L
M
N
O
P
Q
R
S
T
U
V
W
X
Y
Z

Figure **C.21**

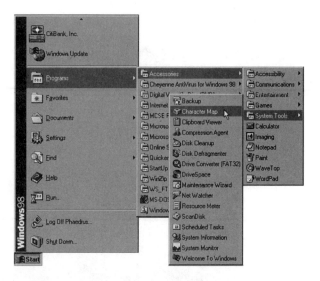

Figure **C.22**

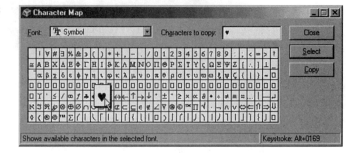

Check Box

In Windows 98 terminology, a check box is a function that permits you to make selections within various Windows 98 accessories, components, and applications. Check boxes normally appear just after the text that explains the purpose of the selections shown.

To select a feature, just click its corresponding check box; a check mark or times sign (×) will usually appear. To deselect a feature, click its check box so that the mark disappears. Many Windows 98 dialog boxes utilize the check box function.

Clipboard

The Clipboard is used as a holding or staging area for graphics or text that has been copied to it. Think of the Clipboard as a spot within the memory of your computer that holds information that you have copied or cut (perhaps through a copy-and-paste or cut-and-paste operation), but have not yet pasted to its new location.

> **note...** Even though you might have pasted whatever was in the Clipboard, a copy remains there until you either copy something else or shut down Windows 98.

The Clipboard Viewer (discussed next) is the Windows 98 utility that permits you to see exactly what is in the clipboard holding area. This can make it easier for you to manage your cutting and pasting operations.

Clipboard Viewer

The Microsoft Clipboard Viewer for Windows 98 enables you to see what items you have copied to the clipboard. Items copied to the clipboard can then be pasted into other Windows applications, such as Microsoft Word, Microsoft PowerPoint, and the like. To use the Clipboard Viewer, follow these steps:

1. Click the **Start** button, choose **Programs**, **Accessories**, **System Tools**, **Clipboard Viewer**, as shown in Figure C.23.

Figure **C.23**

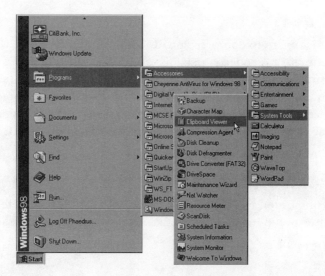

A
B
C
D
E
F
G
H
I
J
K
L
M
N
O
P
Q
R
S
T
U
V
W
X
Y
Z

2. The **Clipboard Viewer** window, shown in Figure C.24, opens. The screen shows all the special characters and graphics presently saved on the Clipboard.

Figure **C.24**

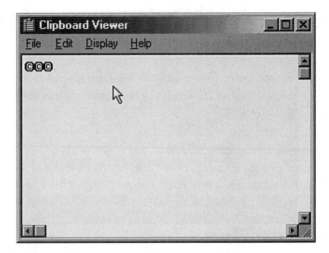

> **tip...**   Whenever Windows 98 is shut down or restarted, all the contents of the Clipboard are discarded. Be sure to save the Clipboard's contents to a Windows application before shutting down your system.

Codec

Codec refers to **co**mpression/**dec**ompression (see how they derived this acronym?). A codec is used for audio and video files in such a manner that it permits your computer to more effectively manage its multimedia functions. You need not worry about codecs; the operating system automatically handles these files for you. But if you want to impress your friends by talking about codecs, one of the more popular codec formats is MPEG.

Communications

As illustrated in Table C.1, Windows 98 comes complete with a variety of communications tools—eight, to be exact—that serve an assortment of functions.

Table C.1   Windows 98 Communications Tools

Tool	Description
Dial-Up Networking	This enables you to connect to other computers via a telephone line using a modem. It supports the TCP/IP, NetBEUI, and IPX/SPX network communications protocols.
Dial-Up Server	This feature enables you to dial in to your PC from another computer.
Direct Cable Connection	Using a parallel- or serial-connected cable between two PCs, you can transfer data files between the two computers.
HyperTerminal	This accessory enables you to connect to other PCs and online services through a modem.
Microsoft Chat 2.1	This software package enables you to conduct chat sessions with other people connected to the same chat server. (This is the client-side piece of software.)
Microsoft NetMeeting	Through NetMeeting, you can call other people on the same LAN or across the Internet. Once connected, you can share files, use a shared whiteboard, and chat.
Phone Dialer	This telephony software permits you to dial a telephone through the modem.
Virtual Private Networking	VPN allows for secure connections to private networks, even though the data is traveling across public networks such as the Internet.

To install any or all of these features, use the Add/Remove Programs option from the Control Panel (refer to the section titled "Add/Remove Programs" for further details about this option):

1. Click the **Start** button, choose **Settings**, **Control Panel**, as shown in Figure C.25.

A
B
C
D
E
F
G
H
I
J
K
L
M
N
O
P
Q
R
S
T
U
V
W
X
Y
Z

Figure **C.25**

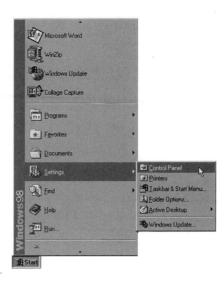

2. In the Control Panel window, shown in Figure C.26, double-click the **Add/Remove Programs** icon.

Figure **C.26**

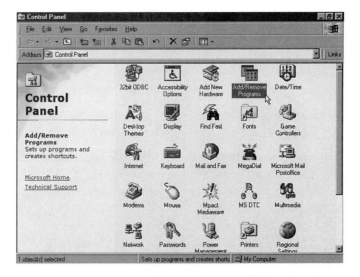

3. In the Add/Remove Programs Properties dialog box, shown in Figure C.27, click the **Windows Setup** tab, select the **Communications** option, and then click the **Details** button.

Figure **C.27**

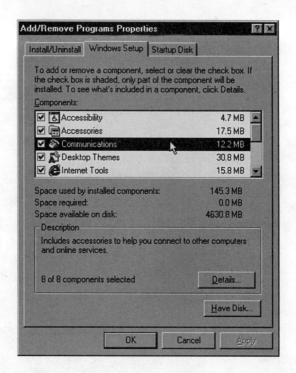

4. In the Communications dialog box, shown in Figure C.28, check any items you want to install and then click the **OK** button. Windows 98 will install the appropriate software files and drivers.

Components

Microsoft tosses around two terms: accessories and components. Now, to the average person, these might seem to be similar terms, but in Windows 98 terminology, they are not. *Accessories* refers only to those features listed in the Accessories area in the Windows Setup tab of the Add/Remove Programs Properties dialog box; *components* refers to everything else. As shown in Table C.2, components fall under 10 categories.

Figure **C.28**

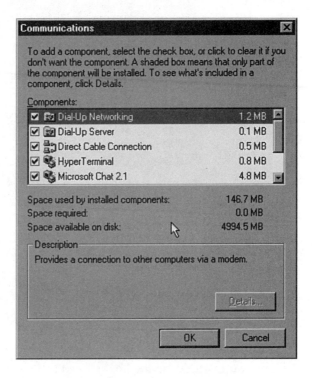

Table C.2   Components of Windows 98

Categories	Components
Accessibility	Accessibility Options
	Accessibility Tools
Communications	Dial-Up Networking
	Dial-Up Server
	Direct Cable Connection
	HyperTerminal
	Microsoft Chat 2.1
	Microsoft NetMeeting
	Phone Dialer
	Virtual Private Networking

Categories	Components
Desktop Themes	Desktop Themes (this component offers 16 graphical themes, including Baseball, Jungle, and Windows 98, as well as the support files for these themes)
Internet Tools	Microsoft FrontPage Express Microsoft VRML 2.0 Viewer Microsoft Wallet Personal Web Server Real Audio Player 4.0 Web Publishing Wizard Web-Based Enterprise Mgmt
Microsoft Outlook Express	Microsoft Outlook Express (includes the Windows Address Book)
Multilanguage Support	Baltic Central European Cyrillic Greek Turkish
Multimedia	Audio Compression CD Player DVD Player Macromedia Shockwave Director Macromedia Shockwave Flash Media Player Microsoft NetShow Player 2.0 Multimedia Sound Schemes Sample Sounds Sound Recorder Video Compression Volume Control
Online Services	America Online (AOL) AT&T WorldNet Service CompuServe Prodigy Internet The Microsoft Network (MSN)

A
B
C
D
E
F
G
H
I
J
K
L
M
N
O
P
Q
R
S
T
U
V
W
X
Y
Z

continues

A
B
C
D
E
F
G
H
I
J
K
L
M
N
O
P
Q
R
S
T
U
V
W
X
Y
Z

Table C.2   Continued

Categories	Components
System Tools	Backup
	Character Map
	Clipboard Viewer
	Driver Converter (FAT32)
	Group Policies
	Net Watcher
	System Monitor
	System Resource Meter
	WinPopup
Web TV for Windows	Wave Top Data Broadcasting
	Web TV for Windows

To install any or all of these Windows 98 components, use the Add/Remove Programs program feature of the Windows 98 Control Panel (refer to the "Add/Remove Programs" section of this book for more details).

Compression Agent

Compression Agent enables you to free hard drive disk space without a adding an extra hard drive. You free disk space with Compression Agent by compressing your files or by altering the level of the current compression rate.

note... Although you can use Compression Agent to compress files, there is a catch: You cannot compress drives using the FAT32 storage format (see the section titled "FAT32 Converter" for more details about FAT32). FAT32 is better than FAT16 in that FAT32 stores information on hard drives much more efficiently, which gives you more drive space. If your hard-disk drive is less than 512 MB (tiny by today's standards), however, FAT16 might be more efficient or at least as efficient as FAT32.

To use Compression Agent, follow these steps:

1. Click the **Start** button, and choose **Programs**, **Accessories**, **System Tools**, **Compression Agent**, as shown in Figure C.29.

Figure **C.29**

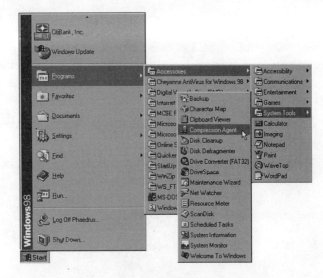

2. The Compression Agent window, shown in Figure C.30, opens. To start the compression process, click the **Start** button.

Figure **C.30**

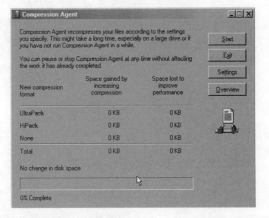

3. This tool can take several hours to run; you should not use your computer for any other functions while this utility is operational.

A
B
C
D
E
F
G
H
I
J
K
L
M
N
O
P
Q
R
S
T
U
V
W
X
Y
Z

Control Panel

The Windows 98 Control Panel is the heart of the configuration area for the operating system. In it, you will find all the major system components and the tools required for their initial configuration and usage. To use the Control Panel, follow these steps:

1. Click the **Start** button, and choose **Settings**, **Control Panel**, as shown in Figure C.31.

2. The Control Panel window, shown in Figure C.32, contains icons representing a number of tools (discussed in Table C.3).

Figure **C.31**

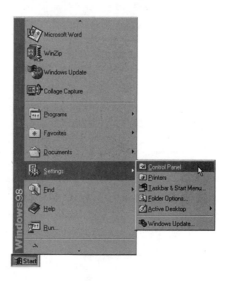

Table C.3   Windows 98 Control Panel Tools

Tool	Description
Add New Hardware	This Windows 98 wizard helps you properly install the necessary software drivers for new hardware components.
Add/Remove Programs	This Windows 98 wizard helps you properly install the necessary software programs for new Windows 98 applications.

Tool	Description
Date/Time	This component helps you set the time, date, and time zone for your personal computer.
Desktop Themes	This component installs as a part of the Desktop Themes accessory. It is used to set up fancy colors, fonts, sounds, backgrounds, and mouse pointers for your PC.
Display	This component prompts you with the Display Properties dialog box, where you configure such features as the monitor, screen saver, Active Desktop, and color schemes.
Find Fast	This Microsoft Office component speeds your computer's capability to locate all of your Microsoft Office-created files.
Fonts	Use this feature to add, change, or delete screen and printer fonts from the Windows 98 operating system.
Game Controllers	Use this feature to configure joysticks, steering wheels, and so forth for use with the Windows 98 operating system.
Internet	Use this feature to configure the Internet Explorer 4 web browser.
Keyboard	Use this feature to configure the language, click blink, and character-speed rate of the PC keyboard for use with the Windows 98 operating system.
Mail and Fax	Use this function to control the property settings of the Inbox, including email, fax, Exchange mail, personal folders, and the Microsoft Outlook client software configurations.

continues

A
B
C
D
E
F
G
H
I
J
K
L
M
N
O
P
Q
R
S
T
U
V
W
X
Y
Z

A
B
C
D
E
F
G
H
I
J
K
L
M
N
O
P
Q
R
S
T
U
V
W
X
Y
Z

Table C.3   Continued

Tool	Description
MegaDial	This is a Cypress Research Corp. component that installs as a part of that telephony application. This component does not ship with the Microsoft Windows 98 operating system software; rather, it is an add-on component provided by the OEM manufacturer of my home computer.
Microsoft Mail Postoffice	Use this feature to set up and configure an email post office for use with a peer-to-peer Windows 98 network group.
Modems	Use this feature to confirm modem settings, as well as to perform basic diagnostic checks on already-installed modems.
Mouse	Use this feature to modify the manner in which the attached PC mouse works, including its pointer attributes.
Mpact Mediaware	This Dolby Laboratories component installs as a part of a multimedia application. This component does not ship with the Microsoft Windows 98 operating system software; rather, it is an add-on component provided by the OEM manufacturer of my home computer's multimedia features.
MS DTC	This icon is used to modify the transactional DTC client software configuration that was created for use with the Windows 98 Personal Web Server.
Multimedia	Use this feature to modify the manner in which the attached audio, video, MIDI, CD music, and other multimedia devices map through the PC system.

Tool	Description
Network	This Windows 98 component is required for the configuration of any networking function, including peer-to-peer, Dial-Up Networking, and connecting a Windows 98 PC to the Internet, or to a NetWare, Windows NT, or Banyan VINES system.
32-bit ODBC	This Microsoft Office component, which is installed as part of the Office software, might also appear in the Control Panel as a result of other installed 32-bit computer applications that require Open Database Connectivity (ODBC) features.
Passwords	Windows 98 passwords, some network passwords, Windows 98 Remote Administration, and user profiles can all be configured through this component.
Power Management	This component is best used with corporate or mobile computers, in that power-saving modes are configurable for hard drives, monitors, and the Windows 98 computer system as a whole. For the home user, this component is probably best left off because it can be rather annoying.
Printers	Windows 98 printers can be configured through use of this Control Panel function. This feature operates in the same manner as the Printers feature that appears in the Start menu.
Regional Settings	This component controls the localization of the Windows 98 operating system, including the system language; time, dates, and currency formats; and the number and calendar types.

continues

A
B
C
D
E
F
G
H
I
J
K
L
M
N
O
P
Q
R
S
T
U
V
W
X
Y
Z

A
B
C
D
E
F
G
H
I
J
K
L
M
N
O
P
Q
R
S
T
U
V
W
X
Y
Z

Table C.3   Continued

Tool	Description
Sounds	Windows 98 system event sounds are configured via this Control Panel option.
System	Use this option to configure full system components such as hardware devices, hardware startup profiles, system performance, cache sizes, and the viewing of system information including IRQs, I/O ports, DMA channels, and memory addresses.
TelePath for Windows with X2	This 3Com component installs as a part of that modem application. This component does not ship with the Microsoft Windows 98 operating system software; rather, it is an add-on component provided by the OEM manufacturer of my home computer's modem.
Telephony	The telephony feature permits you to predefine calling cards, and to configure telephony software drivers and Dial-Up Networking options.
Tweak UI	This Windows 98 component installs as a part of the Windows 98 Resource Kit. It enables you to modify Windows 98's look and feel by changing the desktop and IE4 policies, and so forth. Tweak UI is *not* a supported Windows 98 component, meaning that you cannot call Microsoft's Technical Support line and expect someone there to answer any of your questions or help you with any configuration issues. Tweak UI is aimed at power users who want easier access methods to some of the less-customizable functions of the Windows 98 operating system.

Tool	Description
Users	Use this feature to set up a PC for use with multiple users. It has a wizard feature that walks you step-by-step through its installation process.
Accessibility Options	Use this feature to modify the Windows 98 for users with vision, hearing, or dexterity problems.

Figure **C.32**

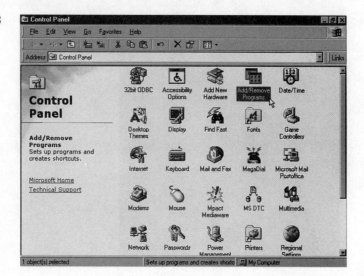

A
B
C
D
E
F
G
H
I
J
K
L
M
N
O
P
Q
R
S
T
U
V
W
X
Y
Z

D

A
B
C

D

E
F
G
H
I
J
K
L
M
N
O
P
Q
R
S
T
U
V
W
X
Y
Z

Date/Time

Windows 98 keeps track of the system date and time for the computer. As shown in Figure D.1, you can easily view the date by hovering your mouse pointer over the time display, which appears on the right end of the taskbar.

Figure **D.1**

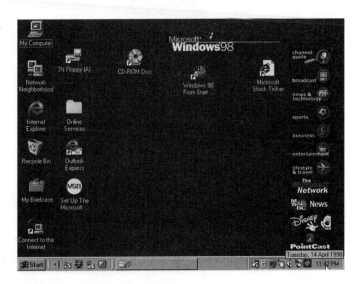

To set the month, day, year, and time zone, follow these steps:

1. Double-click the time display on the taskbar to open the Date/Time Properties dialog box, shown in Figure D.2.

2. To change the date—for example, to February 9, 1998—click **9** in the calendar display, select **February** from the Month drop-down list, and click the up- or down-arrow button next to the Year text box to change the year to 1998.

3. To change the time, click the up- or down-arrow button beneath the clock.

4. To change the time zone, first click the **Time Zone** tab to open the screen shown in Figure D.3.

Figure **D.2**

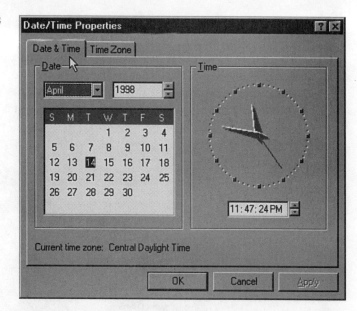

Figure **D.3**

5. If your time zone uses Daylight Saving Time, click the **Automatically Adjust Clock for Daylight Saving Changes** check box. (Note that when these daylight saving days arrive, you will be prompted with a dialog box

A
B
C
D
E
F
G
H
I
J
K
L
M
N
O
P
Q
R
S
T
U
V
W
X
Y
Z

informing you of the change to make sure that you are aware that a date change was performed.) Windows 98 will automatically update itself twice a year to reflect Daylight Saving Time changes. To change the time zone itself, click the down-arrow button near the top of the tab and select another time zone from the drop-down list, as shown in Figure D.4. When you are satisfied with your selection, click **OK**.

Figure **D.4**

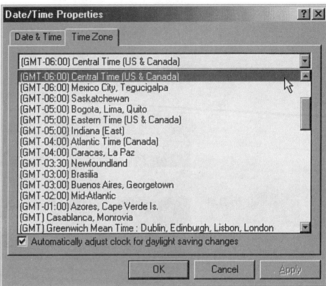

note... Notice the parenthetical items containing the initials GMT that appear in every Time Zone entry. As you might expect, GMT stands for Greenwich Mean Time, and the numeral following it (if any) indicates how many hours that time zone is ahead of or behind Greenwich Mean Time.

Desktop

The Windows 98 desktop is the primary screen from which all activities originate; it is the screen you see when you first enter Windows 98. This screen typically contains a series of icons—including My Computer, Network Neighborhood, and Recycle Bin—as well as a Channel bar that enables you to easily reach Internet content. The desktop can also be enabled as the Windows 98 Active Desktop, a concept that was discussed earlier in this book.

Desktop Themes

Desktop Themes, which are built in to Windows 98, enable you to easily change your desktop background (also known as *wallpaper*), screen saver, sound events, mouse pointer graphics, system colors, desktop icon graphics, and system display fonts. Microsoft is releasing several additional variations to these Desktop Themes in its Windows 98 add-on product known as Microsoft Plus! 98, which should be available about 30 days following the initial Windows 98 release date of June 25 1998. To use these themes, follow these steps:

1. Click the **Start** button, choose **Settings**, **Control Panel**, as shown in Figure D.5.

Figure **D.5**

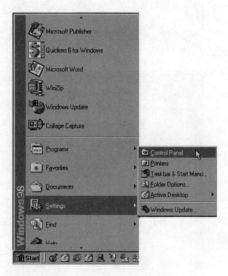

2. In the Control Panel window, shown in Figure D.6, double-click the **Desktop Themes** icon.

3. In the Desktop Themes screen, shown in Figure D.7, notice that all the check boxes in the **Settings** section are grayed out. This indicates that you cannot change any of the current themes' settings.

4. To switch to a different theme, click the down-arrow button to the right of the **Theme** text box, and select a new theme from the list of available themes (as shown in Figure D.8).

A
B
C
D
E
F
G
H
I
J
K
L
M
N
O
P
Q
R
S
T
U
V
W
X
Y
Z

A
B
C
D
E
F
G
H
I
J
K
L
M
N
O
P
Q
R
S
T
U
V
W
X
Y
Z

Figure **D.6**

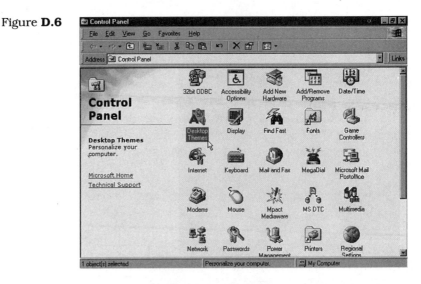

Figure **D.7**

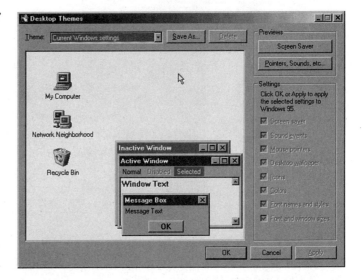

5. As shown in Figure D.9, a preview of the selected theme (in this case, Inside Your Computer) is provided. Notice that the check boxes in the Settings section are no longer grayed out. Uncheck any of the settings to see how the preview changes.

Figure **D.8**

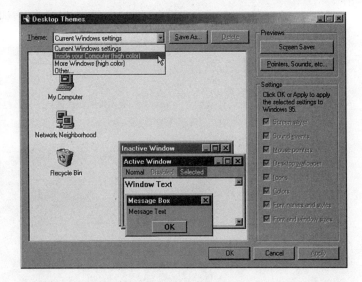

Figure **D.9**

6. After you are satisfied with the theme you have chosen and any modifications you have made, click the **OK** button.

A
B
C
D
E
F
G
H
I
J
K
L
M
N
O
P
Q
R
S
T
U
V
W
X
Y
Z

A
B
C
D
E
F
G
H
I
J
K
L
M
N
O
P
Q
R
S
T
U
V
W
X
Y
Z

Dial-Up Networking

The Dial-Up Networking feature of Windows 98 enables you to connect to a remote network via a modem. To configure a Dial-Up Networking session, follow these steps:

1. Click the **Start** button, choose **Programs**, **Accessories**, **Communications**, **Dial-Up Networking**, as shown in Figure D.10.

Figure **D.10**

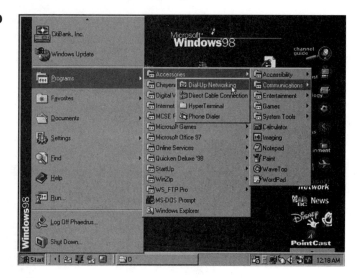

2. Double-click the **Make New Connection** icon in the Dial-Up Networking window, shown in Figure D.11, to start the Make New Connection Wizard. This wizard walks you through the steps of creating a Dial-Up Networking connection.

3. Type a name for the new connection in the text box at the top of the wizard's first screen, shown in Figure D.12. (In this case, leave the name as the default, My Connection.)

4. Select a modem device from the Select a Device drop-down list (click the down-arrow button next to the text box to view the list). The default modem will typically be the one you want to use unless you have multiple modems connected to your PC. When you are satisfied with your selections, click **Next**.

Figure **D.11**

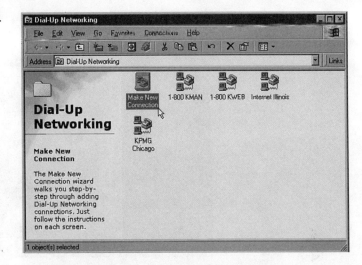

Figure **D.12**

5. In the screen shown in Figure D.13, type the telephone number of the computer to which you will be connecting. (This computer will typically belong to your Internet service provider.) Be sure to select the correct country code. (The one shown here is the default.) Click **Next** to continue.

A
B
C
D
E
F
G
H
I
J
K
L
M
N
O
P
Q
R
S
T
U
V
W
X
Y
Z

A
B
C
D
E
F
G
H
I
J
K
L
M
N
O
P
Q
R
S
T
U
V
W
X
Y
Z

Figure **D.13**

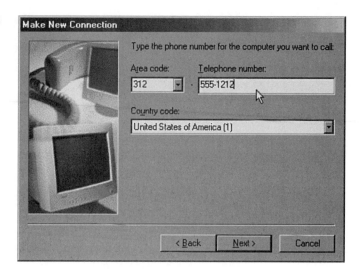

6. Click on the **Finish** button in the wizard's final screen, shown in Figure D.14. Doing so returns you to the Dial-Up Networking window.

Figure **D.14**

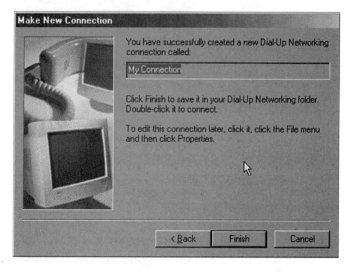

7. Notice that the connection you created using the wizard now appears in the Dial-Up Networking window, as shown in Figure D.15.

Figure **D.15**

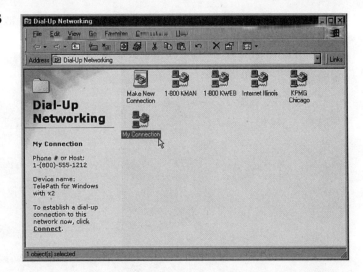

You can either wait until you use this connection to confirm that the default telephony settings suit your needs, or you can confirm that those settings are correct now by viewing them in the My Connection dialog box. To check these settings using the latter technique, follow these steps:

1. Right-click the newly created **My Connection** icon and choose **Properties** from the ensuing shortcut menu, as shown in Figure D.16.

Figure **D.16**

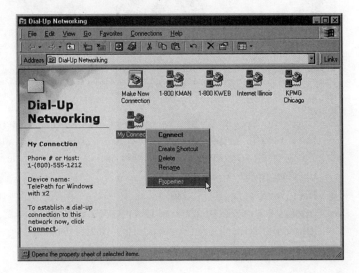

A
B
C
D
E
F
G
H
I
J
K
L
M
N
O
P
Q
R
S
T
U
V
W
X
Y
Z

A

B

C

D

E

F

G

H

I

J

K

L

M

N

O

P

Q

R

S

T

U

V

W

X

Y

Z

2. You can make changes to the telephone number and the modem selection in the General tab of the My Connection dialog box, shown in Figure D.17, but you just entered this information while using the Make New Connection Wizard.

Figure **D.17**

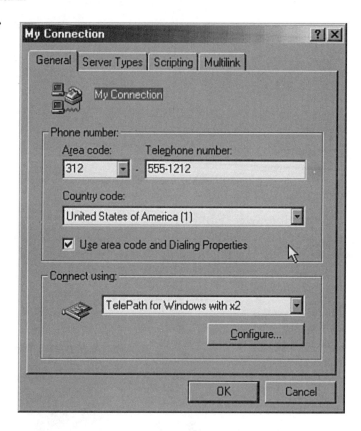

3. Click the **Server Types** tab to view the screen shown in Figure D.18. For most non-Internet connections, this tab's default settings are adequate. If you seek to connect to an Internet service provider (ISP), however, you need to make a few changes.

4. Because the Internet supports only the use of TCP/IP, you should uncheck the **NetBEUI** and **IPX/SPX Compatible** check boxes in the Allowed Network Protocols section of the Server Types tab to free system resources.

Figure **D.18**

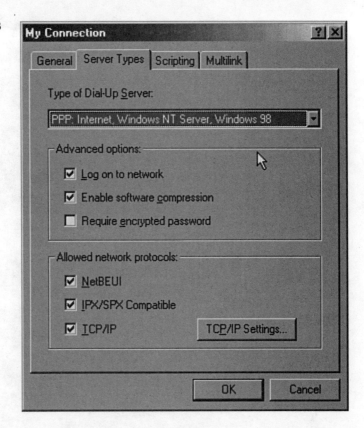

5. To configure your TCP/IP connection, click th **TCP/IP Settings** button. This opens the TCP/IP Setting dialog box, show in Figure D.19.

6. Most likely, the only settings your ISP will ask you to change are the primary and secondary DNS (domain name server) numbers. To do so, select the **Specify Name Server Addresses** option and type the appropriate primary DNS, secondary DNS, primary WINS, and secondary WINS. A typical address might be `10.10.5.100`. The information that goes into these address boxes will be provided by your Internet service provider (or local system administrator, should you be doing this at work). Click **OK** to return to the Server Types tab of the My Connection dialog box.

A
B
C
D
E
F
G
H
I
J
K
L
M
N
O
P
Q
R
S
T
U
V
W
X
Y
Z

Figure **D.19**

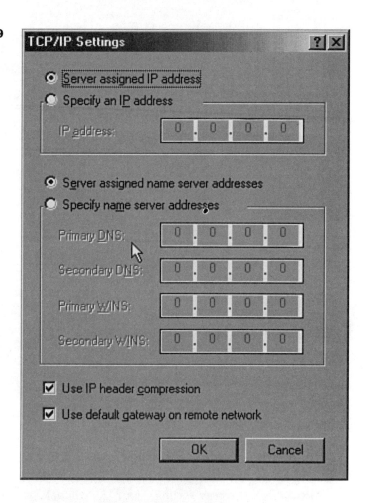

tip...   DNS addresses represent the TCP/IP address for that particular DNS server. When you connect to the Internet via your local ISP, all you usually need is that ISP's DNS addressing scheme. This usually comes in the form of the primary and the secondary DNS addresses.

7. Click the **Multilink** tab to view the screen shown in Figure D.20. This screen enables you to use more than one modem and telephone line at a time to increase bandwidth. To do so, begin by selecting the **Use Additional Devices** option, and then click the **Add** button to place additional modems in the Multilink tab.

Figure **D.20**

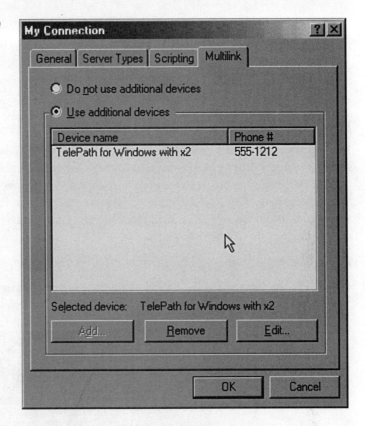

A
B
C
D
E
F
G
H
I
J
K
L
M
N
O
P
Q
R
S
T
U
V
W
X
Y
Z

note... You must have a distinctly separate telephone line for each modem placed in this tab; a party line will not work for this purpose.

note... If you are a home user, you probably will not use this feature.

note... To access the Add button on the Multilink tab, you must have multiple modems already installed and available for use. If the Add button is not grayed out, you can click it and select additional modems to be used with the Multilink process. If it is grayed out, you must add more modems to your Windows 98 installation to use this feature. To do this, and add a modem to the selection list, use either the Add New Hardware or the Modems functions of the Windows 98 Control Panel.

A
B
C
D
E
F
G
H
I
J
K
L
M
N
O
P
Q
R
S
T
U
V
W
X
Y
Z

8. To accept all the changes made in the My Connection dialog box and return to the Dial-Up Networking window, click the **OK** button. Close that window by clicking the **Close button** (×) that appears in the upper-right corner of the window.

Dial-Up Server

The Windows 98 Dial-Up Server feature enables you to use your own PC as a server to which other computers can dial up for remote access. This feature cannot be configured unless you have installed the proper files for the Dial-Up Networking function. (Refer to the "Components" section for information about installing components, and refer to the "Dial-Up Networking" section for more information about this feature.)

To configure the Dial-Up Server feature, follow these steps:

1. Click the **Start** button, choose **Programs**, **Accessories**, **Communications**, and **Dial-Up Networking**, as shown in Figure D.21.

Figure **D.21**

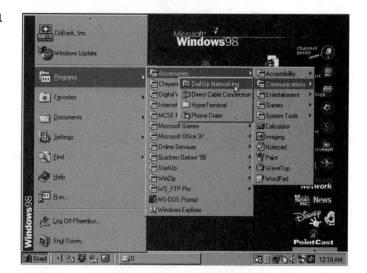

2. Click the **Connections** menu option and select **Dial-Up Server**, as shown in Figure D.22.

Figure **D.22**

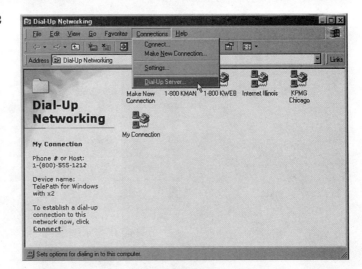

3. The ensuing Dial-Up Server dialog box, shown in Figure D.23, enables you to configure this service. To permit others to dial into your PC, select the **Allow Caller Access** option. Next, click the **Server Type** button to specify what type of dial-up connectivity is supported by your PC.

Figure **D.23**

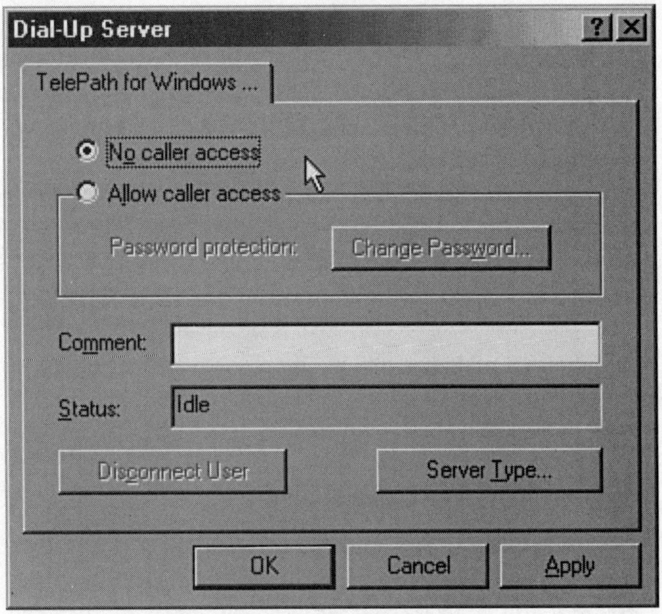

A
B
C
D
E
F
G
H
I
J
K
L
M
N
O
P
Q
R
S
T
U
V
W
X
Y
Z

4. Because you are using Windows 98, select the **PPP: Internet, Windows NT Server, Windows 98** option from the **Type of Dial-Up Server** drop-down list in the Server Types dialog box, as shown in Figure D.24.

Figure **D.24**

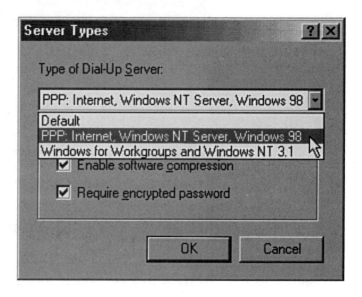

5. If the clients dialing in are not necessarily going to be using Windows 95, Windows 98, or Windows NT, you should uncheck the **Require Encrypted Password** check box because non-Windows clients might have difficulty transmitting an encrypted password.

note... The Enable Software Compression option should be left as is (selected), unless your modem's hardware functions better (that is, it can transmit more data in the same period of time) than the software compression that is built in to Windows 98.

6. Click the **OK** button in the Server Types dialog box, and then in the Dial-Up Server dialog box to complete this process.

Direct Cable Connection

The Direct Cable Connection feature is useful if you want to exchange files between two computers but you don't want to set up a network. To configure a direct cable connection, follow these steps:

1. Click the **Start** button, choose **Programs**, **Accessories**, **Communications**, **Direct Cable Connection**, as shown in Figure D.25.

Figure **D.25**

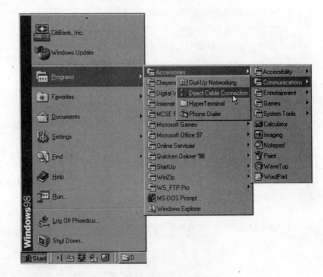

2. The Direct Cable Connection Wizard opens. In the first screen, shown in Figure D.26, you must specify whether you are currently using the Host computer or the Guest computer. After you make your selection (for this example, choose **Guest**), click **Next**.

Figure **D.26**

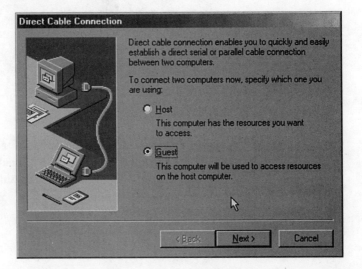

A
B
C
D
E
F
G
H
I
J
K
L
M
N
O
P
Q
R
S
T
U
V
W
X
Y
Z

note... The *host* computer contains the resources that you want to access; the *guest* computer is the system that will be performing the accessing. It is important to note, however, that regardless the connection type, a guest computer can still copy its own files to the host computer. This means that a guest computer can *act* like a host computer even though it is the guest.

note... To begin the connection process, you must have a serial or parallel cable to connect the two computers.

3. In the ensuing screen, shown in Figure D.27, highlight the connection method—parallel or serial—along with the port on which the connection will be made.

Figure **D.27**

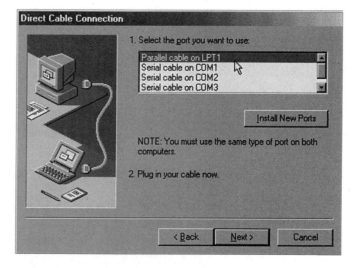

note... A *parallel cable* connects into the parallel port of each computer—on the guest side as well as on the host side. This cable closely resembles a standard parallel printer cable, and transfers data much faster than a serial cable could (average transmission rate is roughly three times faster over a parallel cable than a serial one).

A *serial cable* connects into a serial port of each computer—on the guest side, as well as on the host side. Note that it can be connected to the COM1: port on the guest side, while using the COM2: port on the host side. The serial cable closely resembles a standard modem cable, and provides a relatively slow transmission rate (especially when compared to that of a parallel cable).

4. Connect the serial or parallel cable to both computers. If you do not know how to do this, consult your computer's manuals.

5. Click the **Next** button to view the screen shown in Figure D.28. This dialog box informs you that you have successfully configured the guest computer. Click the **Finish** button.

Figure **D.28**

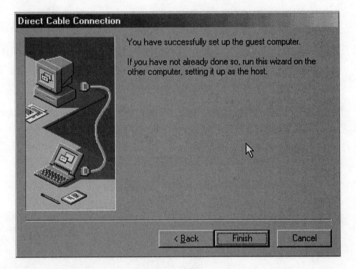

6. Before a direct cable connection can be made, you must run the same wizard process on the other computer and configure it as the host computer (just select the **Host** option in step 2). After you complete the steps in the wizard, click **Finish**.

7. If the dialog box shown in Figure D.29 (or one like it) appears after you click the **Finish** button, you should check to make sure that the cable connections are solid.

A
B
C
D
E
F
G
H
I
J
K
L
M
N
O
P
Q
R
S
T
U
V
W
X
Y
Z

A
B
C
D
E
F
G
H
I
J
K
L
M
N
O
P
Q
R
S
T
U
V
W
X
Y
Z

Figure **D.29**

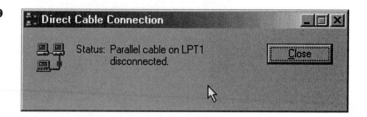

8. After the connection is complete and you have transferred all the data that you want, click on the **Close** button to terminate the direct cable connection. Remember that after you click on the **Close** button, the session will end and you can no longer use that direct cable connection session.

Discover Windows 98

Microsoft's Discover Windows 98 application demonstrates a vast improvement over the online assistance offered in Windows 95. To use this new online tutorial, follow these steps:

1. Click the **Start** button, choose **Programs**, **Accessories**, **System Tools**, **Welcome To Windows**, as shown in Figure D.30.

Figure **D.30**

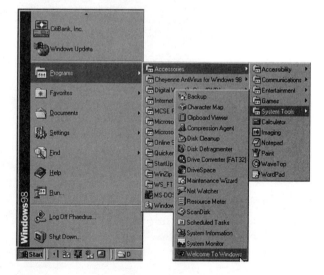

2. To begin the tour, click the **Discover Windows 98** option in the Welcome to Windows 98 screen, shown in Figure D.31.

Figure **D.31**

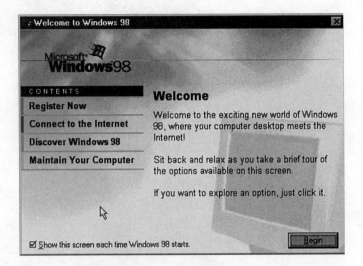

tip...   Note the Show This Screen Each Time Windows 98 Starts check box at the bottom of the screen shown in Figure D.30. If you leave this option checked (the default), you will automatically see this screen every time you start Windows 98. To disable this option, just click it to remove the check box.

3. Click the **Discover Windows 98** option to change the text message to the right of the menu, as shown in Figure D.32.

4. As shown in Figure D.33, the Discover Windows 98 tour is split into four components:

   - Computer Essentials   This section, for people who are new to Windows, walks the user through the basics of using the mouse and keyboard, and teaches basic maneuvering skills.

   - Windows 98 Overview   This section is for people who are familiar with a Windows 3.x environment.

   - What's New   This section is for people who are upgrading to Windows 98 from Windows 95.

   - More Windows 98 Resources

A
B
C
D
E
F
G
H
I
J
K
L
M
N
O
P
Q
R
S
T
U
V
W
X
Y
Z

A
B
C
D
E
F
G
H
I
J
K
L
M
N
O
P
Q
R
S
T
U
V
W
X
Y
Z

Figure **D.32**

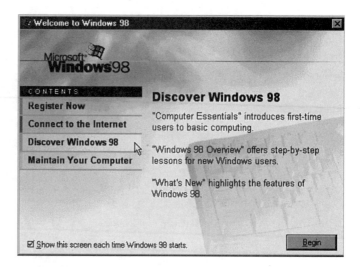

Figure **D.33**

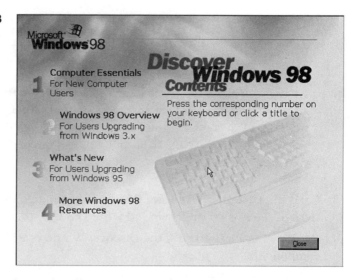

5. Click the **Computer Essentials** option to view the screen shown in Figure D.34. You can continue the tour as long as you like, and can quit at any time.

Figure **D.34**

6. After you finish with the tutorial, you will be presented with a message asking whether you are sure you want to close the Discover Windows 98 tutorial session. Click **Yes** to end the process.

Disk Cleanup

The Disk Cleanup function is an automated way for Windows 98 to delete extraneous files such as temporary Internet files, other temporary files, downloaded ActiveX and Java program applets, documents in the Recycle Bin, temporary Windows 98 files, and remove the Windows 98 uninstall information. To use the Disk Cleanup feature, follow these steps:

1. Click the **Start** button, choose **Programs**, **Accessories**, **System Tools**, **Disk Cleanup**, as shown in Figure D.35.

2. The first Disk Cleanup dialog box, shown in Figure D.36, shows Windows 98's progress as it determines how much hard drive space can be saved by the Disk Cleanup program.

3. After Disk Cleanup determines how much space will be saved, the screen shown in Figure D.37 appears. In the Disk Cleanup tab, place a check mark next to the types of files you want removed, and then click **OK**.

A
B
C
D
E
F
G
H
I
J
K
L
M
N
O
P
Q
R
S
T
U
V
W
X
Y
Z

A
B
C
D
E
F
G
H
I
J
K
L
M
N
O
P
Q
R
S
T
U
V
W
X
Y
Z

Figure **D.35**

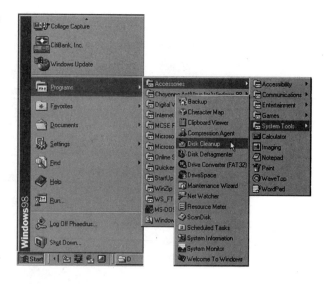

Figure **D.36**

note... Click the **View Files** button to view a list of files contained within the highlighted bin. In the case of Figure D.37, clicking the **View Files** button would reveal the names of the temporary Internet files that you are about to delete. The **View Files** button is only present for use with temporary Internet files, downloaded program files, and the Recycle Bin.

note... If you use the Internet as much as I do (which is about 30 to 45 minutes daily), the Temporary Internet Files entry will probably contain most of the disk-cleanup opportunities.

4. If the Total Space to Be Cleaned section of the Disk Cleanup tab reads 0 MB, click the **More Options** tab, shown in Figure D.38.

Figure **D.37**

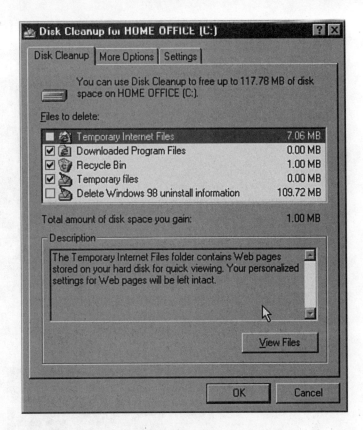

warning... Be very careful about deleting files that you do not understand. In the case of Recycle Bin and temporary Internet files, this warning might not apply. But with the others, please think about what you are doing prior to performing the cleanup process. It is always better to be safe than sorry when it comes to your PC.

5. Click the **Clean Up** button in the Windows Components area to open the Windows Setup tab of the Add/Remove Programs Properties dialog box, shown in Figure D.39. (For more information about this dialog box, refer to the section titled "Add/Remove Programs.") From here, you can safely delete any nice-to-have-but-not-necessary Windows 98 options. If you don't have vision or dexterity problems, for example, consider deleting the Accessibility Options. (Refer to the section titled "Accessibility Options" for more information about this feature.) This can save as much as 6 MB of hard drive space.

A
B
C
D
E
F
G
H
I
J
K
L
M
N
O
P
Q
R
S
T
U
V
W
X
Y
Z

Figure **D.38**

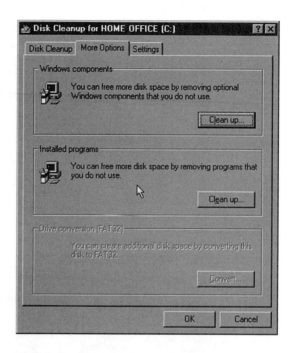

Figure **D.39**

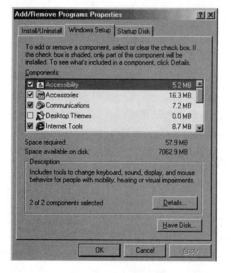

6. After you have made your selections, click the **OK** button to process the changes. This returns you to the Disk Cleanup screen.

7. Click the **Clean Up** button in the Installed Programs area to open the Install/Uninstall tab of the Add/Remove Programs Properties dialog box, shown in Figure D.40 (for more information about this dialog box, refer to the section titled "Add/Remove Programs"). From here, you can safely delete any third-party applications that you do not require by selecting them in the list and clicking the **Add/Remove** button.

Figure **D.40**

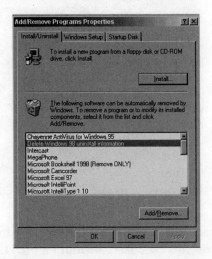

8. After you finish deleting/removing programs, click the **OK** button to exit the dialog box. This returns you to the Disk Cleanup screen.

note... It is strongly recommended that you do not remove applications you do not recognize, unless you are the only user of the PC and it is a computer for home use. Deleting things you do not understand can lead to computing oblivion.

Disk Defragmenter

The Windows 98 Disk Defragmenter enables you to rearrange files on your hard drive so that software programs can find files faster. This, in turn, will help applications run faster. Another plus of the Disk Defragmenter is that it automatically rearranges the free disk space on your hard drive, which might give you more free space to work with. To use the Disk Defragmenter, follow these steps:

A
B
C
D
E
F
G
H
I
J
K
L
M
N
O
P
Q
R
S
T
U
V
W
X
Y
Z

1. Click the **Start** button, choose **Programs**, **Accessories**, **System Tools**, **Disk Defragmenter**, as shown in Figure D.41.

Figure **D.41**

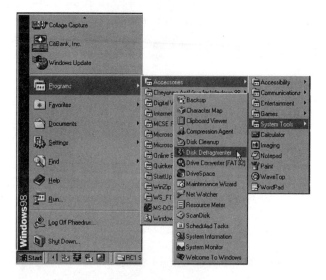

2. Select the drive you want to defragment from the drop-down list in the ensuing Select Drive dialog box, shown in Figure D.42. Click **Settings** to continue.

Figure **D.42**

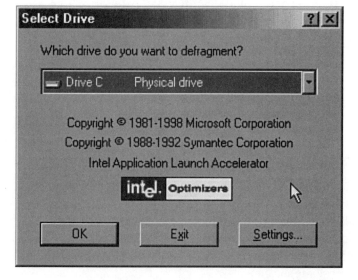

3. Use the Disk Defragmenter Settings dialog box, shown in Figure D.43, to configure the disk defragmentation process either for every defragmentation operation or for only the current one. I recommend that you check both options in the When Defragmenting My Hard Drive section (note, however, that checking these options slows the defragmentation process) and that you use these options every time you defragment your hard drive. After you make your selections, click **OK** to start Defragmenter.

Figure **D.43**

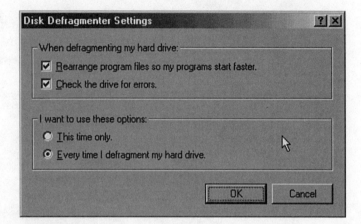

note... Disk Defragmenter's help text states that you can run other programs while using Disk Defragmenter. Although this might technically be a true statement, it is strongly recommended that you run Disk Defragmenter program by itself because Disk Defragmenter greatly affects the performance of other running programs. Even worse, running other programs, such as word processors, alongside Disk Defragmenter can cause Disk Defragmenter to continually lose its place and start over because word processors and other programs write to the hard drive that Defragmenter is trying to defragment. I have seen people use Disk Defragmenter throughout the course of an entire day, never finishing the process while dramatically slowing their PCs.

Even when other applications aren't running, Defragmenter can take a long time to complete. Do not fret if it takes several hours to run the Disk Defragmenter utility, especially if it has been a long time since you last ran this utility. I recommend that you run Defragmenter during

continues

A
B
C

D

E
F
G
H
I
J
K
L
M
N
O
P
Q
R
S
T
U
V
W
X
Y
Z

A
B
C
D
E
F
G
H
I
J
K
L
M
N
O
P
Q
R
S
T
U
V
W
X
Y
Z

continued

a down time, such as during lunch, just as you are leaving work (letting it run overnight while you are out of the office), or just before you go to bed. One way to avoid some of the headaches you are bound for is to use the Task Scheduler component of Windows 98. Refer to the section titled "Task Scheduler" for more information.

4. During the defragmentation process, you will see a dialog box containing a progress bar, as shown in Figure D.44. If you want to end the defragmentation process prior to its completion, click the **Stop** button.

Figure **D.44**

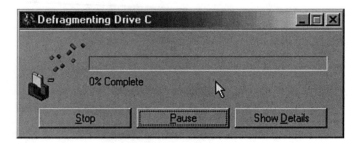

5. You are presented with a completion box. Click **Accept** (it is your only choice), and the program will end automatically.

Disk Management

The art of disk management is only as complex as you make it. That is, how you arrange programs and directories on your hard drive largely depends on your own organizational skills or lack thereof.

The Windows 98 Explorer feature provides a directory-tree structure for finding files and folders (in Windows 98, a subdirectory is known as a *folder*). When viewed through Explorer, a folder looks just as you might expect: like a manila folder. When you click a folder, the icon changes from a closed manila folder to an open one, and the contents of the folder are revealed. The applications you use are typically spread among multiple folders.

Most programs produced by commercial companies (such as Microsoft) probably install in the `C:\Program Files` directory. This, for the most part, is helpful because it leaves you with a common starting point for most of the applications on your hard drive. Some commercial packages, however, do not follow this trend, nor do some applications that you produce yourself. It does not hurt anything to install applications all over the hard drive, but it might make it more confusing to find them by using the Windows 98 Explorer feature.

As a rule of thumb, you should minimize the number of files that you copy or install into your root (**C:**) directory. This will make troubleshooting Windows 98 operating system errors a bit easier, and might limit problems that can occur as a result of copying too many similarly named files to the same directory.

note...   By *file*, I mean documents, spreadsheets, and the like—not file directories.

For more information about disk management, see the following sections in this book:

- Add/Remove Programs
- File Management
- Windows Explorer

Display Options

Windows 98 display options enable you to change how your computer desktop is displayed, as well as to manipulate the various screen fonts and colors that will be present throughout the many Windows applications on your PC. To make changes to the display options, follow these steps:

1. Right-click a blank portion of the desktop and choose **Properties** from the ensuing shortcut menu, as shown in Figure D.45.

2. The Display Properties dialog box appears with the Background tab selected by default, as shown in Figure D.46. Here you can specify an HTML document or picture to use as a background for your desktop.

note...   The tabs in your Display Properties dialog box might differ slightly from the ones shown here. The core tabs—which you will have on your machine—are Background, Screen Saver, Appearance, Effects, Settings, and Web. The STB Vision tab shown in Figure D.46 pertains specifically to the video card that came with my PC. Chances are that your computer will have a vendor-specific tab as well.

A
B
C
D
E
F
G
H
I
J
K
L
M
N
O
P
Q
R
S
T
U
V
W
X
Y
Z

A
B
C
D
E
F
G
H
I
J
K
L
M
N
O
P
Q
R
S
T
U
V
W
X
Y
Z

Figure **D.45**

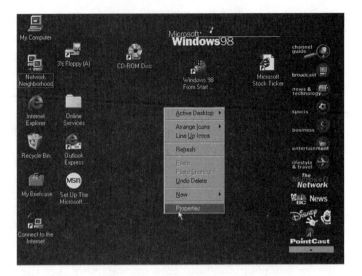

Figure **D.46**

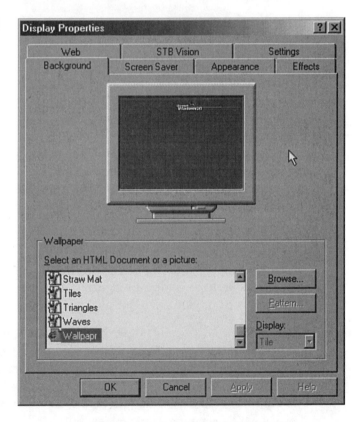

3. Click the **Screen Saver** tab to view the screen shown in Figure D.47.
   Here you can choose a screen saver to be displayed on your machine,
   establish how long your computer must be idle before the screen-saver
   image is displayed, and, if desired, set a password for returning to your
   work after the screen saver has been displayed.

Figure **D.47**

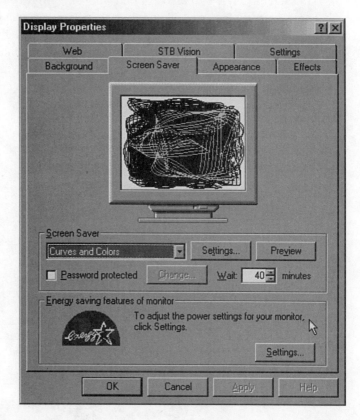

note... The original purpose of screen savers was to prevent a phenomenon
known as *burn-in,* in which a faint image of the contents of your screen
remained present even after you turned off your computer. Although
people with older monitors still use screen savers for this purpose,
screen savers are now used primarily for entertainment value.

A
B
C
D
E
F
G
H
I
J
K
L
M
N
O
P
Q
R
S
T
U
V
W
X
Y
Z

note...   Details on modifying screen-saver components, as well as further instructions on configuring a screen saver, can be found in the section titled "Screen Savers."

4. The Screen Saver tab also enables you to configure your monitor's energy-saving features. To change these settings click the **Settings** button, make your choices in the ensuing dialog box (shown in Figure D.48), and click **OK** to return to the Display Properties dialog box. Note that these same settings can be changed through the Windows 98 Power Management option found in the Control Panel (refer to the "Power Management" section for more information).

Figure **D.48**

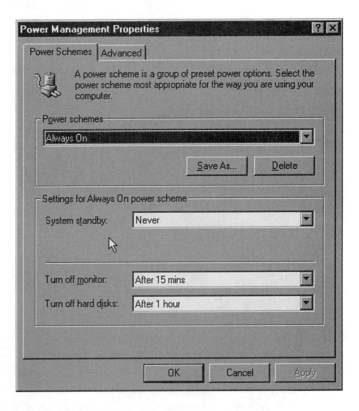

note...   If the Settings button is grayed out, that indicates that your monitor does not support energy-saving features.

5. To modify the PC colors, fonts, and general appearance, click the **Appearance** tab. Click the down-arrow button to the right of the Scheme text box to view the Scheme drop-down list, shown in Figure D.49. Select the scheme you want from the list; a preview of the scheme will appear in the display window above the Scheme text box.

Figure **D.49**

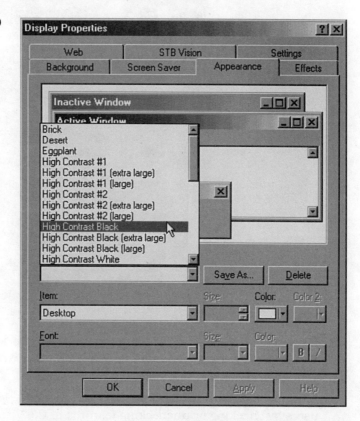

6. Click the **Effects** tab to view the screen shown in Figure D.50. Here you can change the icons associated with various Windows 98 features. Select the icon you want to change in the Desktop Icons area, and then click the **Change Icon** button.

7. The dialog box shown in Figure D.51 prompts you for the name of a file that contains Windows-compatible icon graphics. After you have entered the filename, press the **Enter** key; any available icons will appear in the box. Click **OK** to return to the Effects tab of the Display Properties dialog box after you have made your selection.

A
B
C
D
E
F
G
H
I
J
K
L
M
N
O
P
Q
R
S
T
U
V
W
X
Y
Z

A
B
C
D
E
F
G
H
I
J
K
L
M
N
O
P
Q
R
S
T
U
V
W
X
Y
Z

Figure **D.50**

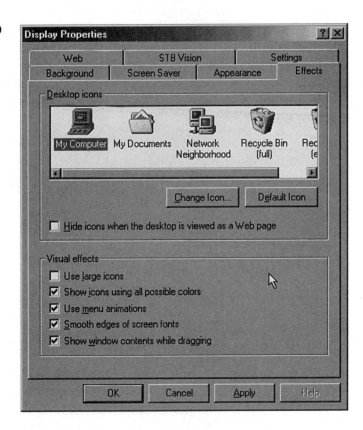

8. If you want to hide icons when using the Active Desktop feature of Windows 98, click the **Hide Icons When the Desktop Is Viewed as a Web Page** check box in the Effects tab.

9. Alter the manner in which icons and the Windows 98 desktop appear to users by checking or unchecking features in the Visual Effects section. Play around with these options to find the effects that please you most.

10. Click the **Web** tab to view the screen shown in Figure D.52. To use the features of the Web from Windows 98, you must first activate the Active Desktop. Do so by checking the **View My Active Desktop as a Web Page** check box. You can now add HTML and Web-related content (such as JPEG and GIF graphics, as well as animated GIF files). To add a file, click the **New** button and pick a file from your local hard drive.

Figure **D.51**

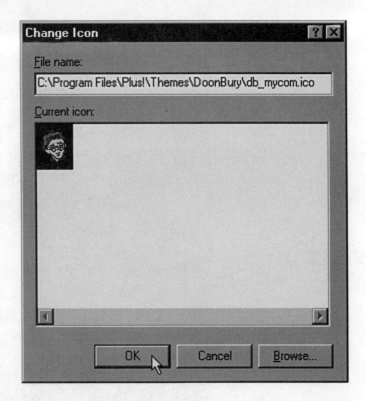

note... When you click the **New** button, you are just telling Windows 98 that you want to use an existing file (regardless of whether it is already on your hard drive). Although the content might already be on your hard drive, it is not in a location that Windows 98 can see. Following this process puts the content into the correct location so that Windows 98 can use it.

11. Click the **Settings** tab to view the screen shown in Figure D.53. This screen enables you to alter the resolution of your monitor, as well as to set the number of colors available for use.

note... The lower the screen resolution (for example, 640×480), the larger the characters and graphics will appear to be. If you were to choose a higher resolution (such as 800×600), the screen characters and graphics would appear to be smaller.

A
B
C
D
E
F
G
H
I
J
K
L
M
N
O
P
Q
R
S
T
U
V
W
X
Y
Z

Figure **D.52**

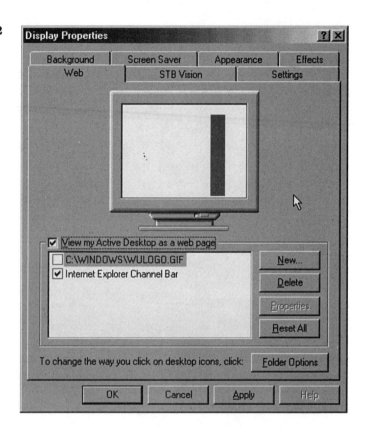

note...   If, in the Colors area, you specify that a large number of colors be used, as is the case when you select **High Color (16 bit)**, it might negatively impact your system's overall performance.

12. To accept your changes in the Display Properties dialog box and return to the desktop, click **OK**.

Document Templates

A document template is a file that permits you to easily create a certain type of document for a specific Windows 98 application. Windows 98 comes with several predefined templates, including the following:

- Microsoft HTML templates
- Notepad text files
- Bitmap images

- WordPad files
- Bricfcases

If you create your own document templates, you can better customize the starting point for document creation. The Microsoft Word template, for instance, just gives you a blank document. If you make your own template within Microsoft Word (a DOT file) and save it into the Document Templates folder for Microsoft Office (usually `C:\Program Files\Microsoft Office\Templates`), you can apply this template to your Microsoft Word documents. This becomes very useful if you create the same types of documents over and over, such as office memos that have a standard letterhead.

Documents

In Windows 98, document refers to any file you generate using a Windows 98-compatible application. For example, a document could be a business letter typed in WordPad, a spreadsheet generated in Excel, or a picture created in Paint.

Figure **D.53**

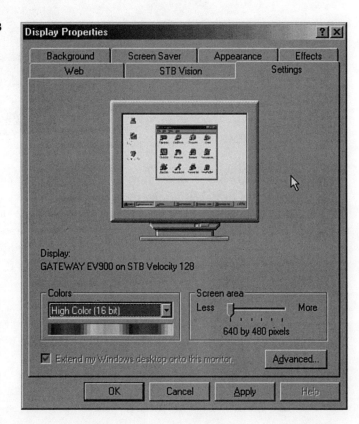

Documents Menu

The Documents menu selection found in the Windows 98 Start menu, shown
in Figure D.54, provides a quick way to access a recently used document.
To use the Documents menu, click the **Start** button and then choose
Documents. You can click a folder appearing above the solid line at the top of
the Documents menu to open that folder's window. The filenames appearing
below the solid line are the files that you have used most recently on your
computer. You can open one of these files by clicking it; Windows 98 will then
automatically start the file's application and opens that file inside the application.

Figure **D.54**

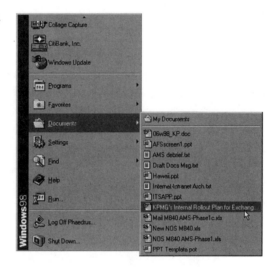

note... Not all applications are capable of putting their most recently accessed
files into this area. Typically, only 32-bit Windows applications with the
Windows 95 (or later) seal of approval will place the names of their
most recently accessed files into this holding area. It is, for the most
part, safe to assume that most Microsoft-built applications will place
their most recently used files here.

note... To learn how to delete filenames from this area, see the section titled
"Taskbar Properties."

Driver Converter (FAT32)

The purpose of the FAT32 driver converter is to help you convert your existing 16-bit FAT drives to FAT32. FAT32 is an improvement of the file allocation table (FAT) file system that improves hard drive disk space efficiency on drives larger than 512 MB. FAT32 is not recommended for users whose hard drives are smaller than 512 MB or for users who need to dual-boot between Windows 98 and another operating system (you cannot dual-boot after FAT32 has been installed).

To use Drive Converter, follow these steps:

1. Click the **Start** button, choose **Programs**, **Accessories**, **System Tools**, **Drive Converter (FAT32)**, as shown in Figure D.55.

Figure **D.55**

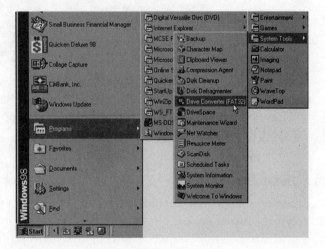

2. This starts the Drive Converter Wizard, the first screen of which is shown in Figure D.56. Click **Next** to continue.

Figure **D.56**

A
B
C
D
E
F
G
H
I
J
K
L
M
N
O
P
Q
R
S
T
U
V
W
X
Y
Z

3. In the next screen, shown in Figure D.57, click the hard drive that you want upgraded to the FAT32 format, and then click **Next**.

Figure **D.57**

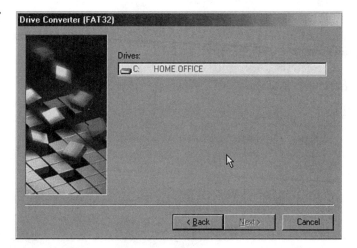

4. Carefully follow the rest of the wizard's prompts. When you finish, you will have a hard drive whose contents are now properly converted into the FAT32 format.

DriveSpace

DriveSpace enables you to artificially expand the size of your hard drive, which enables you to save more information on that hard drive, even though its physical size has not changed. DriveSpace might seem a bit like magic; it just uses a different storage algorithm for mapping bytes of information to a drive.

note... DriveSpace 3 is not compatible with a FAT32-formatted hard drive. Therefore, if you are using FAT32, this application is not for you. When you run out of space on FAT32, you will need to purchase another hard drive.

To use DriveSpace, follow these steps:

1. Click the **Start** button, choose **Programs**, **Accessories**, **System Tools**, **DriveSpace**, as shown in Figure D.58.

2. This opens the DriveSpace 3 window. To compress a drive, click the **Drive** menu and choose **Compress**, as shown in Figure D.59.

3. This starts the Compression Wizard. Carefully follow each of the steps to complete the process.

4. After you complete the wizard, you will have considerably more free hard drive space, as well as two hard drives. (One is a physical drive; the other is a logical drive.) This new *logical* drive is actually your C: drive, and the physical hard drive becomes known as another drive letter (probably H:). Continue to use your C: drive just as you have in the past, and try not to place any files or applications on your new drive.

Figure **D.58**

Figure **D.59**

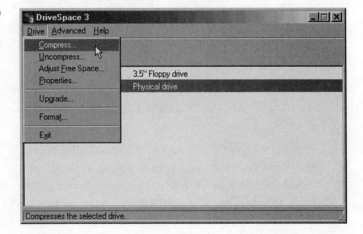

A B C D E F G H I J K L M N O P Q R S T U V W X Y Z

A
B
C
D
E
F
G
H
I
J
K
L
M
N
O
P
Q
R
S
T
U
V
W
X
Y
Z

note...   You do not want to put files on the new drive because that would actually lower the amount of free space available on the C: drive.

Sound confusing? It is. Think of it this way: Pretend you have a cup of water (your C: drive) floating in a bowl of water (your H: drive). As you add more water (files) to the cup (your C: drive), it begins to fill. That is okay, as long as the water in the bowl (the H: drive) doesn't overflow (signifying that the hard—H:—drive is completely full). If you add water (files) to the bowl (the H: drive), it directly relates to how much water (files) you can add to the cup (your C: drive) before the bowl (your hard drive) overflows.

Another choice is to create a new drive from your current drive's free space. This process eliminates the need to compress any of your current drive's files or applications, but will result in less free hard drive space upon completion. To compress just the free space on a drive, follow these steps:

1. Click the **Advanced** menu option and choose **Create Empty**, as shown in Figure D.60.

Figure **D.60**

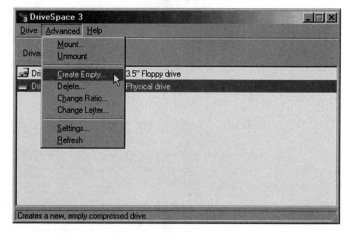

2. This starts the Compression Wizard. Follow each of the steps carefully to complete the process. Upon completion, you will have approximately double the free hard drive space as you did before, as well as the two hard drives. (One is a physical drive; the other is the logical drive.)

note... For the nonbelievers in the crowd: Yes, DriveSpace is a safe application that will not corrupt your data at whim.

Drop-Down List Box

Windows 98 uses a software programming feature known as a drop-down list box throughout the operating system. This list box usually contains a list of items or options from which you are to select. The primary purpose of a drop-down list box is to limit the choices for whatever you are attempting to do. In the "Desktop Themes" section of this book, for example, you had to choose which theme you wanted for your PC. The list containing the themes was a drop-down list box. (See? You have already used them like an expert!)

DVD Player

The Digital Versatile Disc (DVD) Player uses a revolutionary new format for DVD discs. DVD discs look and act just like CD-ROMs, except that they can store quite a bit more data (roughly 2600 MB on DVD versus 640 MB on CD-ROM). As the DVD standards evolve, this storage level is expected to increase immensely (at least double). Both DVD discs and CDs can be read by the DVD-ROM drive, and the drive will function just as your old CD-ROM drive did.

The most noticeable difference will be in the operation of a DVD-ROM drive. Because a DVD disc can store not only audio and computer data (the two things a CD-ROM can store), but video as well, you must have special hardware and software to access this video portion. The hardware is called an MPEG decoder card (MPEG stands for *Moving Picture Experts Group*). The DVD software required is the DVD Player that is built in to Windows 98.

To start the DVD Player, click the **Start** button, choose **Programs**, **Accessories**, **Entertainment**, **DVD Player**, as shown in Figure D.61.

Because most DVD-ROM players require specialized software specific to their decoder card, the DVD software support built in to Windows 98 might not be sufficient for your DVD-ROM drive. For this reason, you are generally better off using the custom DVD playing software that came with your DVD-ROM drive than you would be using the Windows 98 DVD Player software.

A
B
C
D
E
F
G
H
I
J
K
L
M
N
O
P
Q
R
S
T
U
V
W
X
Y
Z

A

B

C

D

E

F

G

H

I

J

K

L

M

N

O

P

Q

R

S

T

U

V

W

X

Y

Z

Figure **D.61**

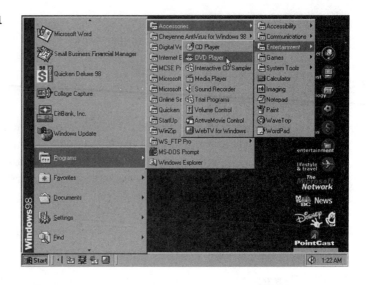

E

A
B
C
D
E
F
G
H
I
J
K
L
M
N
O
P
Q
R
S
T
U
V
W
X
Y
Z

Emergency Boot Disk

Emergency boot disk is the informal name for the Windows 98 StartUp disk (see the "StartUp Disk" entry for details). The purpose of the StartUp disk is to help you get back into your computer should the Windows 98 operating system fail for any reason. The StartUp Disk contains specialized boot files that will start the operating system from a single floppy disk, and then will attempt to restore operations to your PC as best as possible. Use of the StartUp disk should be as a last resort, because it is possible that it may overwrite some critical system information, possibly forcing you to reinstall one or more of your applications.

Explorer (Windows)

Explorer is the informal term for the Windows Explorer application that is used to maneuver throughout the Windows 98 file system. For further details, see the section titled "Windows Explorer."

Extranet

An extranet can be defined as a private network that usually uses the public telephone systems with Internet technology to share information or with others either within your organization or on the outside. An extranet is sometimes an extension of an organization's intranet that makes internal information "public" to a specific audience.

F

A

B

C

D

E

F

G

H

I

J

K

L

M

N

O

P

Q

R

S

T

U

V

W

X

Y

Z

FAT32 Converter

The FAT32 converter is a hard disk file storage format that has been especially designed for drives with more than 512 MB of space. Because FAT32 is a new 32-bit file allocation table format, it does not support a dual-boot functionality with the other Windows operating systems available today. For further details on converting your hard drive to FAT32, see the section titled "Driver Converter (FAT32)."

Favorites

Windows 98 Favorites are *hyperlinks* to Internet/intranet/extranet web sites. To use the Favorites list, follow these steps:

1. Click the **Start** button, and choose **Favorites**, as shown in Figure F.1.

Figure **F.1**

2. Click any entry in the Favorites menu (you might need to click a folder or two to reach the web site you want to visit) to start your default web browser. The default web browser will probably be Microsoft Internet Explorer because it is integrated into the Windows 98 operating system. The browser automatically opens the file, folder, or web site that you have selected.

tip... You must establish a connection to the Internet prior to opening a web browser; otherwise, the browser will not be able to find any sites. Although opening Favorites within Windows 98 starts the default web browser, it does not automatically complete the Internet connection.

When inside the Microsoft Internet Explorer Web browser, you can view the Favorites links that are available from the Start menu. As an added advantage, you can organize your favorites into various folders, as shown in Figure F.2.

Figure **F.2**

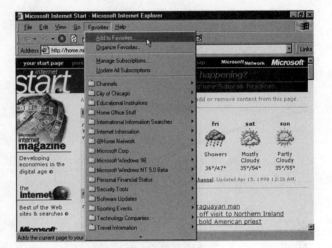

To organize your Favorites list, follow these steps:

1. To add a new site to your Favorites list, first visit the site you want to add (an example is shown in Figure F.3).

2. Click the **Favorites** menu option, and select **Add to Favorites**, as shown in Figure F.4.

3. The Add Favorite dialog box, shown in Figure F.5, appears. Click the **Create In** button if you want to add this favorite to an existing folder or to create a new folder within the Windows 98 Favorites section. In this instance, I plan to place the site I have selected in an existing folder named United States Government.

A
B
C
D
E
F
G
H
I
J
K
L
M
N
O
P
Q
R
S
T
U
V
W
X
Y
Z

Figure **F.3**

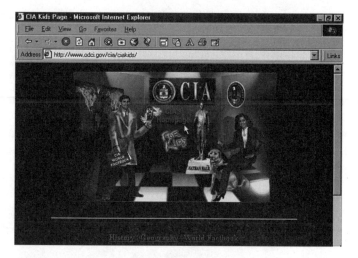

Figure **F.4**

4. The dialog box shown in Figure F.5 expands to show the folder structure of your current Favorites area, as shown in Figure F.6. Scroll down until you find the folder in which you want to place the site, and then click it.

5. Click the **OK** button to insert this web site into your Favorites section.

6. Click the **Favorites** menu option to confirm that the Favorite you just added has been successfully placed in the list. As shown in Figure F.7, the CIA home page for kids has been successfully placed in the United States Government folder of my Favorites list.

Figure **F.5**

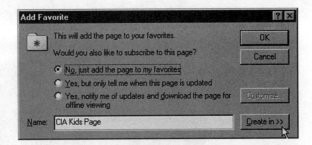

Figure **F.6**

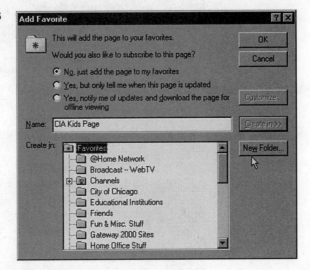

To organize sites already in your Favorites list into folders, follow these steps:

1. Click the **Favorites** menu item and select **Organize Favorites**, as shown in Figure F.8.

2. The **Organize Favorites** dialog box, shown in Figure F.9, appears. Here you move, rename, delete, or open an existing Favorite.

A
B
C
D
E
F
G
H
I
J
K
L
M
N
O
P
Q
R
S
T
U
V
W
X
Y
Z

A
B
C
D
E
F
G
H
I
J
K
L
M
N
O
P
Q
R
S
T
U
V
W
X
Y
Z

Figure **F.7**

Figure **F.8**

note...   When organizing your Favorites folders, be practical and logical. Don't stuff everything into one spot, but at the same time, do not try to over-organize and create so many different folders that it becomes impossible to find anything. You can use the standard file-management techniques for your Windows 98 Favorites just as you do for the rest of your computer.

Figure **F.9**

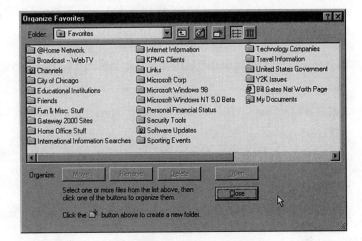

Files

Files are the software creations that make all things possible in PC computing today. Every folder, word processing document, software application, and operating system feature is actually nothing more than a file. Thousands of files come with the Windows 98 operating system and with each software application that you load on your PC. Even more are created by these very same applications (in the form of word processing documents, spreadsheets, and the like).

File Management

It is strongly recommended that you devise some scheme for organizing and managing the files stored on your computer. Much like Microsoft organizes most of the applications installed on your computer in the Program Files folder, you can organize your own files in a manner that will make it easier to locate them for future use. If you had a folder called DATA that contains a series of subdirectories, each of which was named after the application that created its contents, for example, it would be very easy to find, use, modify, and back up these files as necessary. This file structure might look something like this:

```
C:\DATA
C:\DATA\EXCEL
C:\DATA\POWERPOINT
C:\DATA\PUBLISHER
```

A
B
C
D
E
F
G
H
I
J
K
L
M
N
O
P
Q
R
S
T
U
V
W
X
Y
Z

```
C:\DATA\QUICKEN
C:\DATA\WORD
```

To organize and manage your files, you need to know how to do the following:

- Copy files
- Delete files
- Move files
- Swap files over a direct cable connection

Copying Files

Copying a file from one location on a PC to another is simple. To copy a file, follow these steps:

1. First, you must find the file you want to copy (suppose for this example that you want to copy the Microsoft Word shortcut file). In this example, double-click the **My Computer** icon, shown in Figure F.10, on the desktop.

Figure **F.10**

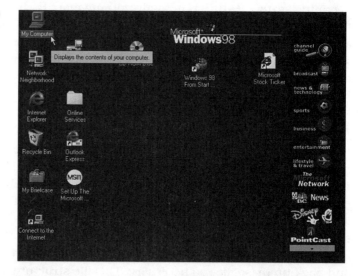

2. The My Computer window, shown in Figure F.11, opens. If your window does not look like the one shown here, click the **View** menu option and then click **Details** to alter the screen layout so that it matches the one in the example.

Figure **F.11**

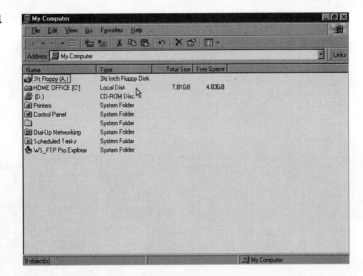

tip...   The My Computer window displays a variety of information, including the total size of your hard drive (see the Total Size column) as well as how much free space is available (see the Free Space column).

tip...   Viewing the My Computer window is a quick way to determine what the drive letter assignments are for each drive within the system. For example, the 3 1/2-inch floppy drive on the picture shows it with the drive letter assignment as A:. The CD-ROM drive (which already has a music CD inserted in it) is labeled Audio CD and has been given the drive letter assignment of D:.

3. Double-click the drive in which the file that you want to copy exists. If in doubt, start with the C: drive; it is usually the primary (if not the only) hard drive in a PC. This opens a window like the one shown in Figure F.12.

4. Double-click any folder to open it. Depending on how your files are organized on your computer, you might need to click a few folders to reach the one you're looking for. Wherever it is located, click the **Microsoft Office** folder to view a screen like the one shown in Figure F.13.

A
B
C
D
E
F
G
H
I
J
K
L
M
N
O
P
Q
R
S
T
U
V
W
X
Y
Z

Figure **F.12**

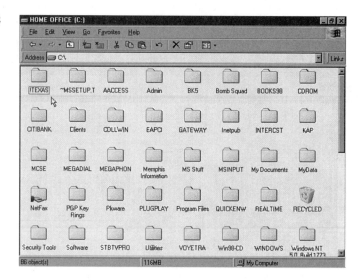

Figure **F.13**

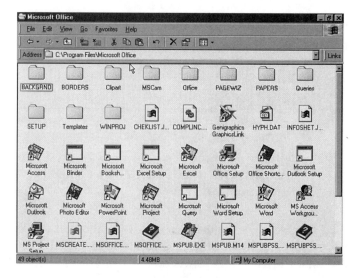

5. Here you will find the file you want to copy—the shortcut for Microsoft Word (you can learn more about shortcuts in the section titled "Shortcuts"). Select this file by clicking it once with the left mouse button; then right-click the selected file and choose **Copy** from the ensuing shortcut menu, as shown in Figure F.14. The file you have selected is copied to the clipboard.

Figure **F.14**

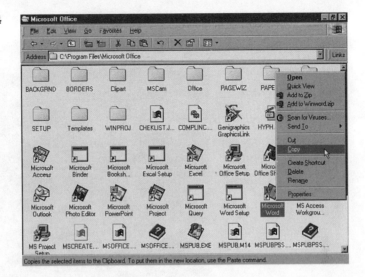

6. Move to the place where you want to paste the copy of the file—in this example, the Windows 98 desktop (you can reach this spot by minimizing or closing one or more of your open windows).

7. Right-click a blank portion of the desktop and choose **Paste** from the ensuing shortcut menu, as shown in Figure F.15.

Figure **F.15**

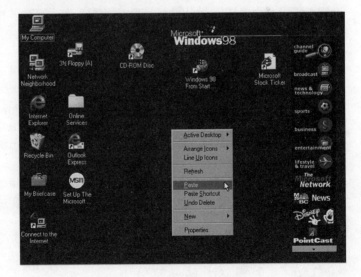

A
B
C
D
E
F
G
H
I
J
K
L
M
N
O
P
Q
R
S
T
U
V
W
X
Y
Z

8. As shown in Figure F.16, the Microsoft Word shortcut file is pasted to the desktop.

Figure **F.16**

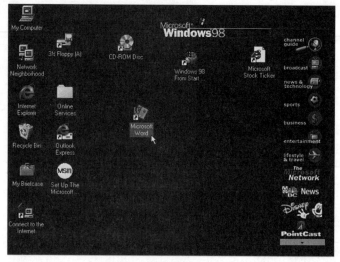

Deleting Files

Removing files (documents, pictures, programs, and so on) from your computer can seem intimidating to a first-time user. But under Windows 98, this process is easier to understand and perform. To delete a file, follow these steps:

1. First, you must find the file you want to delete. In this example, double-click the **My Computer** icon, shown in Figure F.17, on the desktop.

2. The My Computer window, shown in Figure F.18, opens. If your window does not look like the one shown here, click the **View** menu option and then click **Details** to alter the screen layout so that it matches the one in the example.

3. Double-click the drive in which the file that you want to delete exists. If in doubt, start with the C: drive; it is usually the primary (if not the only) hard drive in a PC.

4. When you find the file you want to delete, click it to select it, as shown in Figure F.19. (In this example, the selected file is a graphics file named `Frank & Genevieve Snow.TIF`.)

Figure **F.17**

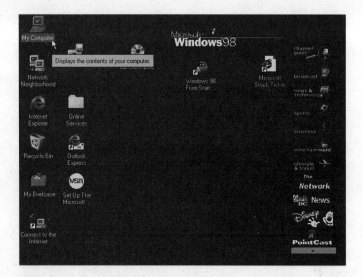

Figure **F.18**

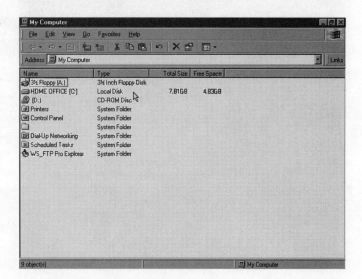

5. Right-click the selected file and select **Delete** from the ensuing shortcut menu, as shown in Figure F.20. This will remove the selected file from the window.

A
B
C
D
E
F
G
H
I
J
K
L
M
N
O
P
Q
R
S
T
U
V
W
X
Y
Z

A
B
C
D
E
F
G
H
I
J
K
L
M
N
O
P
Q
R
S
T
U
V
W
X
Y
Z

Figure **F.19**

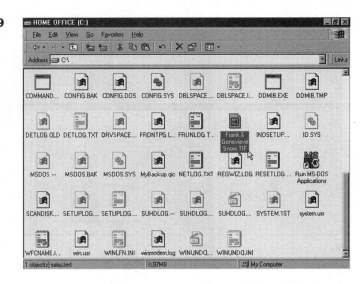

Figure **F.20**

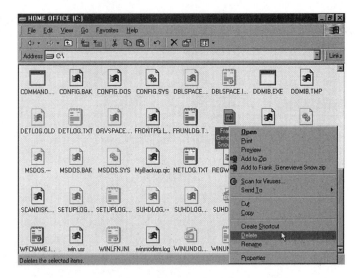

tip... An easier way to delete a file is to select it and then press the **Delete** key on your keyboard.

6. Close the C: window and return to the desktop by closing or minimizing all open windows. Then double-click the **Recycle Bin** icon on your desktop, shown in Figure F.21.

Figure **F.21**

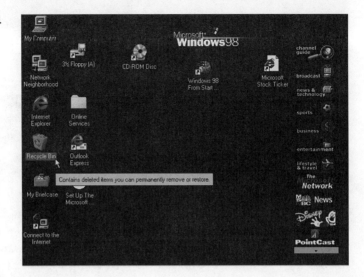

7. The file you deleted appears in the Recycle Bin. To delete it permanently from your system, right-click the **Recycle Bin** icon on the desktop, and choose **Empty Recycle Bin** from the ensuing shortcut menu, as shown in Figure F.22.

Figure **F.22**

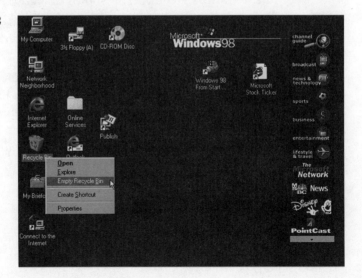

A
B
C
D
E
F
G
H
I
J
K
L
M
N
O
P
Q
R
S
T
U
V
W
X
Y
Z

A
B
C
D
E
F
G
H
I
J
K
L
M
N
O
P
Q
R
S
T
U
V
W
X
Y
Z

8. You will see a message box like the one shown in Figure F.23, asking you whether you really want to delete the files in the Recycle Bin. Click the **Yes** button to complete the deletion process.

Figure **F.23**

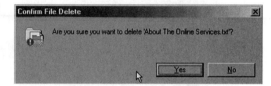

Moving Files

To move a file such as a picture, a word processing document, or a spreadsheet from one folder to another on your computer is not as difficult as you might think. To move files around on your computer, you use a technique known as *drag and drop*. That is, you drag a file from one location and literally drop it into a new one. To move files around within Windows 98, follow these steps:

1. Start Windows Explorer by clicking the **Start** button, and choosing **Programs**, **Windows Explorer**, as shown in Figure F.24.

2. The Explorer window, shown in Figure F.25, opens. To find the file you seek, first find the folder where it resides. You might have to click a series of folders to reach the file you seek.

3. For the sake of example, suppose that the file you seek—a Word document—is found in a subfolder of the Program Files folder: C:\Program Files\KMAN\DOWNLOAD. To reach this subfolder, click the plus sign (+) next to the Program Files folder, which can be found in the left pane, and then click the **KMAN** folder, which can be found in the right pane.

Figure **F.24**

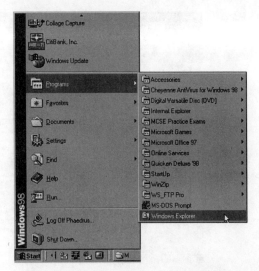

Figure **F.25**

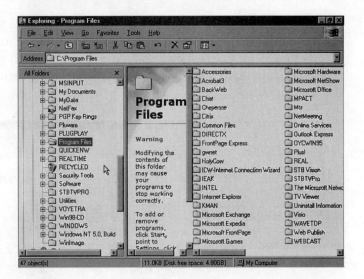

4. Click the **DOWNLOAD** folder in the left pane, and then click the file you want to move (**Adolphson, Dave.doc**), as shown in Figure F.26. (Notice that if you leave the mouse pointer over a Microsoft Word file, the name of the file's author appears.)

A
B
C
D
E
F
G
H
I
J
K
L
M
N
O
P
Q
R
S
T
U
V
W
X
Y
Z

A
B
C
D
E
F
G
H
I
J
K
L
M
N
O
P
Q
R
S
T
U
V
W
X
Y
Z

Figure **F.26**

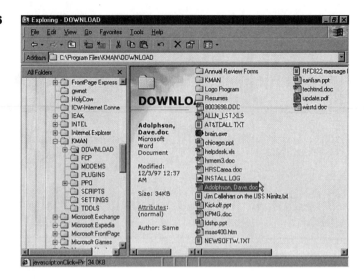

5. Using the scrollbar in the left pane, scroll to the folder where you want the file to be moved. Hold down the left mouse button and drag the file to its new location, as shown in Figure F.27. When the destination folder (in this example, KPMG-Styled Resumes) becomes highlighted, release the mouse button.

Figure **F.27**

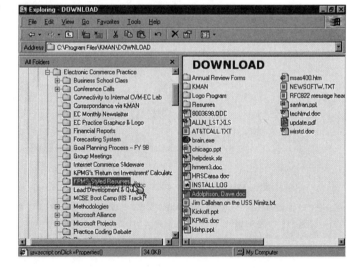

6. The file that you moved no longer resides in the DOWNLOAD file; it now resides in the KPMG-Styled Resumes folder, as shown in Figure F.28.

Figure **F.28**

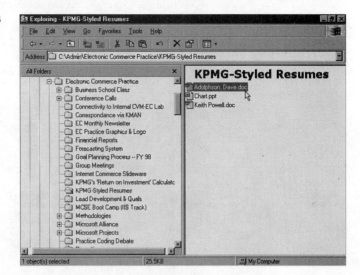

Swapping Files over a Direct Cable Connection

Files can be copied between two computers through the use of the Direct Cable Connection feature of Windows 98. After the two computers are connected, you just drag and drop files from one computer to the other (see the preceding section titled "Moving Files" for more information about drag and drop). The only difference is that although you drag and drop files between computers, you are actually leaving the original file on the first computer intact. In other words, this is a copy operation, not a move operation.

Find

The Find command under Windows 98 is greatly improved compared to the command in earlier versions of Windows. Not only can you search for files and folders, you can also search for friends on the Internet, computers on your network, and items in your address book.

Finding Files and Folders

To find files or folders on your computer, follow these steps:

A
B
C
D
E
F
G
H
I
J
K
L
M
N
O
P
Q
R
S
T
U
V
W
X
Y
Z

A
B
C
D
E
F
G
H
I
J
K
L
M
N
O
P
Q
R
S
T
U
V
W
X
Y
Z

1. Click the **Start** button, and then choose **Find**. You will see the Find menu, which contains the various Find options, as shown in Figure F.29.

   Figure **F.29**

   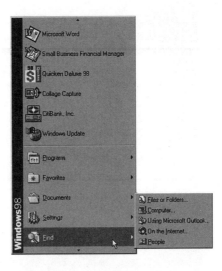

2. Click the first item, **Files or Folders**, to open the Find: All Files screen (with the Name & Location tab displayed), as shown in Figure F.30.

   Figure **F.30**

   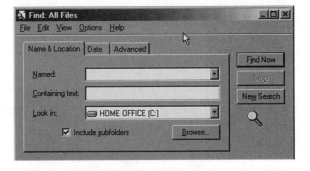

3. If you know the name of the file you seek, or if you can type some of the text that the file contains, the Name & Location tab is the screen for you. Type the name of the file you're looking for with its extension (.DOC, .PPT, .XLS, and so on) if you know it, and select the drive in which the

file resides (such as the C: drive) from the Look In drop-down list. Alternatively, type some text that the file contains in the Containing Text text box.

4. To narrow a search, you can enter the date your file was created, last modified, or last accessed. To do so, click the **Date** tab of the Find: All Files dialog box, as shown in Figure F.31.

Figure **F.31**

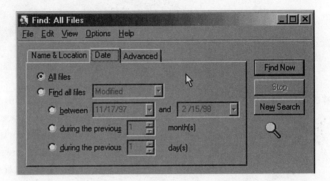

note... Although this screen will search by a series of days or dates, you should still enter either a file name or a text string on the previous tab. Otherwise, you probably won't locate the file that you are looking for, because many files are automatically modified or accessed by the operating system without your realizing it.

5. If you leave this screen at its default setting, All Files, it instructs Windows 98 to search through all files from all dates, which doesn't exactly take advantage of this screen's functions. Instead, select the **Find All Files** option, and select either **Created**, **Accessed**, or **Modified** from the corresponding drop-down list box.

6. Click the **Between xx and xx** button to instruct Find to search the range of dates that you specify; click the **During the Previous xx Month(s)** button to instruct Find to search backward over the number of months you specify; click the **During the Previous xx Day(s)** button to instruct Find to search backward over the number of days you specify.

7. To narrow your search even further by searching by the file's size and type, click the **Advanced** tab, as shown in Figure F.32.

A B C D E F G H I J K L M N O P Q R S T U V W X Y Z

Figure **F.32**

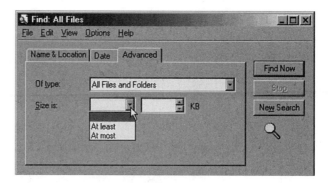

note...   Entering information about the file's size is a quick way to limit a
search. If you're looking for a graphic file, for example, you could select
At Least from the **Size Is** drop-down list and enter **3** in the KB spinner
box (because most graphic files exceed this size). This will speed the
search, because the computer will not bother itself with the hundreds
of files that are smaller than 3 KB.

8. Click the **Find Now** button to instruct Windows 98 to look for the file in
question. Locations of matches are placed in the box that appears immediately below the Find screen, as shown in Figure F.33.

Figure **F.33**

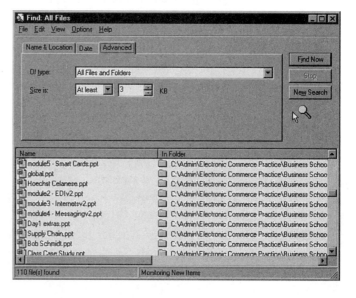

tip... If you need to stop a search in progress, click once on the **Stop** button to end it.

Finding a Computer on Your Network

Just as you can search for files on your computer, you can search for computers on your network. To use this search capability, follow these steps:

1. Click the **Start** button, and then choose **Find**. You will see the Find menu, which contains the various Find options, as shown in Figure F.34.

Figure **F.34**

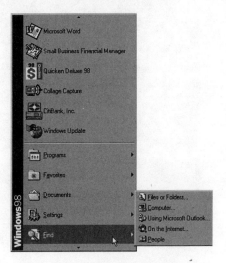

2. Click the second item, **Computer**, to open the Find: Computer screen, shown in Figure F.35.

Figure **F.35**

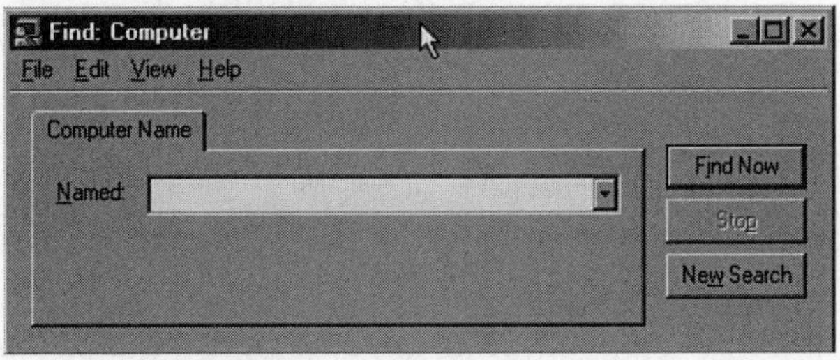

A
B
C
D
E
F
G
H
I
J
K
L
M
N
O
P
Q
R
S
T
U
V
W
X
Y
Z

3. Type the name of the computer you are looking for in the **Named** field, and then click the **Find Now** button to initiate the search. When the Windows 98 search engine finds the computer that matches the search criteria, it places its name and location, as well as any comments about the computer (for Windows-based machines only), in the **Found** box at the bottom of the search screen. In the example shown in Figure F.36, the computer is named phaedrus2, and the search process has located it in the Network Neighborhood.

Figure **F.36**

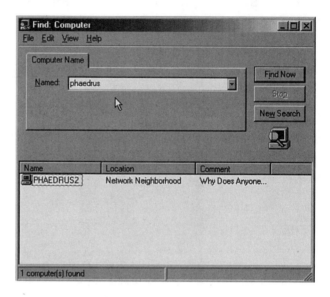

note... Don't worry if you can't remember the entire name of the computer you're looking for; Windows 98 is forgiving. Suppose, for example, that you are looking for a computer named Phaedrus2 but, because you're unsure of the spelling, you just type **Pha**. The Find Computer option will still come up with the correct answer.

Finding Files on the Internet

Windows 98 enables you to find files on the Internet directly from your desktop. To use this Find option, follow these steps:

1. Connect to the Internet either via the Windows 98 Dial-Up Networking feature or an online service such as AOL, MSN, or Prodigy.

tip... If you do not have any type of Internet connection, this search is not for you.

2. Click the **Start** button, and then choose **Find**. You will see the Find menu, which contains the various Find options, as shown in Figure F.37.

Figure **F.37**

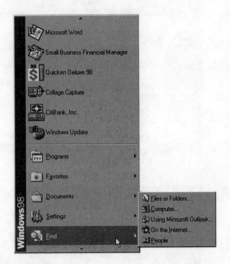

3. Click the fourth item, **On the Internet**, to start your default Internet browser (probably Internet Explorer). Because you connected to the Internet in step 1, your web browser automatically connects to Microsoft's World Wide Web site, which contains various Internet search engine options, as shown in Figure F.38.

note... Notice that this time the Infoseek search engine is at the top of the list that appears on the left side of the page. If you were to exit the browser and then re-enter it, you would find the next search engine product on the list (AOL NetFind) at the top. Talk about equality for search engines....

4. Click the engine that you want to use (to follow along with this example, try **Infoseek**), and then type the search text in the box on the right side of the screen (in this example, as shown in Figure F.39, I have typed **Silver American Eagle**, which refers to a platinum coin that is minted by the U.S. Mint, but that normally does not circulate to the public). Click the **Seek** button to start the search.

A
B
C
D
E
F
G
H
I
J
K
L
M
N
O
P
Q
R
S
T
U
V
W
X
Y
Z

A
B
C
D
E
F
G
H
I
J
K
L
M
N
O
P
Q
R
S
T
U
V
W
X
Y
Z

Figure **F.38**

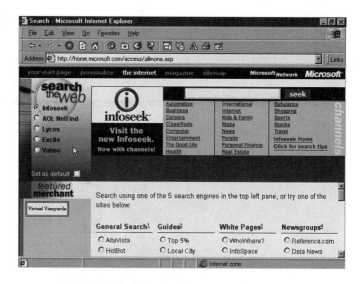

Figure **F.39**

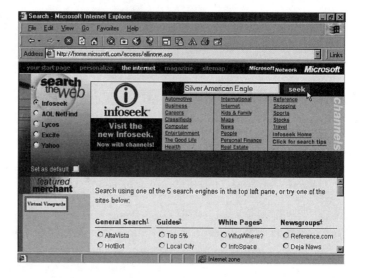

tip...   If your search engine finds too many web sites that match your search criteria, you can narrow your search. In the case of Infoseek, you just click the **Tips** hyperlink (depending on which search engine you use, this hyperlink might have a different name) to view information about making your search more effective.

5. Because your search has returned a manageable number of matches, click the **Search Only Within These 32 Pages** button, shown in Figure F.40.

Figure **F.40**

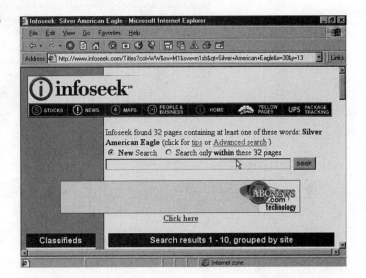

6. Scroll down the resulting screen—shown in Figure F.41—to determine whether your search has been successful. When you reach the bottom of the screen, click the **Next 10** hyperlink to view the next 10 matches.

Figure **F.41**

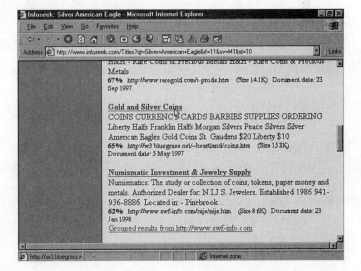

A
B
C
D
E
F
G
H
I
J
K
L
M
N
O
P
Q
R
S
T
U
V
W
X
Y
Z

A
B
C
D
E
F
G
H
I
J
K
L
M
N
O
P
Q
R
S
T
U
V
W
X
Y
Z

7. When you find a web site that looks promising, such as the one shown in Figure F.42, view it by clicking its hyperlink.

Figure **F.42**

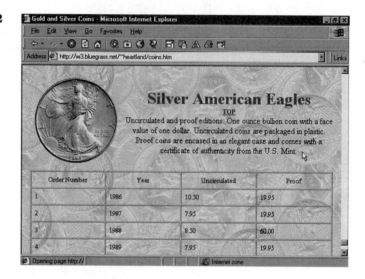

Finding People

The final Find option provided by Windows 98 is for finding people. You can use this option to find people in your Windows 98 address book, or to find people on the Internet.

Finding People in Your Address Book

To use Find to find people in your address book, follow these steps:

1. Click the **Start** button, and then choose **Find**. You will see the Find menu, which contains the various Find options, as shown in Figure F.43.

2. Click the fifth item, **People**, to open the Find People screen, shown in Figure F.44.

3. Type the name, email address, street address, or telephone number of the person you're looking for, and then click the **Find Now** button to start the search.

4. To hasten a search, you can enter information into multiple fields, such as entering a person's name as well as his or her phone number.

Figure **F.43**

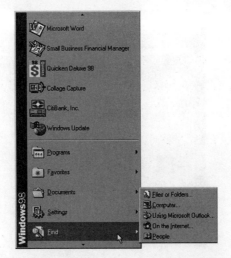

Figure **F.44**

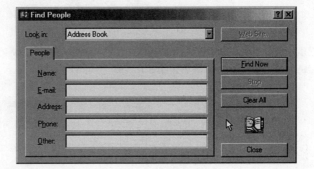

Finding People over the Internet

To use Find to find people on the Internet, follow these steps:

1. Connect to the Internet either via the Windows 98 Dial-Up Networking feature or an online service such as AOL, MSN, or Prodigy.

tip... If you do not have any type of Internet connection, the Internet People option is not for you.

2. Click the **Start** button, and then choose **Find**. You will see the Find menu, which contains the various Find options, as shown in Figure F.45.

A
B
C
D
E
F
G
H
I
J
K
L
M
N
O
P
Q
R
S
T
U
V
W
X
Y
Z

A
B
C
D
E
F
G
H
I
J
K
L
M
N
O
P
Q
R
S
T
U
V
W
X
Y
Z

Figure **F.45**

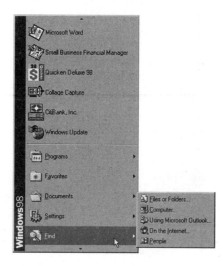

3. Open the Find People screen by clicking the **People** item in the Find menu.

4. Click the down-arrow button to the right of the Look In text field to view the list box shown in Figure F.46.

Figure **F.46**

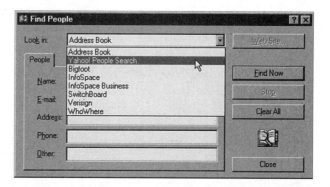

5. Select any of the available search services (for this example, I have selected Bigfoot) to enable the **Web Site** button. The name of the search engine you have chosen will also appear at the bottom of the screen, as shown in Figure F.47.

Figure **F.47**

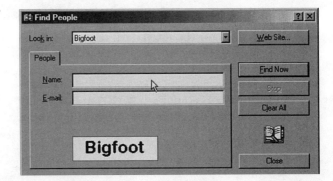

note... You can click the **Web Site** button to access the web site for the search service shown, provided that you have already established a connection to the Internet.

6. Type the name or email address of the person you want to find, and then click the **Find Now** button to initiate the search.

7. If the person is found, you will see his or her name in the box that appears at the bottom of the screen, as shown in Figure F.48. After the name appears, you can click the **Add to Address Book** button to add that person's email address to your personal address book.

Figure **F.48**

A
B
C
D
E
F
G
H
I
J
K
L
M
N
O
P
Q
R
S
T
U
V
W
X
Y
Z

note... These search engines are only as good as their information (garbage in, garbage out). For the most part, they contain accurate and updated information, but not always.

note... You might want to click the **Web Site** button for some or all of these search engines so that you can add your information to each site's database. This will make it easier for long-lost friends or relatives to find you on their Windows 98 computers.

Folders

In the parlance of Windows 98, directories and subdirectories are known as folders. Simply put, folders are where all files and other directories are stored within Windows 98. To explore your folder structure, follow these steps:

1. Right-click the **My Computer** icon and choose **Explore**, as shown in Figure F.49.

Figure **F.49**

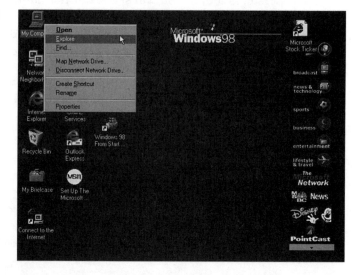

2. The My Computer window of Windows Explorer, shown in Figure F.50, opens. This window shows all the drives installed on this computer: a 3 1/2-inch floppy drive (the A: drive), a hard drive labeled HOME OFFICE (the C: drive), and a CD-ROM or DVD-ROM drive with a music CD in it (the D: drive). You will also find shortcuts to four of the more popular

folders: Printers, Control Panel, Dial-Up Networking, and Scheduled Tasks.

Figure **F.50**

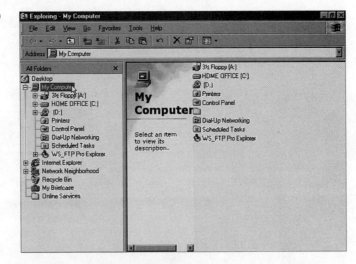

A B C D E F G H I J K L M N O P Q R S T U V W X Y Z

note... You use Windows Explorer to maneuver around your hard drive. Explorer enables you to move, copy, create, and delete files and folders as necessary. For more information about Explorer, see the section titled "Windows Explorer."

3. Click the **C:** drive (labeled HOME OFFICE) entry in the left column; the pane on the right will change accordingly, as shown in Figure F.51. All the icons you see in this view are folders.

Fonts

Fonts are used within Windows 98 to control how letters, numbers, and special characters look onscreen as well as when they are printed.

Installing Fonts

To install a font, follow these steps:

1. Click the **Start** button, choose **Settings**, **Control Panel**, as shown in Figure F.52.

Figure **F.51**

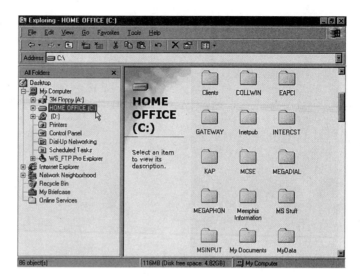

Figure **F.52**

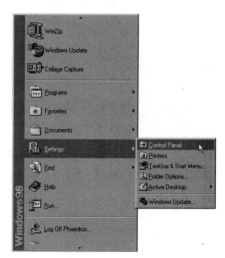

2. Double-click the **Fonts** icon in the Control Panel window, shown in Figure F.53.

3. The Fonts window opens. Listed here are all the screen and print fonts that are already installed on your system. To add a new font to your system, click the **File** menu option, and choose **Install New Font**, as shown in Figure F.54.

Figure **F.53**

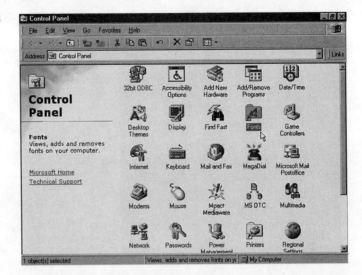

Figure **F.54**

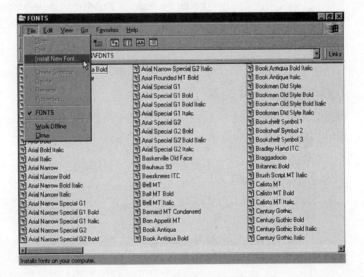

4. The Add Fonts dialog box, shown in Figure F.55, appears. In the bottom half of the window, find the folder or drive where the new font is to be installed.

5. In the List of Fonts box, click any font that you want to install (click the **Select All** button if you want them all).

A
B
C
D
E
F
G
H
I
J
K
L
M
N
O
P
Q
R
S
T
U
V
W
X
Y
Z

A
B
C
D
E
F
G
H
I
J
K
L
M
N
O
P
Q
R
S
T
U
V
W
X
Y
Z

Figure **F.55**

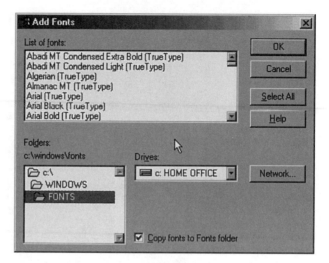

6. Check the **Copy Fonts to Fonts Folder** check box to create a copy of all the fonts that you are installing and to put that copy into the C:\Windows\Fonts folder.

7. Click the **OK** button to proceed with the installation.

Deleting Fonts

Deleting a font that you no longer want is just as easy as installing a new font. To delete a font, follow these steps:

1. Click the **Start** button, choose **Settings**, **Control Panel**, as shown in Figure F.56.

2. Double-click the **Fonts** icon in the Control Panel window, shown in Figure F.57.

3. The **Fonts** window opens. Listed here are all the screen and print fonts that are already installed on your system. Right-click the font you want to delete, and choose **Delete** from the ensuing shortcut menu, as shown in Figure F.58.

Figure **F.56**

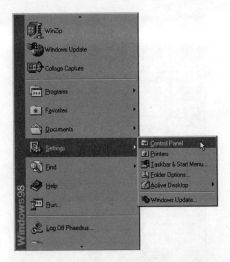

Figure **F.57**

A
B
C
D
E
F
G
H
I
J
K
L
M
N
O
P
Q
R
S
T
U
V
W
X
Y
Z

A

B

C

D

E

F

G

H

I

J

K

L

M

N

O

P

Q

R

S

T

U

V

W

X

Y

Z

Figure **F.58**

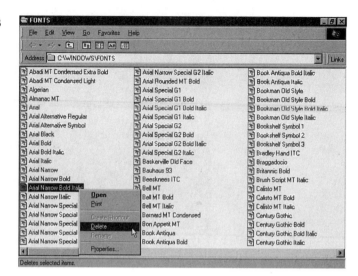

G

A
B
C
D
E
F
G
H
I
J
K
L
M
N
O
P
Q
R
S
T
U
V
W
X
Y
Z

A
B
C
D
E
F
G
H
I
J
K
L
M
N
O
P
Q
R
S
T
U
V
W
X
Y
Z

Games

Windows 98 comes with four built-in games:

- FreeCell
- Hearts
- Minesweeper
- Solitaire

To play any of these games, do the following:

1. Click the **Start** button, choose **Programs**, **Accessories**, and then **Games**; then choose whichever game you want to play. As shown in Figure G.1, I've chosen **FreeCell**.

Figure **G.1**

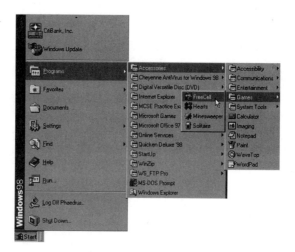

2. If you selected FreeCell as I did, the game opens on the desktop. To start a new game, click the **Game** menu option and choose **New Game**, as shown in Figure G.2. If you need help learning how to play the game, click the **Help** menu option.

note... As an alternative, you can press the **F2** key on your keyboard to begin a new game.

note... Starting any of Windows 98's other built-in games is pretty much the same as starting FreeCell, except that when you want to start a new game of Solitaire, you select the **Deal** option in the **Game** menu.

Figure **G.2**

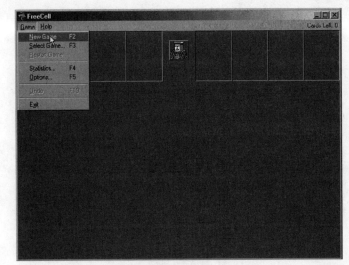

Any additional games you install on your PC might not be placed in the same folder structure as FreeCell, Solitaire, Minesweeper, and Hearts. Many games install into their own default locations, as shown in Figure G.3.

Figure **G.3**

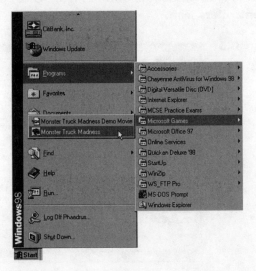

Game Controllers

In Windows 98, game controllers are devices such as joysticks, stick and rudder control systems, steering wheels, and the like. To configure game controllers in Windows 98, do the following:

A
B
C
D
E
F
G
H
I
J
K
L
M
N
O
P
Q
R
S
T
U
V
W
X
Y
Z

A
B
C
D
E
F
G
H
I
J
K
L
M
N
O
P
Q
R
S
T
U
V
W
X
Y
Z

1. Click the **Start** button, choose **Settings**, and then **Control Panel**, as shown in Figure G.4.

    Figure **G.4**

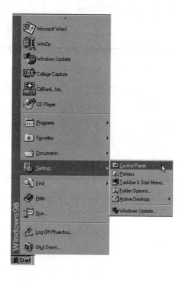

2. The Control Panel window, shown in Figure G.5, opens. Double-click the **Game Controllers** icon.

    Figure **G.5**

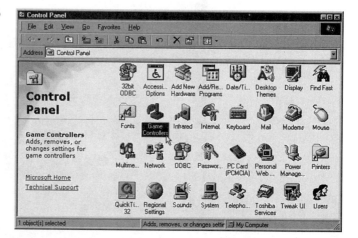

3. If you have no game controllers connected to your computer, then the Game Controllers dialog box is empty, as shown in Figure G.6.

Figure **G.6**

A

B

C

D

E

F

G

H

I

J

K

L

M

N

O

P

Q

R

S

T

U

V

W

X

Y

Z

4. If you are adding a game controller for the first time, you can use the **Add New Hardware** feature; refer to the section titled "Add New Hardware" for more information. Otherwise, you can click the **Add** button on the **Game Controllers** screen. This takes you to the **Add Game Controller** screen, shown in Figure G.7.

Figure **G.7**

5. Click on the game controller that you are connecting to your PC and then click on the **OK** button to install the chosen controller. If your game controller is not listed, click the **Add Other** button to view the screen shown in Figure G.8.

6. Select the hardware you want to install or click the **Have Disk** button to install the necessary device drivers from the floppy disk(s) or CD-ROM disc that came with that particular game controller. Click the **Next** button to continue the installation process.

A

B

C

D

E

F

G

H

I

J

K

L

M

N

O

P

Q

R

S

T

U

V

W

X

Y

Z

Figure **G.8**

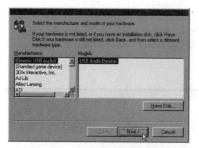

7. As shown in Figure G.9, the **Game Controllers** dialog box displays the hardware you've added (I added the SideWinder Precision Pro device). Click the **Properties** button to test each of the buttons, levers, and movement functions of your game controller.

Figure **G.9**

8. To make port or controller changes to your game controller configuration, click the **Advanced** tab to view the screen shown in Figure G.10. The most important thing to keep in mind here is that if you do not understand the change that you are making, then do not make the change. It is always better to consult the technical support information that came with the game controller or call the device manufacturer's help desk for further details.

note...   Most of the settings on this screen were probably established when you installed your game controller device for the first time. This is especially true if your device came with its own installation software (such as the Microsoft SideWinder Precision Pro joystick seen in this example).

Figure **G.10**

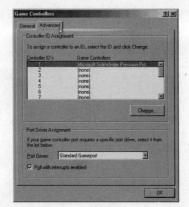

Getting Started

Getting Started is the name of the Windows 98 online book. This book comes with Windows 98 when you purchase the operating system from Microsoft Corporation. To access and use it, do the following:

1. Click the **Start** button and choose **Help**, as shown in Figure G.11.

Figure **G.11**

2. The **Windows Help** window, shown in Figure G.12, opens. Click the **Getting Started Book: Online Version** entry; the book icon to the left of this entry opens to reveal the **Microsoft Windows 98 Getting Started Book** hyperlink.

A
B
C
D
E
F
G
H
I
J
K
L
M
N
O
P
Q
R
S
T
U
V
W
X
Y
Z

A
B
C
D
E
F
G
H
I
J
K
L
M
N
O
P
Q
R
S
T
U
V
W
X
Y
Z

Figure **G.12**

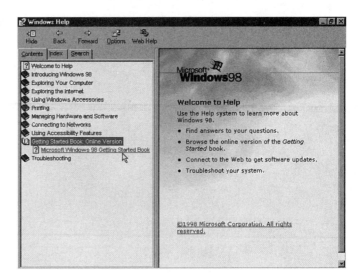

3. Click this hyperlink to view information about the book in the right-hand pane, as shown in Figure G.13.

Figure **G.13**

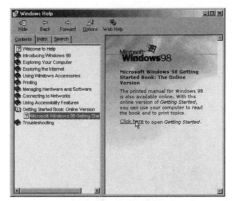

4. Click the **Click Here** hyperlink to open the screen shown in Figure G.14. Click any of the closed-book icons in the left pane to read the corresponding sections.

note...   The three tabs—**Contents**, **Index**, and **Search**—all permit users to find additional information as needed (see the section titled "Windows 98 Help" for more information about using Windows Help).

Figure **G.14**

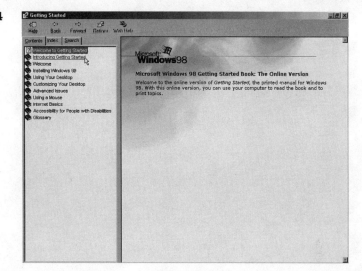

5. To exit the online book, click the × located in the upper-right corner of the window.

Group Policies

Group policies are tools for securing a Windows 98 installation on a network so that the individuals running the connected Windows 98 client PCs do not change things that the system administrator does not want altered. Typically, you would never install group policies on your home PC, but this is not to say that you could not do so.

By using group policies, the system administrator can lower the total cost of ownership of each computer because these policies make it easier to configure each PC to look and act just like the one next to it. That is, a group policy enables you to lock down the user interface, system security, and the PC's underlying infrastructure in such a way as to permit the easier maintenance and support of that computer. When this cost savings is multiplied over hundreds or even thousands of PCs, it does become a substantial number!

A
B
C
D
E
F
G
H
I
J
K
L
M
N
O
P
Q
R
S
T
U
V
W
X
Y
Z

H

Hardware System Requirements

HyperTerminal

A
B
C
D
E
F
G
H
I
J
K
L
M
N
O
P
Q
R
S
T
U
V
W
X
Y
Z

A
B
C
D
E
F
G
H
I
J
K
L
M
N
O
P
Q
R
S
T
U
V
W
X
Y
Z

Hardware System Requirements

The hardware requirements for a Windows 98 computer are roughly the same as those for Windows 95:

- A computer that already has a DOS file allocation table created and has been formatted. This requirement is satisfied if your PC already has another version of Windows installed on it—such as Windows 95 or Windows 3.*x*—or if you are able to get to a DOS command prompt—such as `C:\`.

- An Intel or Intel-compatible 486SX-66 MHz or faster microprocessor CPU.

- A hard disk drive that has at least 110 MB of free space.

- 16 MB of memory (commonly referred to as *RAM* or *DRAM*).

- VGA or higher-resolution monitor (preferably a color one).

- A high-density, 3 1/2-inch floppy disk drive.

- A CD-ROM disk drive, if you plan to install Windows 98 from its CD packaging instead of from an endless series of floppy disks. (Using the Windows CD-ROM is the easiest method, and should be used if at all possible.)

- A Microsoft mouse or compatible pointing device.

note... If you are installing Windows 98 over an existing version of Windows, you are really performing an *upgrade* installation and not a new install. This can be important when you consider that in the past, Microsoft has charged less for *upgrade* versions of its operating systems than it has for full-blown *new* versions.

HyperTerminal

HyperTerminal permits you to connect to another computer system via a telephone line. Although HyperTerminal is similar to Dial-Up Networking (covered in the section titled "Dial-Up Networking"), which is also built into Windows 98, it is different in a few key aspects:

- HyperTerminal provides you with a fully functioning terminal window that can be used for controlling remote systems without any additional software.

HyperTerminal

179

📧 HyperTerminal enables you to easily transfer files between you and another computer user, even if that other user has an old DOS-based PC.

To use the HyperTerminal application, do the following:

1. Click the **Start** button and choose **Programs**, **Accessories**, **Communications**, and then **HyperTerminal**, as shown in Figure H.1.

Figure **H.1**

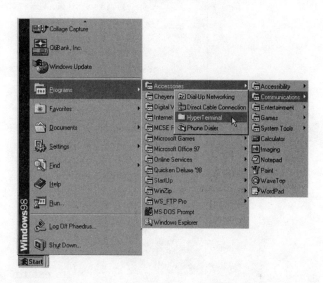

2. The **HyperTerminal** application window, shown in Figure H.2, opens. Icons representing three HyperTerminal contact points are already present in the folder: **AT&T Mail**, **MCI Mail**, and **CompuServe**. The fourth icon, **HYPERTRM.EXE**, represents the application you use to create new points of access. Double-click the **HYPERTRM.EXE** icon.

3. The HyperTerminal *splash screen* shown in Figure H.3 is the first screen to appear. It is displayed only for a few seconds.

note... *Splash screen* is a slang term for an entry screen—usually a pretty picture—to an application program.

The splash screen is replaced by the **Connect To** dialog box, shown in Figure H.4. Here you enter the information for the computer that you are attempting to contact. Click **OK** when you are certain that the information you've provided is correct.

A
B
C
D
E
F
G
H
I
J
K
L
M
N
O
P
Q
R
S
T
U
V
W
X
Y
Z

Figure **H.2**

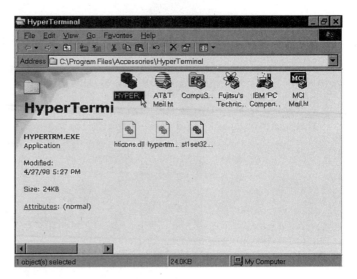

Figure **H.3**

Figure **H.4**

note... For your convenience, information in the **Country Code**, **Area Code**, and **Connect Using** sections of the **Connect To** dialog box is pulled from information you provided when you enabled Windows 98 Dial-Up Networking features. You can alter any of this information simply by typing over the information provided.

4. In the **Connect** dialog box, shown in Figure H.5, you can accept the default dialing properties or alter them as needed (review the section titled "Dial-Up Networking" for further details). Click the **Dial** button to initiate the connection.

Figure **H.5**

5. The **Connect** dialog box shown in Figure H.6 tracks the status of the connection.

Figure **H.6**

note...   Upon connection to the remote system, you can perform a variety of tasks, including transferring files, online chatting, and controlling remote terminal connectivity. For more information about these topics, refer to a good telecommunications manual.

After the connection is made, you are brought to the main HyperTerminal screen (with the name of your connection in the top border of the window), shown in Figure H.7. This is where all contact with the remote system is made.

note...   HyperTerminal can get confusing here: You are connected, but the screen is blank and there is no icon or message telling that you have connected to the remote system correctly. To determine whether you have connected, press **Enter** once or twice (depending on who you are connecting to, it may take two strokes of the **Enter** key to initiate the screen information).

A
B
C
D
E
F
G
H
I
J
K
L
M
N
O
P
Q
R
S
T
U
V
W
X
Y
Z

Figure **H.7**

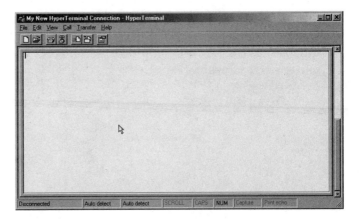

After you are connected, the screen should begin to display information about your connection, as shown in Figure H.8.

Figure **H.8**

6. You will probably be prompted to enter some sort of user ID and password identification in order to access a remote system. Unfortunately, the password information is repeated back to you clearly onscreen, with no security implemented to keep your information secret.

7. After you have been established as a valid user, most systems prompt you for specific information regarding the features that your PC can handle (such as the number of lines per screen and characters per line that your PC screen is capable of showing, and whether your system can handle ANSI support), as shown in Figure H.9.

Figure **H.9**

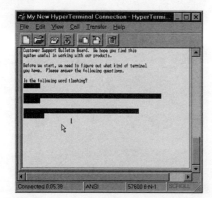

8. After this screen configuration is complete, you may be prompted for more detailed personal information, or you may be taken directly into the practical aspects of the system to which you are connecting.

9. When you finish with the remote system, disconnect from that session. To do this, click the **Disconnect** icon, shown in Figure H.10.

Figure **H.10**

As shown in Figure H.11, it looks as though nothing has happened even though the telephone connection has been terminated.

10. To exit the HyperTerminal application, click the **File** menu option and choose **Exit**.

11. The message box shown in Figure H.12 appears, prompting you to save your connection configuration. Fill in a name for your connection in order to save it to your hard disk.

Figure **H.11**

Figure **H.12**

12. You are returned to the HyperTerminal window from where you started, but now you are able to see the icon, shown in Figure H.13, that represents your new connection.

Figure **H.13**

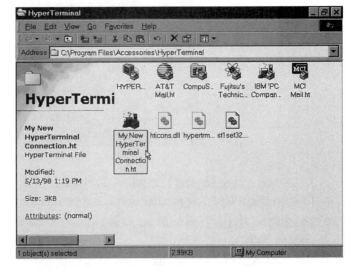

13. To reconnect at a later date, return to the screen shown in Figure H.13 and double-click one of the HyperTerminal connection files (these files are the ones with **.ht** extensions).

I

A
B
C
D
E
F
G
H
I
J
K
L
M
N
O
P
Q
R
S
T
U
V
W
X
Y
Z

A
B
C
D
E
F
G
H
I
J
K
L
M
N
O
P
Q
R
S
T
U
V
W
X
Y
Z

Imaging

The imaging component of Windows 98 has a variety of uses:

- It acts as the software for scanning information into your PC.
- It enables you to view, print, and manipulate received faxes.
- It enables you to view and print several types of graphical images.

> **note...** Eastman Software company, a division of Kodak, Inc., wrote the imaging software that Microsoft licensed and integrated into its Windows 98 product.

To use the imaging software, do the following:

1. Click the **Start** button, and choose **Programs**, **Accessories**, and then **Imaging**, as shown in Figure I.1.

Figure **I.1**

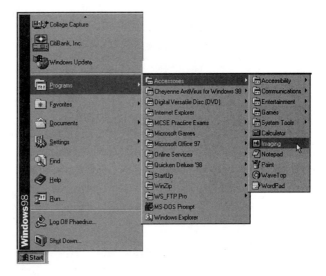

2. The main **Imaging** window is shown in Figure I.2. It is from this main screen that all of your viewing, editing, and/or printing of graphical images is done.

3. To view or print a graphical image that you already have on your computer, click **File** and then choose **Open**.

Figure **I.2**

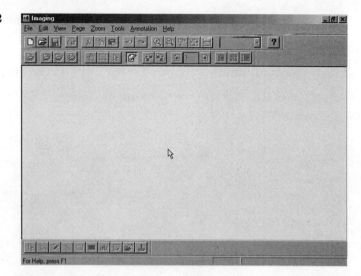

4. Navigate to the Windows 98 folder that contains the image you want to view or print. In the example shown in Figure I.3, I have selected a file named **Harry Caray & Cubs.bmp** from the **WINDOWS** folder.

Figure **I.3**

5. Click the **Open** button to open the file that you have selected, and voila! The image appears inside the **Imaging** window. Print the image by selecting **File** and then **Print**.

A
B
C
D
E
F
G
H
I
J
K
L
M
N
O
P
Q
R
S
T
U
V
W
X
Y
Z

A
B
C
D
E
F
G
H
I
J
K
L
M
N
O
P
Q
R
S
T
U
V
W
X
Y
Z

Playing with the various features and functions of the imaging software is probably the best way to learn to use this tool. Additionally, you can consult the Imaging tool's built-in help system, or you can contact Kodak for assistance. To obtain Kodak's contact information, do the following:

1. Click **Help**, and then click **About Imaging** to open the screen shown in Figure I.4.

Figure **I.4**

2. Click the **Contact Info** button to obtain the necessary information.

Infrared

The infrared component of Windows 98 is used to enable wireless communication between your PC and another computer. The catch here is that your computer must have a physical infrared port or device that can then be configured for this type of communication. To install the infrared device, review the section titled "Add New Hardware." To configure an installed infrared device, do the following:

1. Click the **Start** button, and choose **Settings**, then **Control Panel**, as shown in Figure I.5.

2. The Control Panel window, shown in Figure I.6, opens. Double-click the **Infrared** icon.

Figure I.5

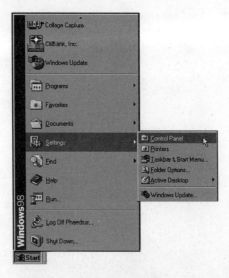

Figure I.6

3. The **Status** tab of the **Infrared Monitor** dialog box opens, as shown in Figure I.7. The message that appears in this example simply indicates that no compatible infrared devices are within range of this computer.

A
B
C
D
E
F
G
H
I
J
K
L
M
N
O
P
Q
R
S
T
U
V
W
X
Y
Z

A
B
C
D
E
F
G
H
I
J
K
L
M
N
O
P
Q
R
S
T
U
V
W
X
Y
Z

Figure **I.7**

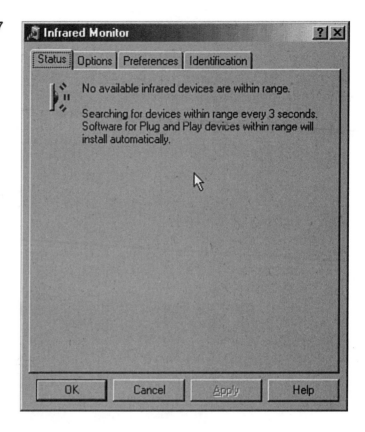

note... The term *within range* can mean different things to different computers. In general, the standard infrared range is 3–6 feet. Infrared ports
should not have any obstructions between them.

4. Click the **Options** tab to reveal the screen shown in Figure I.8. The
   check boxes marked are the set defaults for a generic Windows 98
   infrared device. The second line, **Providing Application Support on
   COM5 and LPT3**, appears so you can easily tell from where your
   infrared device will be "listening" for other infrared devices (serial and/or
   parallel ports are where printers are found).

5. Click the **Preferences** tab to reveal the screen shown in Figure I.9.
   Among other things, this tab permits you to display an **Infrared Monitor**
   icon on the Windows 98 taskbar; you can double-click this icon to quickly return to the **Infrared Monitor** configuration screen.

Figure **I.8**

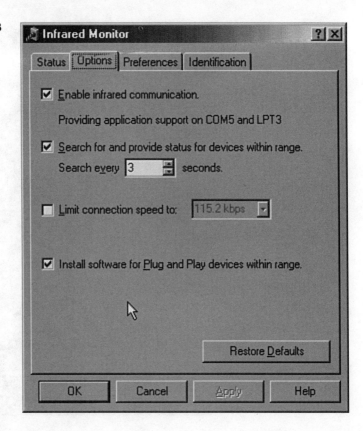

6. Click the **Identification** tab to view the screen shown in Figure I.10. This screen enables you to change your computer's name and to provide a brief description of it.

note... Both of the infrared devices that are attempting to communicate with each other must have unique computer names. If a **duplicate name found** error occurs, then you should change your computer's name in the **Identification** tab of the **Infrared Monitor** dialog box.

note... The **Computer Description** area is just an informational field that other users with infrared devices can scan to make sure that they are connecting to the correct computing device.

A
B
C
D
E
F
G
H
I
J
K
L
M
N
O
P
Q
R
S
T
U
V
W
X
Y
Z

Figure **I.9**

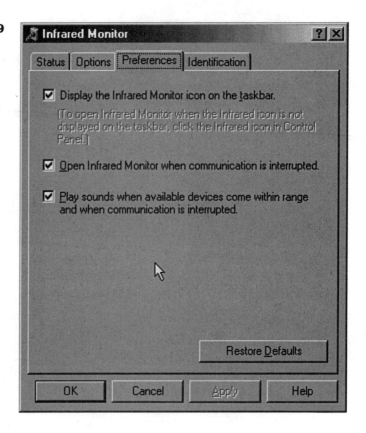

7. Click the **OK** button. Windows 98 accepts any changes to the infrared configuration and returns you to the desktop. If you checked the **Display the Infrared Monitor Icon on the Taskbar** check box in the **Preferences** tab, you should see the **Infrared Monitor** icon on the taskbar, as shown in Figure I.11.

Figure **I.10**

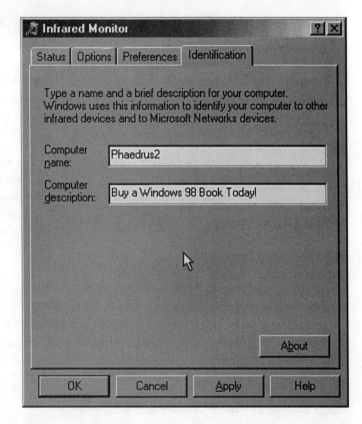

Figure **I.11**

Installing Windows 98

Windows 98 is very easy to install. It can be installed either from a CD-ROM or from a network installation point (this book deals only with the CD-ROM method—it is assumed that your firm's Networking or Information Services groups handles the network installation methods).

To install Windows 98 from a CD-ROM, you must have either DOS or some previous version of Windows (version 3.1 or newer) already installed.

note... If your computer system is new and the hard drive is not yet formatted, consult the manuals that came with the PC for information on formatting the hard drive.

A
B
C
D
E
F
G
H
I
J
K
L
M
N
O
P
Q
R
S
T
U
V
W
X
Y
Z

Before you begin installing Windows 98, you should do the following:

1. Make sure your computer meets the minimum hardware requirements for the Windows 98 operating system. This means that you must have at least 120 MB of free hard drive space and 16 MB of RAM (memory) on a PC with an Intel (or compatible) CPU. Your computer's *CPU* (Central Processing Unit, or "brain") must be at least equal to an Intel 80486-DX processor that runs at least 66 MHz.

note...   **Depending on your installation method (that is, whether you are upgrading from Windows 95 or Windows 3.*x*, whether this is a new installation with the FAT16 file system, or whether it's a new installation with the FAT32 file system), you will probably require more drive space. Plan on the typical installation taking somewhere from 165–225 MB of drive space.**

2. Confirm the existence of at least a disk operating system such as Microsoft DOS (the Windows GUI such as Windows 95 is preferred, because it makes the installation process that much easier).

3. Prepare a formatted, blank, high-density, 3 1/2-inch, 1.44 MB floppy disk to use for the creation of the Startup Disk during the installation process.

Upgrading from Windows 95

To upgrade to Windows 98 from Windows 95, do the following:

1. Start your PC and let it boot completely into Windows 95.

2. Place the Windows 98 CD in your CD-ROM drive.

note...   **All terminate-and-stay-resident (TSR) programs such as virus scanners and protectors, calendars, address books, and the like must be exited prior to the start of the Windows 98 installation process. Consult the help manuals for each program for assistance in stopping these extra services. Additional information can be obtained from the Windows 98 Setup.Txt file that comes on the Windows 98 CD.**

3. Click the **Start** button, then choose **Run**.

4. In the ensuing **Run** dialog box, type the following:

    `x:\Setup`

x equals the disk drive letter of the CD-ROM disk drive, as shown in
Figure I.12.

Figure **I.12**

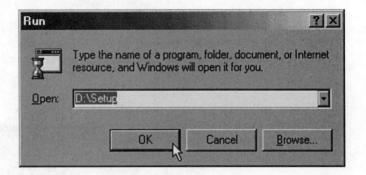

5. Click **OK** to begin the installation process. This starts the Windows 98
    Setup Wizard. Follow all the prompts precisely as they are given on the
    screen, paying strict attention to the section on the creation of the
    Startup Disk.

note... Although the Startup Disk might seem inconsequential, you'll need one
in case Windows 98 fails to boot at some point in the future. Without
the Startup Disk, you would not be able to get back into your computer
(short of rerunning the Windows 98 installation process).

note... The Windows 98 Setup Wizard usually takes 30–60 minutes to complete, and might require you to reboot your computer several times. Do
not worry—this is normal.

note... The installation process takes its default information from your present Windows 95 installation, but most of the precise configuration settings can be altered once the base Windows 98 operating system has
been installed on your PC.

6. After the installation is complete and the system has been rebooted, you
    will be presented with a **Welcome to Windows** logon screen such as the
    one shown in Figure I.13. Enter your name and password (if no pass-
    word is entered, you are not presented with this screen in the future),
    and then click **OK** to enter the Windows 98 operating system.

A
B
C
D
E
F
G
H
I
J
K
L
M
N
O
P
Q
R
S
T
U
V
W
X
Y
Z

A
B
C
D
E
F
G
H
I
J
K
L
M
N
O
P
Q
R
S
T
U
V
W
X
Y
Z

note...   You set your system's user ID and password the first time you enter a
user ID and password into Windows 98. Also, if you do not use a password now, you are not prompted for a user ID to log on in the future.

Don't worry about typing in a password and then forgetting it. If you do
not remember your password (or do not care to type one in), press the
Esc key to bypass this whole logon process (so much for system security).

Figure **I.13**

note...   If your PC has a network card, then the window shown in Figure I.13
contains a third line that prompts you for a server or domain name (if
you do not know the server/domain name, contact your network administrator for further assistance).

Upgrading from Windows 3.1*x*

To upgrade to Windows 98 from Windows 3.1*x*, do the following:

1. Start your PC and let it boot completely into the DOS operating system.

2. Proceed to the Windows 3.1*x* graphical user interface (GUI) application.

note...   All terminate-and-stay-resident (TSR) programs such as virus scanners
and protectors, calendars, address books, and the like must be exited
prior to the start of the Windows 98 installation process. Consult the
help manuals for each program for assistance in stopping these extra
services. Additional information can be obtained from the Windows 98
Setup.Txt file that comes on the Windows 98 CD.

3. Click the **File** menu on the **Program Manager** screen and then click
Run.

4. In the ensuing **Run** dialog box, type the following:

   x:\Setup

   x equals the disk drive letter of the CD-ROM disk drive.

5. Click **OK** to begin the installation process. This starts the Windows 98 Setup Wizard. Follow all the prompts precisely as they are given on the screen, paying strict attention to the section on the creation of the Emergency Startup Disk.

note... The Windows 98 Setup Wizard usually takes 30–60 minutes to complete, and might require you to reboot your computer several times. Do not worry—this is normal.

note... The installation process takes its default information from your present Windows 95 installation, but most of the precise configuration settings can be altered once the base Windows 98 operating system has been installed on your PC.

6. After the installation is complete and the system has been rebooted, you are presented with a **Welcome to Windows** logon screen such as the one shown in Figure I.14. Enter your name and password (if no password is entered, you are not presented with this screen in the future), and then click **OK** to enter the Windows 98 operating system.

Figure **I.14**

note... You set your system's user ID and password the first time you enter a user ID and password into Windows 98. Also, if you do not use a password now, you are not prompted for a user ID to log on in the future.

Don't worry about typing in a password and then forgetting it. If you do not remember your password (or do not care to type one in), press the **Esc** key to bypass this whole logon process (so much for system security).

A
B
C
D
E
F
G
H
I
J
K
L
M
N
O
P
Q
R
S
T
U
V
W
X
Y
Z

A
B
C
D
E
F
G
H
I
J
K
L
M
N
O
P
Q
R
S
T
U
V
W
X
Y
Z

note...   If your PC has a network card, then the window shown in Figure I.14 contains a third line that prompts you for a server or domain name (if you do not know the server/domain name, contact your network administrator for further assistance).

Upgrading from DOS

When you are upgrading from DOS, installing Windows 98 can be a little trickier than when you upgrade from an existing Windows 3.1x/95 implementation. To upgrade to Windows 98 from a DOS prompt (with just the DOS operating system installed), do the following:

1. Start your PC and let it boot completely into the DOS operating system.

note...   All terminate-and-stay-resident (TSR) programs such as virus scanners and protectors, calendars, address books, and the like must be exited prior to the start of the Windows 98 installation process. Consult the help manuals for each program for assistance in stopping these extra services. Additional information can be obtained from the Windows 98 **Setup.Txt** file that comes on the Windows 98 CD.

2. Insert the Windows 98 CD into the CD-ROM drive or the **Setup Disk 1** floppy disk into the **A:** drive.

3. Type the following statement:

   `x:\Setup`

   x equals the disk drive letter of the CD-ROM or floppy setup disk drive.

4. Press **Enter** to begin the installation process. This starts the Windows 98 Setup Wizard.

5. Follow all the prompts precisely as they are given on the screen, paying strict attention to the section on the creation of the Startup Disk.

note...   Any applications on your computer might need to be reinstalled after the Windows 98 operating system is installed. In addition, it is possible that a few of your applications will not run at all under Windows 98. For a partial listing of applications that have trouble in the Windows 98 environment, review the **Programs.Txt** file on the Windows 98 installation disk(s).

note... The Windows 98 Setup Wizard usually takes 30–60 minutes to complete, and might require you to reboot your computer several times. Do not worry—this is normal.

6. You are prompted for various default information, such as the name of the installation directory. It is strongly recommended that you leave the default choice of **C:\Windows** as the directory selection.

7. After the installation is complete and the system has been rebooted, you are presented with a **Welcome to Windows** logon screen such as the one shown in Figure I.15. Enter your name and password (if no password is entered, you are not presented with this screen in the future), and then click **OK** to enter the Windows 98 operating system.

Figure **I.15**

note... You set your system's user ID and password the first time you enter a user ID and password into Windows 98. Also, if you do not use a password now, you are not prompted for a user ID to log on in the future.

Don't worry about typing in a password and then forgetting it. If you do not remember your password (or do not care to type one in), press the **Esc** key to bypass this whole logon process (so much for system security).

note... If your PC has a network card, then the window shown in Figure I.15 contains a third line that prompts you for a server or domain name (if you do not know the server/domain name, contact your network administrator for further assistance).

A
B
C
D
E
F
G
H
I
J
K
L
M
N
O
P
Q
R
S
T
U
V
W
X
Y
Z

IntelliMouse

The IntelliMouse, invented by Microsoft, looks much like a normal mouse, except that it has a little wheel located between the two mouse buttons. The purpose of this wheel is to make scrolling within Windows applications much easier—you no longer need to move your mouse pointer from the specific location in a document to the scrollbars to view a different portion of that document.

note...   For further discussion on general mouse terms and movements, see the section titled "Mouse."

Internet

The Internet, also known as Cyberspace, the Information Superhighway, and a billion other nicknames, is not just one giant network. It consists of tens of thousands or perhaps even millions of interconnected (or *internetworked*) networks. It was originally designed by the U.S. military as a post-nuclear war survival tool.

There are many components to the Internet, but the most commonly known ones are the World Wide Web (WWW), File Transfer Protocol (FTP), and Gopher sites (though Gopher is beginning to die off as of late).

To move to a site on the Internet, all you need to know is the TCP/IP address of the remote computer that houses the site, or that computer's domain name address (such as **microsoft.com**). With the advent of Internet browsers, GUI-based FTP software, and the sheer graphical nature of the WWW, maneuvering around the Internet has become much easier for the average lay person.

Internet Explorer 4.*x*

Internet Explorer (IE) 4 is the Web browser that is built into Windows 98. To use Internet Explorer, do the following:

1. Double-click the **Internet Explorer** icon located on the Windows 98 desktop, as shown in Figure I.16.

2. If you have not yet connected to the Internet—either through a Dial-Up Networking client or through a direct connection—an error message such as the one shown in Figure I.17 appears.

Figure **I.16**

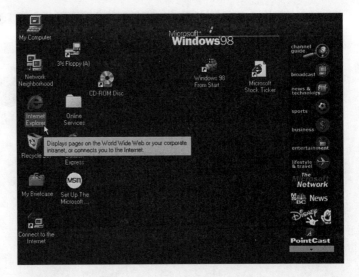

Figure **I.17**

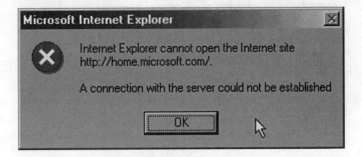

note... For more information about connecting to the Internet, refer to the section titled "Dial-Up Networking."

If you have already connected to the Internet, you'll see a screen such as the one shown in Figure I.18. Click the **Favorites** menu option to display a list of sites that you've saved as favorites, as shown in Figure I.19.

note... For a more detailed discussion of the **Favorites** menu, refer to the section titled "Favorites."

A
B
C
D
E
F
G
H
I
J
K
L
M
N
O
P
Q
R
S
T
U
V
W
X
Y
Z

A
B
C
D
E
F
G
H
I
J
K
L
M
N
O
P
Q
R
S
T
U
V
W
X
Y
Z

Figure **I.18**

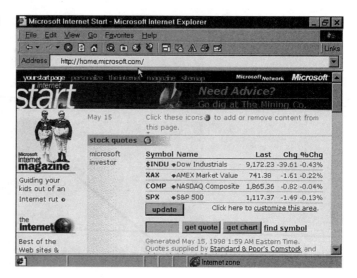

Figure **I.19**

3. Click the **View** menu option to examine Internet Explorer's View options. These options enable you to configure how various features of Internet Explorer are displayed. For example, you can select the **Text Labels** option from the **Toolbars** sub-menu (as shown in Figure I.20) to place text labels on the IE toolbar (this places the text name of each icon directly below that icon's picture on the toolbar).

Figure **I.20**

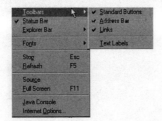

4. Click the **Help** menu option to reveal and configure the available help options, as shown in Figure I.21. One of my favorite help options, **Microsoft on the Web**, enables you to connect directly to Microsoft's web site for timely information and product support.

Figure **I.21**

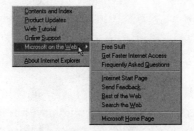

Playing with the features and functions of the IE browser software is probably the best way to learn to use it. For more in-depth information about using Internet Explorer, you might want to consult any number of books dedicated to this topic. A great place to find books about Internet Explorer is Macmillan Computer Publishing's Internet web site (**www.mcp.com**).

Internet Explorer Menu

Many Internet tools come with the full Windows 98 installation. To access these tools, click the **Start** button, choose **Programs**, and then **Internet Explorer**. The following tools areavailable:

- Address Book
- Connection Wizard
- FrontPage Express
- Internet Explorer

A
B
C
D
E
F
G
H
I
J
K
L
M
N
O
P
Q
R
S
T
U
V
W
X
Y
Z

- Microsoft Chat
- Microsoft NetMeeting
- NetShow Player
- Outlook Express
- Personal Web Server
- Web Publishing Wizard

Internet Mail Services

Built into Windows 98 is a series of messaging services such as Internet Mail, Internet News, and NetMeeting. These services are integrated into the Outlook Express software package. Outlook Express enables you to send and receive email to and from other users across the Internet—provided that you already have an established email account with an Internet service provider (ISP) such as Internet Illinois, or with an online service provider such as The Microsoft Network (MSN).

After you have connected to the Internet, it is possible to use Outlook Express to send and receive all email, as well as to read and participate in newsgroups (see the section titled "Outlook Express" for more information).

Intranet

An *intranet* looks, acts, feels, and works just like the Internet, but access to an intranet is limited to a select group of individuals.

ISDN Tools

ISDN stands for Integrated Services Digital Network, and is a special digital telephone line whose bandwidth can be much larger than that of the fastest analog modem. Typical bandwidths are 128 Kbps (which translates to 131,072 bps), as opposed to the fastest analog modem of 56 Kbps (or roughly 57,600 bits per second). Most non-metropolitan areas (population centers with fewer than 100,000 people) in the United States do not yet support ISDN, so check with your local telephone company before going out and spending a few hundred dollars on an ISDN modem.

I know of no computer manufacturers that ship ISDN modems with their PCs. However, if you do happen to own an ISDN modem, then use the Windows 98 ISDN Configuration Wizard application to properly configure it for use with the Windows 98 operating system environment.

ISDN Configuration Wizard

You can use the Windows 98 ISDN Configuration Wizard to configure an ISDN modem for use with Windows 98. This wizard cannot be run until the hardware is installed in your computer, so make sure this has been done before starting the wizard (refer to the section titled "Add New Hardware" for more information).

To use the wizard, do the following:

1. Click the **Start** button, choose **Programs**, **Accessories**, **Communications**, and then **ISDN Configuration Wizard**, as shown in Figure I.22.

Figure **I.22**

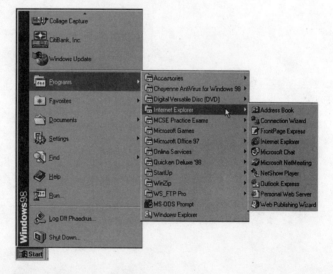

2. If you start the ISDN Configuration Wizard but do not have an ISDN modem, the error message shown in Figure I.23 will appear.

   If an ISDN modem is installed, the wizard should work without a hitch. Follow all the prompts closely to complete the configuration of your ISDN modem.

A
B
C
D
E
F
G
H
I
J
K
L
M
N
O
P
Q
R
S
T
U
V
W
X
Y
Z

Figure **I.23**

note... If you run this wizard and your modem still does not operate properly, then you should consult the technical manuals that came with the ISDN hardware. Additional assistance can be obtained through your local telephone company or the manufacturer of the ISDN hardware.

JKL

A
B
C
D
E
F
G
H
I
J
K
L
M
N
O
P
Q
R
S
T
U
V
W
X
Y
Z

Java

Java, originally developed by Sun Microcomputers, Inc., is one of the latest computer languages for the Internet. It allows small programs—such as a stock ticker—to execute on your computer through an Internet web browser (such as Microsoft Internet Explorer). Java is not meant to be a full-blown development language like Visual Basic or COBOL; it is more like a scripting language such as VBScript.

Java Console

The **Java Console** menu option available in **Internet Explorer** is not a Java development editor. Rather, its purpose is to give you a chance to see some basic information about the Microsoft virtual machine (VM) for Java, which is built into Windows 98. To use the Java Console, do the following:

1. In an **Internet Explorer** window, click **View** and choose **Java Console**, as shown in Figure J.1.

Figure **J.1**

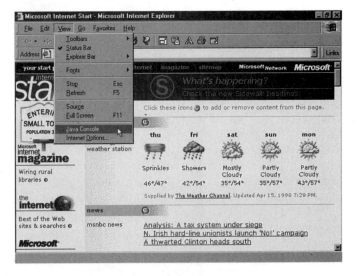

2. The **Java Console** window, shown in Figure J.2, appears. Here you can view some basic information about system priorities, threads, and memory usage. Type the first letter of any of these options to cause that option to execute. For further details on any of these options, type a question mark (**?**) to start the Help feature.

Figure **J.2**

Keyboard

The keyboard that came with your PC is a very important piece of hardware. Without it, it would be virtually impossible to use your PC or any of the programs installed on it.

Although your keyboard might appear to be working just fine, Windows 98 provides a few configuration options that can help you tweak your keyboard to make it a bit more to your liking. To configure your keyboard, do the following:

1. Click the **Start** button, select **Settings**, and then click **Control Panel**, as shown in Figure K.1.

Figure **K.1**

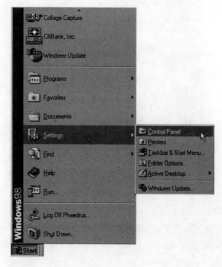

A
B
C
D
E
F
G
H
I
J
K
L
M
N
O
P
Q
R
S
T
U
V
W
X
Y
Z

A
B
C
D
E
F
G
H
I
J
K
L
M
N
O
P
Q
R
S
T
U
V
W
X
Y
Z

2. The **Control Panel** window, shown in Figure K.2, opens. Double-click the **Keyboard** icon.

Figure **K.2**

3. The **Keyboard Properties** dialog box appears opened to the **Speed** tab, shown in Figure K.3. Configure the **Character Repeat** and **Cursor Blink Rate** settings.

Figure **K.3**

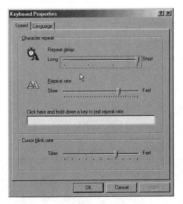

note... The **Character Repeat** section of the **Speed** tab enables you to specify how quickly or slowly a character repeats itself on your computer's monitor if you hold down that character's key. Use the test box on the screen to determine through trial and error which setting is best suited to your tastes.

note... The **Cursor Blink Rate** area enables you to specify how quickly or slowly the mouse cursor shown on your computer monitor blinks on and off. Play around with this setting until you discover the right one for you.

4. Click the **Language** tab to view the screen shown in Figure K.4. Here you can specify what language you want to use on your PC (the default setting is **English (United States)**.

Figure **K.4**

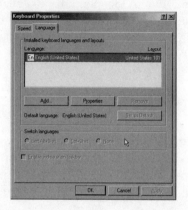

note... You can specify that any of a number of languages be used, and you can increase the number of available languages by installing Windows 98's five additional language-support features (Baltic, Central European, Cyrillic, Greek, and Turkish). For information about installing these features, refer to the sections titled "Add/Remove Programs" and "Multilanguage Support."

5. To add another language, click the **Add** button and follow the prompts.

note... If you install a language that you don't understand, it is possible to completely mess up your computing environment. This can be fixed only through this **Keyboard Properties** screen, so either memorize where the various buttons you'll need to use on that screen are placed, or make sure that you are fluent in the language you are installing.

6. When you are satisfied with your settings, click the **OK** button to exit the **Keyboard Properties** dialog box.

A
B
C
D
E
F
G
H
I
J
K
L
M
N
O
P
Q
R
S
T
U
V
W
X
Y
Z

A
B
C
D
E
F
G
H
I
J
K
L
M
N
O
P
Q
R
S
T
U
V
W
X
Y
Z

LAN

A LAN (an acronym for *local area network*) usually consists of a small group of PCs used to control file and print services, user access permissions, and the like. Typically, a LAN's purpose is to facilitate the sharing of files and data in a local group of PCs (such as a human resources department), and to permit many people to print to a limited number of networked printers.

note...   A LAN without at least one server is considered to be a peer-to-peer network, which means that all logon and access security must be controlled on each individual PC. Likewise, a LAN with one or more servers usually has the LAN's security authentication and printer access controlled by just a few of the servers.

List Box

Windows 98 uses a software programming feature known as a list box throughout the operating system. List boxes usually contain a list of items or options from which you are to select one. The primary purpose of a list box is to limit the choices for whatever you are attempting to do.

Local Printer

A local printer is one that is physically attached to your computer, and may be any type of Windows 98-compatible printer. This is not a printer that you would find by using the **Network Neighborhood** icon on the Windows 98 desktop.

Log Off

The logoff process for Windows 98 is useful only when multiple persons use the same computer. If only one user works on a certain PC, the shutdown process would be used.

In the event that multiple users use your PC, you should log off by doing the following:

1. To log off of a Windows 98 PC, click once on the **Start** button and then click **Log Off *User Name***, as shown in Figure L.1 (in this case, ***User Name*** equals **Phaedrus**).

Figure **L.1**

note... The current user's name automatically appears, so you do not need to figure out who is already logged on to the computer.

2. You'll see the screen shown in Figure L.2. Click **Yes** to confirm that you want to log off of Windows.

Figure **L.2**

Windows 98 shuts down all active programs and returns you to the logon screen, shown in Figure L.3. Here the next user can log on to Windows.

Figure **L.3**

M

A
B
C
D
E
F
G
H
I
J
K
L
M
N
O
P
Q
R
S
T
U
V
W
X
Y
Z

A
B
C
D
E
F
G
H
I
J
K
L
M
N
O
P
Q
R
S
T
U
V
W
X
Y
Z

Macromedia Shockwave

Macromedia Shockwave is a multimedia Internet technology experience supported by the major Internet Web browsers on the market today, including Microsoft Internet Explorer and Netscape Navigator. Macromedia permits Microsoft to integrate its base Shockwave technology directly into the Internet Explorer 4 Web browser. Because Macromedia is constantly updating its plug-ins (a *plug-in* is an add-on component you can download and install for use directly with your Web browser), you might want to cruise over to Macromedia's Web site (www.macromedia.com/) and pick up the latest and greatest plug-ins as soon as you install your copy of Windows 98.

Mail

Electronic mail (email) is the method by which you can communicate in writing with another user anywhere on the planet. Email can occur via a corporate network or series of internetworks, or via the Internet. To configure how email is handled by your Windows 98 system, do the following:

1. Right-click the **Internet Explorer** icon on the Windows 98 desktop and choose **Properties** from the ensuing shortcut menu, as shown in Figure M.1.

Figure **M.1**

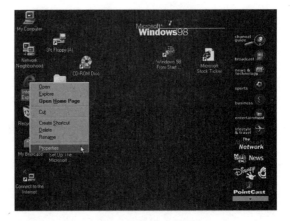

2. Click the **Programs** tab in the **Internet Properties** dialog box to view the screen shown in Figure M.2.

Figure **M.2**

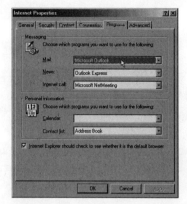

note... The **Messaging** area enables you to choose which email package you want to use with the Internet Explorer browser, as well as which Internet news and call software you want to use.

3. Click the down-arrow button of the **Mail** text box to view the drop-down list box that lists the available email software packages that are compatible with the IE browser (see Figure M.3).

Figure **M.3**

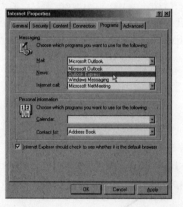

note... If you have a full Windows 98 installation, you are presented with the **Outlook Express** and the **Windows Messaging** options. If you have Office installed on your machine, you'll also have the option of selecting **Microsoft Outlook**, as shown in Figure M.3.

note... Outlook Express is my favorite, because it makes sending and receiving mail very easy.

note... The Windows Messaging client software is also known as the *Inbox* or *Exchange* client, which can be very cumbersome and difficult to configure and use.

4. Click the email package of your choice to select it, and then click the **OK** button to accept the changes and to close the **Internet Properties** dialog box.

Check out the section titled "Microsoft Outlook Express" for information about reading and sending mail.

Menus

The menus found throughout Windows 98 enable you to easily access applications, data, and system utilities by using either your mouse or keyboard. When using your mouse to navigate menus, you simply click the menu and command you want. To use your keyboard, you must first determine which keyboard shortcut accesses the menu you need. To do this, simply look for the underlined *hotkey* in the menu's name. For example, the letter *F* in the **File** menu is underlined, indicating that *F* is the hotkey. Pressing the Alt+F key combination opens the **File** menu.

Media Player

Windows 98 Media Player enables you to play several types of files including ActiveMovie, Mpact MPEG Decoder, Video for Windows, Sound (WAV), MIDI Sequencer, and CD Audio files (you might be able to play a few other types, depending upon your computer's sound equipment). To use Media Player, do the following:

1. Click the **Start** button, choose **Programs**, **Accessories**, **Entertainment**, and then **Media Player**, as shown in Figure M.4.

2. The **Media Player** window, shown in Figure M.5, opens. To quickly determine which types of files are supported by your equipment, click the **Device** menu option to view a list of acceptable devices.

Figure **M.4**

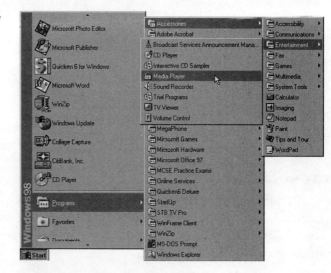

A
B
C
D
E
F
G
H
I
J
K
L
M
N
O
P
Q
R
S
T
U
V
W
X
Y
Z

Figure **M.5**

3. To select a media file for playing, click the **File** menu option and choose **Open**. The **Open** dialog box, shown in Figure M.6, appears.

Figure **M.6**

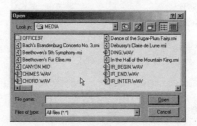

4. Navigate to the folder containing the file you want to view, select the file, and then click the **Open** button. As shown in Figure M.7, you are returned to the **Media Player** window, and the file you selected (in this case, Beethoven's *Fur Elise*) is ready to be played.

5. Click the **Play** button (the one on the far left that resembles a single right arrow). When the music starts, the marker on the timeline moves to show how much time has elapsed and how much is remaining, as shown in Figure M.8.

A
B
C
D
E
F
G
H
I
J
K
L
M
N
O
P
Q
R
S
T
U
V
W
X
Y
Z

Figure **M.7**

Figure **M.8**

Microsoft Chat 2.1

Microsoft Chat enables you to "chat" (using your keyboard) with others in an Internet chat room. Microsoft Chat is special because it's very visual—everyone appears as a comic book character. You can modify your own character so it demonstrates a range of emotions.

note... If your computer is not powerful enough to support Microsoft Chat's visual elements (that is, its comic-book characters and so on), you can configure it to operate in plain-text format. However, if you change it to operate in plain-text mode, then the primary purpose for using Comic Chat (its visual elements) is lost.

To use the Microsoft Chat application, do the following:

1. Connect to the Internet (refer to the sections titled "Dial-Up Networking" and "Network" for details).

2. Click the **Start** button, choose **Programs**, **Internet Tools**, and then **Microsoft Chat**, as shown in Figure M.9.

3. In the **Enter New Nickname** dialog box, shown in Figure M.10, type a descriptive name (your real name is okay, too), and then click the **OK** button.

note... If you've used Microsoft Chat on your machine before, you bypass the screen shown in Figure M.10.

4. The **Connect** screen, shown in Figure M.11, appears. Unless you know of other chat servers or chat rooms that you want to visit, leave the defaults in place and click **OK** to continue.

Figure **M.9**

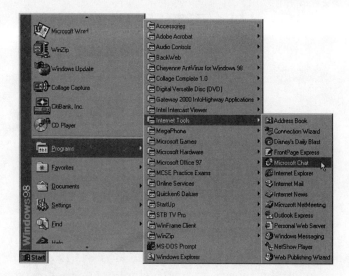

Figure **M.10**

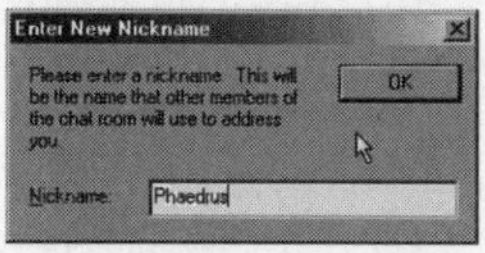

Figure **M.11**

5. When you enter the Comic Chat room, you first see the "Message of the Day" pop-up window. To move beyond this screen, simply click **OK**. If you never want to be bothered with this screen during future connections, uncheck the **Show This Whenever Connecting** check box.

6. Your character, whose name is the same as the nickname specified in the **Enter New Nickname** screen, now enters an active chat room. Right-click the character and choose **Get Profile** from the ensuing shortcut menu, as shown in Figure M.12. The result of this query appears in the chat window.

A
B
C
D
E
F
G
H
I
J
K
L
M
N
O
P
Q
R
S
T
U
V
W
X
Y
Z

A
B
C
D
E
F
G
H
I
J
K
L
M
N
O
P
Q
R
S
T
U
V
W
X
Y
Z

Figure **M.12**

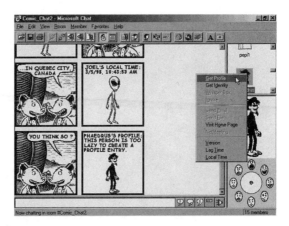

note... The shortcut menu shown in Figure M.12 provides many options. You can obtain a user profile, identity information, software version, lag time, local time, and email options. If you right-click another user's comic-book character, then the options that are grayed out in Figure M.12 are available for use.

7. To view your Microsoft Chat options, click the **View** menu item and choose **Options**. This opens the **Personal Info** tab of the **Microsoft Chat Options** dialog box, shown in Figure M.13.

Figure **M.13**

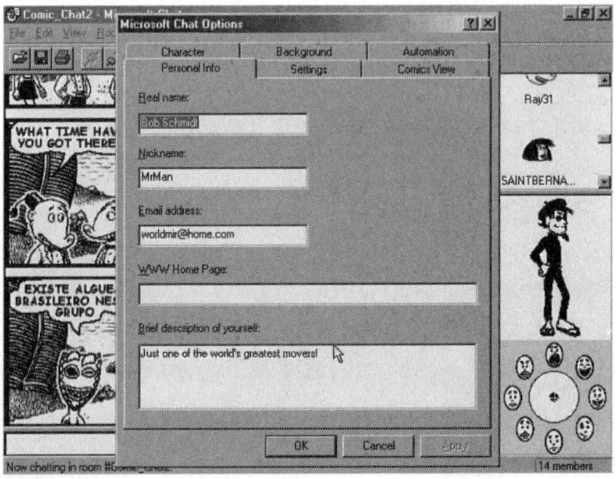

8. The only field you are required to fill out in this screen is **Nickname**. (If you've filled in your information but want to change your nickname, simply type over the name you've already supplied in the **Nickname** field. In this example, I've changed my nickname from **Phaedrus** to **MrMan**.) If you want to provide more information about yourself, you can fill out the **Real Name**, **Email Address**, **WWW Home Page**, and **Brief Description of Yourself** fields.

note... Microsoft Chat does not accept the use of spaces, punctuation marks, and special characters in nicknames. Refrain from using characters other than letters and numbers.

note... If you choose not to enter a personal profile in the **Brief Description of Yourself** field, your system displays the phrase **This Person is too Lazy to Create a Profile Entry** by default.

9. Click the **Settings** tab to view the screen shown in Figure M.14. Here you can configure how Microsoft Chat behaves, including whether Microsoft Chat-specific information is sent to other users, whether users of your machine can visit certain types of chat rooms, whether you hear sounds, and whether you want to receive chat invitations.

Figure **M.14**

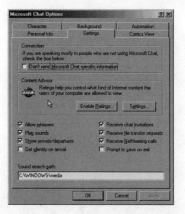

10. Click the **Comics View** tab to view the screen shown in Figure M.15. Here you can customize the fonts used in Microsoft Chat, and you can change the layout of the Chat window.

A
B
C
D
E
F
G
H
I
J
K
L
M
N
O
P
Q
R
S
T
U
V
W
X
Y
Z

A
B
C
D
E
F
G
H
I
J
K
L
M
N
O
P
Q
R
S
T
U
V
W
X
Y
Z

Figure **M.15**

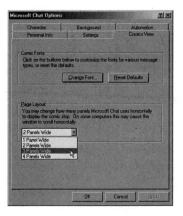

note... If you make your screen four panels wide, the size of each pane in your viewer area will be smaller than if your screen is one panel wide.

11. Click the **Character** tab to view the screen shown in Figure M.16. When you click a character name in the **Character** list, that character appears in the **Preview** box. Click one of the facial expressions in the area below the **Preview** box to change the expression—and thus, convey the mood— of your character. Select the character and expression that you want to use in your chat sessions.

Figure **M.16**

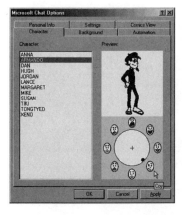

12. Click the **Background** tab to view the screen shown in Figure M.17. When you click a background name in the **Background** list, that background appears in the **Preview** area.

Figure **M.17**

13. Click the **Automation** tab to view the screen shown in Figure M.18. This screen enables you to set a greeting to be displayed each time someone enters a chat room that you are hosting (to host a chat room, you must be the first person to arrive in a room).

Figure **M.18**

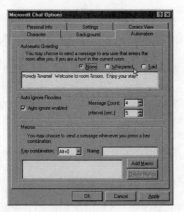

note... The **Macros** area of the **Automation** tab enables you to create a macro that you can use to send messages. For more information about this feature, click the **Help** button in the upper-right corner of the dialog box.

14. Click the **Apply** button to apply your changes.

15. Click **OK** to exit the **Microsoft Chat Options** dialog box and return to your chat room.

A
B
C
D
E
F
G
H
I
J
K
L
M
N
O
P
Q
R
S
T
U
V
W
X
Y
Z

A
B
C
D
E
F
G
H
I
J
K
L
M
N
O
P
Q
R
S
T
U
V
W
X
Y
Z

16. Type what you want your character to say in the long white box at the bottom of the screen, press **Enter**, and *voilà!* As shown in the bottom-left pane in Figure M.19, your character starts speaking to everyone else in the chat room.

Figure **M.19**

17. To exit Chat, either click the × button in the upper-right corner of this screen or click the **File** menu option and choose **Exit**.

note...   You can print Chat sessions by clicking the **File** menu option and choosing **Print**. To save your Chat session for future use, click the **File** menu and choose **Save As**. You will be prompted to type a descriptive name for your Chat session, which is saved with a **.ccc** file extension.

Microsoft FrontPage Express

Microsoft FrontPage Express provides a quick and easy way for you to create your own web page that can be viewed on your PC (see the section titled "Personal Web Server" for more information) or on the Internet (assuming your ISP can host your pages). To use Microsoft FrontPage Express, do the following:

1. Click the **Start** button, choose **Programs**, **Internet Tools**, and then **FrontPage Express**, as shown in Figure M.20.

Figure **M.20**

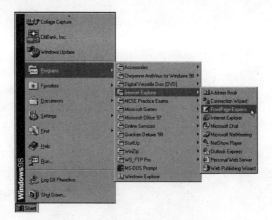

2. The **FrontPage Express** window, shown in Figure M.21, opens. If you are an HTML programming wizard, then you can just start typing and create yourself a web site. But if you are like the rest of us, you will probably find it easier to modify an existing web site to get the hang of things. To open a web site, click the **File** menu and choose **Open**.

Figure **M.21**

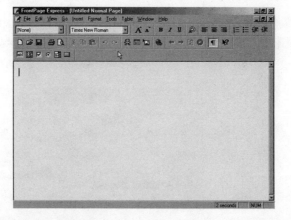

note... Remember that the text and graphics of web sites belonging to both companies and individuals are their own and that copyright and trademark laws do apply. Although I do suggest you use other web sites for learning purposes, I strongly recommend that you never use anyone else's work on your own web site. The only time it's acceptable to borrow from other web sites is if you have written permission to do so. Failure to do so is, well, a bad thing.

A
B
C
D
E
F
G
H
I
J
K
L
M
N
O
P
Q
R
S
T
U
V
W
X
Y
Z

A

B

C

D

E

F

G

H

I

J

K

L

M

N

O

P

Q

R

S

T

U

V

W

X

Y

Z

3. The **Open File** dialog box, shown in Figure M.22, opens. If you want to find an existing web page or site on your local computer or network, select the **From File** option button and then enter the path name to the file in the corresponding text box (click **Browse** if you don't know the path name). Select the **From Location** option button if you want to pull a copy of a web page from the Internet or from an intranet/extranet, and then type the URL of the site you want to access (in this example, I've typed http://www.microsoft.com).

Figure **M.22**

4. Click the **OK** button to retrieve the web page and return to the **FrontPage** window, as shown in Figure M.23. The screen is filled with graphics and strange-looking characters.

Figure **M.23**

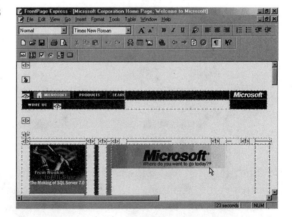

5. To examine the HTML code that makes the graphical features of the site possible, click the **View** menu option and select **HTML**.

6. The **View or Edit HTML** window, shown in Figure M.24, opens. View the contents of this window to get a feel for how HTML operates.

Figure **M.24**

note... HTML code is not as difficult or complex as it looks. HTML simply uses tags to format text and other elements of a Web page. For example, to place a title on your Web page, you enclose the title text with the **<title></title>** tags (in other words, simply type whatever text you want to appear as your title between these two tags). To take a closer look at HTML, pick up *Sams Teach Yourself HTML 3.2 in 24 Hours* by Dick Oliver.

note... If your goal is to quickly and easily create your own web sites, I urge you to purchase a book on HTML (*The Complete Idiot's Guide to HTML* by Paul McFedries is a good one). Alternatively, I recommend upgrading to the full Microsoft FrontPage 98 software package. This package provides many of the very advanced features found in web sites around the Internet.

Microsoft NetMeeting

Microsoft NetMeeting permits you to host or join virtual meetings across the Internet, without having to incur the expense of long-distance telephone calls or purchasing additional software.

A
B
C
D
E
F
G
H
I
J
K
L
M
N
O
P
Q
R
S
T
U
V
W
X
Y
Z

A
B
C
D
E
F
G
H
I
J
K
L
M
N
O
P
Q
R
S
T
U
V
W
X
Y
Z

Configuring NetMeeting

To configure NetMeeting for use, do the following:

1. Click the **Start** button, choose **Programs**, **Internet Tools**, and then **Microsoft NetMeeting**, as shown in Figure M.25.

Figure **M.25**

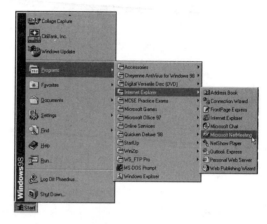

note... If you've used NetMeeting on your machine before, then you are taken directly into the primary NetMeeting screen shown in Figure M.36.

2. If this is the first time you've used NetMeeting, the Microsoft NetMeeting Configuration Wizard is automatically started. The first screen of this wizard, shown in Figure M.26, simply describes what you can accomplish by using NetMeeting. Click the **Next** button to continue.

Figure **M.26**

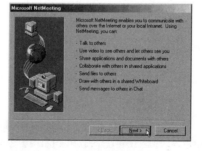

3. The wizard's second screen, shown in Figure M.27, enables you to specify whether you are logged on to a directory server when NetMeeting

starts and, if so, which server you want to use. After you make your selections, click **Next** to continue.

Figure **M.27**

note... The *directory server* is the computer that hosts the Internet conference call meeting, and all intended participants must use the same one. It is suggested that you use the default server provided by Microsoft until you find or create others for your own purposes.

4. The wizard's third screen, shown in Figure M.28, enables you to enter information about yourself in order to identify you to the other participants on the meeting server. You must enter information in the **First Name**, **Last Name**, and **E-mail Address** fields before clicking the **Next** button in order to continue.

Figure **M.28**

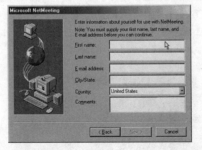

note... Before you get riled up about putting your personal information on the Internet for all to see, just remember that you need not provide accurate information. You could, for example, enter **Chicago** as your first name, **Cubs** as last name, and **WorldSeries@1998** as your email address if you so desired. NetMeeting does not verify that the information you provide is correct.

A
B
C
D
E
F
G
H
I
J
K
L
M
N
O
P
Q
R
S
T
U
V
W
X
Y
Z

A
B
C
D
E
F
G
H
I
J
K
L
M
N
O
P
Q
R
S
T
U
V
W
X
Y
Z

5. The fourth screen of the wizard, shown in Figure M.29, enables you to categorize your information. This screen is important if children share your computer with you, because it allows you to filter content that is inappropriate. After you make your selection, click the **Next** button to continue.

Figure **M.29**

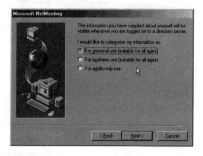

note... If you select the **For Adults-only Use** radio button, you will encounter dozens of NetMeeting participants whose only purpose appears to be for the trafficking or discussion of pornography.

6. In the fifth screen of the wizard, shown in Figure M.30, you specify the speed of your network connection. If the type of connection you use does not appear on this screen, click the option that most closely matches the speed of your connection device. For example, because I use a cable modem, which is much faster than any of the listed options, I have selected the **Local Area Network** option because it is the fastest one available. After you select your connection speed, click **Next** to continue.

Figure **M.30**

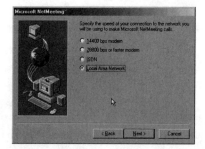

note...   If you specify a speed that is too fast for your modem, the graphics and content might be forwarded to you in a manner that your modem cannot handle. This, in turn, can lead to lost information.

7. The sixth screen of the wizard, shown in Figure M.31, enables you to specify which video capture device (camera) you will use to display your picture to others in the NetMeeting session. Choose the name of your camera from the drop-down list and then click **Next**.

Figure **M.31**

8. The first screen of the **Audio Tuning** wizard, shown in Figure M.32, appears. Before continuing with this wizard, you must close all applications that play or record sounds, such as CD Player or Sound Recorder. Click **Next** to continue.

Figure **M.32**

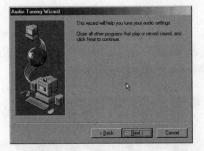

9. Use the second screen of the Audio Tuning wizard, shown in Figure M.33, to adjust your sound card's playback volume. Simply move the **Volume** slider and then click the **Test** button to hear a sample sound. When you are satisfied with the playback volume, click the **Next** button.

A
B
C
D
E
F
G
H
I
J
K
L
M
N
O
P
Q
R
S
T
U
V
W
X
Y
Z

A
B
C
D
E
F
G
H
I
J
K
L
M
N
O
P
Q
R
S
T
U
V
W
X
Y
Z

Figure **M.33**

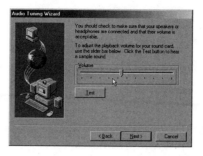

10. In the third screen of the Audio Tuning wizard, shown in Figure M.34, you can test and adjust sound input levels. Simply move the **Record Volume** slider and speak the test phrase shown in the screen into the microphone (you'll probably need to play with this setting until you find one you like). Click the **Next** button to continue.

Figure **M.34**

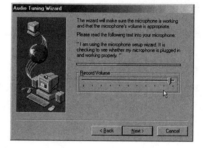

11. The final screen of the Audio Tuning wizard, shown in Figure M.35, appears. To confirm your configuration settings, click **Finish**. You'll see the Microsoft NetMeeting main window.

Figure **M.35**

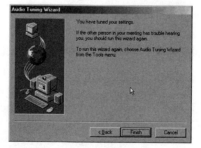

Using NetMeeting

Once NetMeeting is configured for use, you can use it to video conference with others. To use NetMeeting, follow these steps:

1. When you first enter the NetMeeting window (either by completing the NetMeeting and Audio Tuning Wizards or by clicking the **Start** button, choosing **Programs**, **Internet Tools**, and then **Microsoft NetMeeting**), you'll notice that you are not yet connected to any conference calls or directory servers. Click the down-arrow button to the right of the **Category** text field and choose a category from the drop-down list.

note... The available categories are **Business**, **Personal**, and **Pleasure**. The **Business** and **Personal** options are for persons of all ages and tastes. The **Pleasure** category, also known as the **Adult Content** category, is definitely not for children.

2. Click the down-arrow button to the right of the **Server** text field and choose a server from the drop-down list. Until you become more familiar with Microsoft NetMeeting, I recommend that you stick with one of the default Microsoft servers, as shown in Figure M.36.

Figure **M.36**

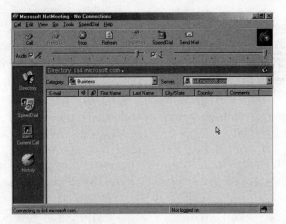

3. Press the **Enter** key to initiate the connection, and your screen lists the other users on this directory server, as shown in Figure M.37.

A
B
C
D
E
F
G
H
I
J
K
L
M
N
O
P
Q
R
S
T
U
V
W
X
Y
Z

Figure **M.37**

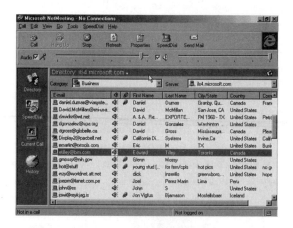

note... Be aware that your children may encounter some folks on the business- and family-oriented servers who are trolling for their own pornographic interests, as shown in Figure M.37 (look at the fifth entry from the bottom to get a clearer idea of what I mean). The best solution is close parental supervision when younger children use NetMeeting across the Internet.

note... You must have established a connection to the Internet if the server you are attempting to contact is located somewhere else in cyberspace (that is, if you are attempting to connect to a server not found on your local intranet). This includes all the Microsoft servers as well.

4. To join a call in progress, double-click any entry that sports an asterisk on the left-hand side of its computer monitor icon.

note... The people in the call you are attempting to join can reject your entry if they so choose. Do not be surprised if you are unable to join in a call.

5. To make your own call, click the **Call** toolbar button and follow the prompts.

Changing NetMeeting Settings

If you need to reconfigure any of the settings you specified in the NetMeeting Configuration Wizard, do the following:

1. Click the **Call** menu option and choose **Change My Information**. This opens the **My Information** tab of the Options dialog, shown in Figure M.38.

Figure **M.38**

2. Enter your contact information and specify how your information should be categorized.

note...   You are free to use fictional names in NetMeeting if you prefer to remain anonymous.

3. Click the **General** tab to view the screen shown in Figure M.39. Here you can reconfigure many of the options set in the NetMeeting Configuration Wizard, including the speed of the connection and the basic NetMeeting operations. You can also specify the Windows 98 folder that you want to use to store files transmitted to you during the course of a NetMeeting conference call.

Figure **M.39**

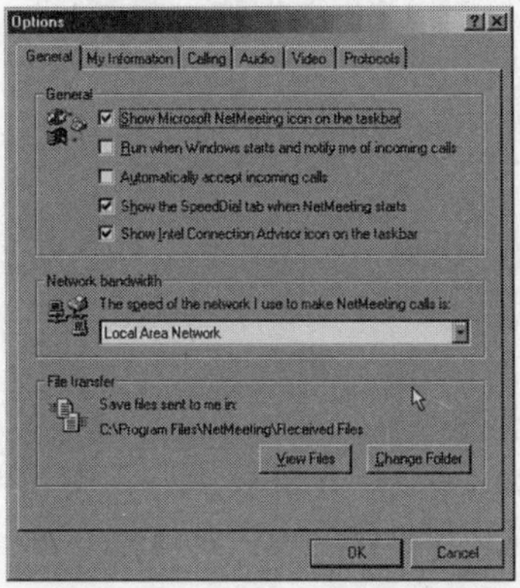

A
B
C
D
E
F
G
H
I
J
K
L
M
N
O
P
Q
R
S
T
U
V
W
X
Y
Z

A

B

C

D

E

F

G

H

I

J

K

L

M

N

O

P

Q

R

S

T

U

V

W

X

Y

Z

4. Click the **Calling** tab to view the screen shown in M.40. Here you can set the name of the directory server that should be used when you first enter NetMeeting. You can also specify that, for privacy, your name not be listed in the directory; people who already know your email address will still be able to contact you.

Figure **M.40**

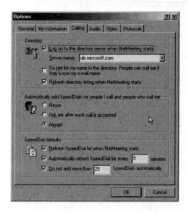

5. Click the **Audio** tab to view the screen shown in Figure M.41. Because you set many of these options in the Audio Tuning Wizard (which you used while configuring NetMeeting for use), it is recommended that the options on this screen should not be modified. However, you can rerun the Audio Tuning Wizard by clicking the **Tuning Wizard** button.

Figure **M.41**

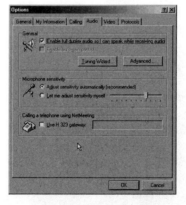

6. Click the **Video** tab to view the screen shown in Figure M.42. Here you can configure the level of video quality, the size of the image you send, and whether you send or receive video at the start of each call.

Figure **M.42**

note... The better the quality and the larger the size of the video images sent and received, the slower the NetMeeting call appears to operate. Unless you have a high-speed network connection, it is recommended that you specify **Faster Video** instead of **Better Quality** in the **Video Quality** area, and either **Small** or **Medium** in the **Send Image Size** area.

note... If you do not have a camera attached to your PC, then the settings in this screen do not pertain to you.

7. Click the **Protocols** tab to view the screen shown in Figure M.43. Here you can add or remove protocols (such as TCP/IP and the like) and set the properties of protocols by clicking the **Properties** button.

Figure **M.43**

8. Click the **OK** button to accept changes and to return to the primary NetMeeting window.

Using NetMeeting Tools

NetMeeting offers a variety of tools to make conference calling more efficient. To access these tools, click the **Tools** menu option, as shown in Figure M.44. Available tools enable you to do the following:

- Switch audio and video
- Improve video
- Share applications
- Collaborate
- Chat
- Use a whiteboard
- Transfer files
- Tune your audio settings
- Reconfigure various other settings

Figure **M.44**

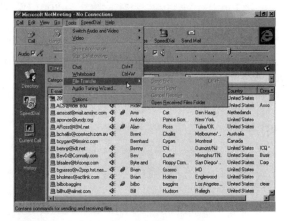

Microsoft NetShow Player

NetShow enables the transmission of multimedia communications across networks such as the Internet. It can support live audio and video to users on the network without consuming the network's available bandwidth. NetShow Player enables you to view this content on your PC. To use NetShow Player, do the following:

1. Click the **Start** button, choose **Programs**, **Internet Explorer**, and then **NetShow Player**, as shown in Figure M.45.

Figure **M.45**

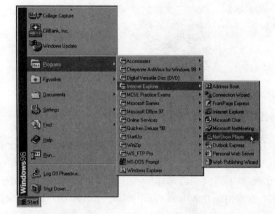

2. The **Microsoft NetShow Player** window, shown in Figure M.46, appears. To open a file to view with NetShow Player, click the **File** menu option and then choose **Open**.

Figure **M.46**

3. Navigate to the file you want to view and then click the **Open** button.

4. Click the **Play** button in the **NetShow Player** window (this button resembles a right arrow) to begin playing the NetShow content, as shown in Figure M.47.

Figure **M.47**

If the screen looks a little fuzzy or the sound isn't good, you can modify NetShow Player's settings by doing the following:

A
B
C
D
E
F
G
H
I
J
K
L
M
N
O
P
Q
R
S
T
U
V
W
X
Y
Z

A
B
C
D
E
F
G
H
I
J
K
L
M
N
O
P
Q
R
S
T
U
V
W
X
Y
Z

1. Click the **View** menu option and choose **Play Settings**, as shown in Figure M.48.

Figure **M.48**

2. The **Settings tab** of the **Microsoft NetShow Player Properties** dialog box opens, as shown in Figure M.49. This tab enables you to change how many times the NetShow file you are viewing plays, whether the stream should be rewound when if finishes playing, the size of the playing window, and the available controls.

Figure **M.49**

3. Click the **Codecs** tab to view the screen shown in Figure M.50. Here you can see which CODECs are operational on your computer (for more information about CODECs, refer to the section titled "CODECs").

note...   Microsoft provides a web site where you can obtain more information regarding NetShow CODECs at http://www.microsoft.com /netshow/codecs.htm.

4. Click the **Advanced** tab to view the screen shown in Figure M.51. This tab enables you to modify the manner in which data is transmitted and received by the NetShow Player software.

Figure **M.50**

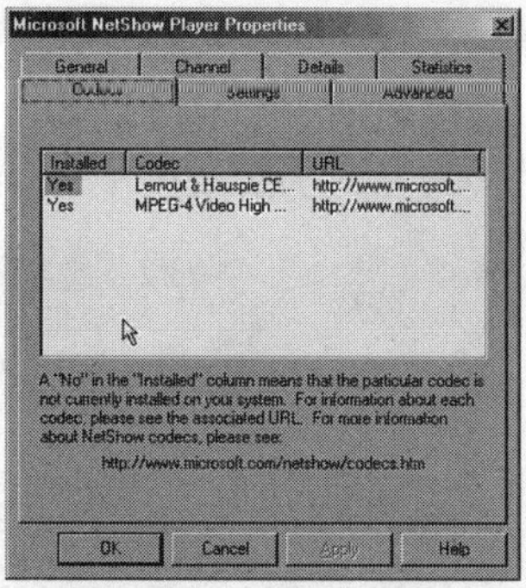

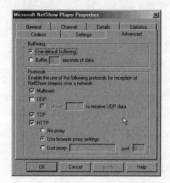

Figure **M.51**

A
B
C
D
E
F
G
H
I
J
K
L
M
N
O
P
Q
R
S
T
U
V
W
X
Y
Z

note... Unless you are very well acquainted with the TCP/IP protocol suite, the HTTP protocol, and data buffering, I suggest that you leave the default settings in place for this screen.

note... If you are using the Microsoft NetShow Player in a corporate environment, contact your network administrator(s) for further assistance in tuning the Advanced settings for your NetShow Player environment.

5. Click **OK** to accept changes and to close the **Microsoft NetShow Player Properties** dialog box.

The **Microsoft NetShow Player Properties** dialog box also includes various informational screens. Although you cannot enter new information into these screens, viewing them can be helpful if you encounter problems with a file.

A
B
C
D
E
F
G
H
I
J
K
L
M
N
O
P
Q
R
S
T
U
V
W
X
Y
Z

The **General** tab, shown in Figure M.52, contains information regarding the NetShow file being played, including its title, author, copyright, rating (if specified by the author), and description.

Figure **M.52**

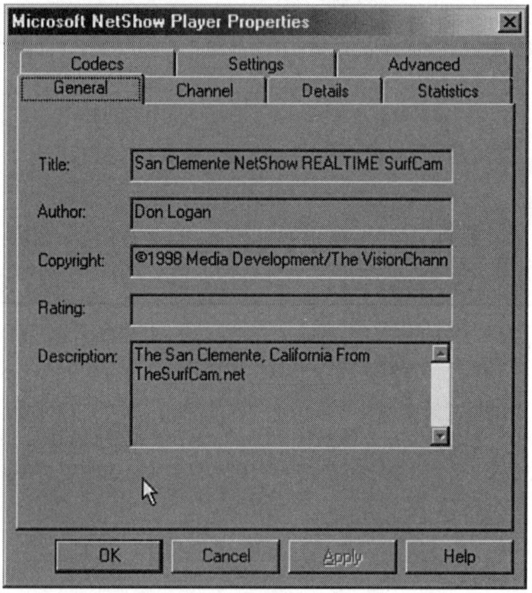

The **Channel** tab, shown in Figure M.53, contains information about the channel from which the file has been accessed.

Figure **M.53**

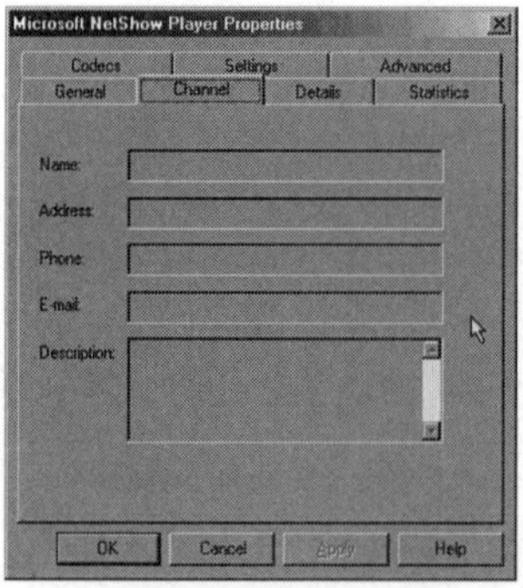

🖝 The **Details** tab, shown in Figure M.54, contains data about the NetShow file in use, including its protocol, creation date, duration, bandwidth, error correction, image width, and image height. A source link is also listed (this link shows where the file is located on the Internet).

Figure **M.54**

🖝 The **Statistics** tab, shown in Figure M.55, provides a graphical view of how the NetShow file in use has been received, including information about the TCP data packets that have been received, recovered, or lost during the transmission of the file across the Internet.

Figure **M.55**

Microsoft Office

Microsoft Office is the most popular of the three major office suites presently available in the computer marketplace (the other two are Lotus SmartSuite and Corel Office). Microsoft Office has two flavors: standard and professional. The standard version comes with Microsoft Word (a word processor), Microsoft Excel (a spreadsheet application), Microsoft PowerPoint (a business

A
B
C
D
E
F
G
H
I
J
K
L
M
N
O
P
Q
R
S
T
U
V
W
X
Y
Z

presentation program), and Microsoft Outlook (a personal information manager/email client). The professional edition contains all the applications offered by the standard version, plus Microsoft Access (a database program).

Microsoft Office works very well with Windows 98, providing some additional integration in the realm of electronic messaging that you normally would not find in other office suites's products.

Microsoft Outlook Express

Microsoft Outlook Express is a slimmed-down version of the full-blown Microsoft Outlook email package that comes with Microsoft Office. Outlook Express provides a fully functional POP3 email client that can also access Internet newsgroups.

Outlook Express is able to handle multiple Internet mail connection points simultaneously, a feature not found in most other Internet email software. Suppose, for example, that you have an Internet mail account at work, another one at home, and a third at your spouse's school. Outlook Express enables you to send and receive email to and from all three Internet connections simultaneously instead of requiring you to log in and log out of each one individually.

Starting Outlook Express

To access Outlook Express, click the **Start** button and then choose **Programs**, **Internet Explorer**, and **Outlook Express**, as shown in Figure M.56. The Inbox folder of main **Outlook Express** window, shown in Figure M.57, opens.

Figure **M.56**

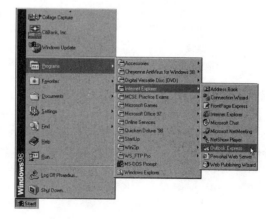

Figure **M.57**

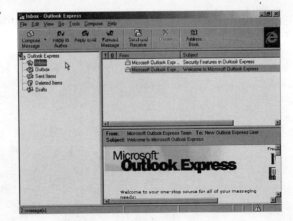

Composing a New Message

To compose a message to be sent to another user on your LAN or across the Internet, do the following:

1. Click the **Compose** menu option and choose **New Message Using**. As shown in Figure M.58, a submenu of stationery options appears.

Figure **M.58**

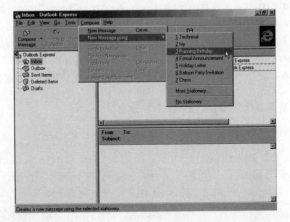

note... If you want to send a message without using stationery, simply choose **New Message** from the **Compose** menu.

2. Click the stationery you want to use.

A
B
C
D
E
F
G
H
I
J
K
L
M
N
O
P
Q
R
S
T
U
V
W
X
Y
Z

3. In the ensuing **Compose New Message** screen, shown in Figure M.59, type the recipient's email address and then type your message.

Figure **M.59**

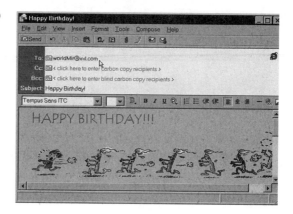

4. Click the **Send** button to move the message to your Outlook Express Outbox folder.

Sending and Receiving Mail

To transmit messages from Outlook Express to other people on your LAN or across the Internet, and to receive messages that others have sent to you, click the **Tools** menu option and choose **Send and Receive**. All the messages in your Outbox folder are sent, and all messages waiting for you at your ISP or local post office are received and placed in your Inbox folder.

Reading and Replying to Mail

Reading email within Outlook Express is very easy:

1. Click the **Inbox** icon (located under the **Outlook Express** icon in the left pane) to select it. A list of messages (if there are any) appears in the right-hand pane, as shown in Figure M.60.
2. Double-click any of the messages that appear in the list. The message you selected opens, as shown in Figure M.61.
3. To reply to this message, click either the **Reply to Author** or the **Reply to All** button, as shown in Figure M.62.
4. A Message Reply screen opens, as shown in Figure M.63. Type your reply and then click the **Send** button.

Figure **M.60**

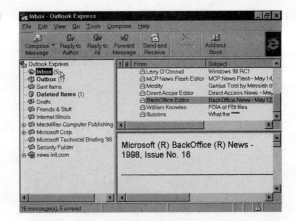

Figure **M.61**

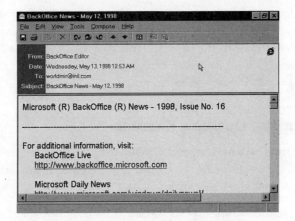

Figure **M.62**

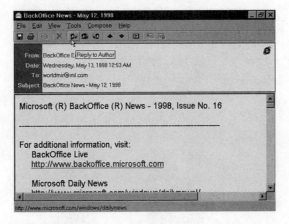

A
B
C
D
E
F
G
H
I
J
K
L
M
N
O
P
Q
R
S
T
U
V
W
X
Y
Z

A
B
C
D
E
F
G
H
I
J
K
L
M
N
O
P
Q
R
S
T
U
V
W
X
Y
Z

Figure **M.63**

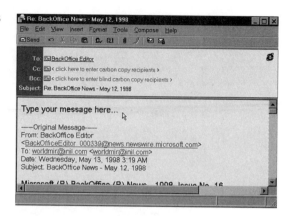

note... You can send one or more message attachments with any email message from Outlook Express. To attach a file, either click the paper-clip icon or click the **Insert** menu option and choose **File Attachment**. You are then prompted to select the file you want to attach. Do so and then send the message as normal.

Configuring Outlook Express

To reach the Outlook Express **Options** dialog box, where you can configure Outlook Express to better suit your needs, click **Tools** and then **Options**. The following screens are available:

- The **General** tab, shown in Figure M.64, enables you to configure how often Outlook Express checks for new messages, whether Outlook Express plays sounds when new messages arrive, and other aspects of how it performs.

Figure **M.64**

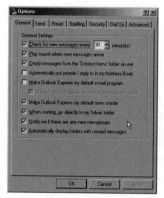

🖐 The **Send** tab, shown in Figure M.65, enables you to instruct Outlook Express as to how you want email and newsgroup messages to be creat ed and sent, and to specify that a copy of all sent messages be logged.

Figure **M.65**

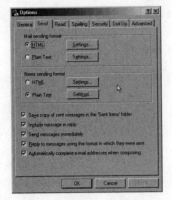

🖐 The **Read** tab, shown in Figure M.66, enables you to specify how incoming messages are downloaded and viewed.

Figure **M.66**

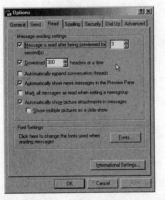

note... The **Download *xxx* Headers at a Time** option enables you to specify how many email message headers (that is, author and subject lines) you want to download during a single connection session. This can be useful in the event you get *spammed* (barraged with electronic junk mail). For example, suppose a spammer sends you dozens of messages

continues

A
B
C
D
E
F
G
H
I
J
K
L
M
N
O
P
Q
R
S
T
U
V
W
X
Y
Z

A
B
C
D
E
F
G
H
I
J
K
L
M
N
O
P
Q
R
S
T
U
V
W
X
Y
Z

continued

about free trips, free cash, or whatever. If you download the header files for these types of messages, you can delete them on your ISP's mail server without downloading the full text of their messages to your PC.

note... Click the **Fonts** button to specify the font in which all messages are displayed. Click the **International Settings** button to configure Outlook Express for use with other languages.

The **Spelling** tab, shown in Figure M.67, enables you to configure how the built-in spellchecker for Outlook Express works. (If you are familiar with Microsoft Office applications such as Word, Excel, and PowerPoint, this screen will look familiar.)

Figure **M.67**

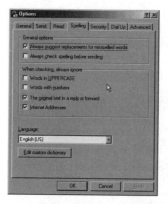

The **Security** tab, shown in Figure M.68, enables you to set security zones (like the ones in Internet Explorer), which permit you to configure how scripts and active content are used within HTML messages (click the **Settings** button to set these options). The **Secure Mail** and **Digital IDs** sections enable you to hide the content of your email messages.

note... Click the **More Info** button in the **Digital IDs** section for information on this very complex topic.

The **Dial Up** tab, shown in Figure M.69, enables you to automatically connect to the Internet or your email post office via a telephone line.

Simply click the **Dial this Connection** checkbox and enter the name of the connection in the adjacent text box (you can get this information from your ISP).

Figure **M.68**

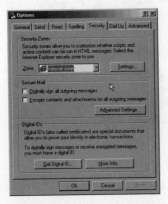

Figure **M.69**

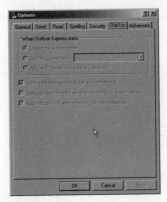

note... If you have a network (LAN/WAN) connection to the Internet or to your email post office, or if you do not use a modem, you should skip this section.

● The **Advanced** tab, shown in Figure M.70, enables you to set message logging options.

A
B
C
D
E
F
G
H
I
J
K
L
M
N
O
P
Q
R
S
T
U
V
W
X
Y
Z

A
B
C
D
E
F
G
H
I
J
K
L
M
N
O
P
Q
R
S
T
U
V
W
X
Y
Z

Figure **M.70**

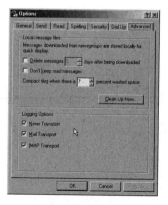

Establishing an Email Account

You cannot participate in newsgroups or send email until you've established an account with an ISP. To establish an account, do the following:

1. In the main Outlook Express window, click the **Tools** menu option and select **Accounts**.

2. Click the **Mail** tab in the ensuing **Internet Accounts** screen to view any existing accounts (if you don't have an account, this tab is empty, as shown in Figure M.71).

Figure **M.71**

3. Click the **Add** button and select **Mail** from the ensuing shortcut menu. The first screen of the Internet Connection Wizard, shown in Figure M.72, appears.

4. Type the **Display Name** for your Internet mail account (this is the name that appears in the **From** field of outgoing messages) and click **Next** to continue.

Figure **M.72**

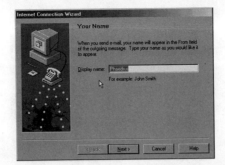

note... I usually refrain from using my real name in this field, but if you are a corporate environment, this might not be a wise decision. (In other words, use your real name if you are at work.)

5. In the **Internet E-mail Address** window, shown in Figure M.73, type the email address assigned to you by your ISP or company email administrator, and then click **Next** to continue.

Figure **M.73**

6. Enter the names of your email servers in the **E-mail Server Names** window, shown in Figure M.74. You must also specify the type of your incoming email server. If this is an ISP account, the email server is probably a POP3 mail server (when in doubt, use POP3 as your default). Click **Next** to continue.

note... Contact your ISP or local email administrator if you need help filling out this screen.

A
B
C
D
E
F
G
H
I
J
K
L
M
N
O
P
Q
R
S
T
U
V
W
X
Y
Z

Figure **M.74**

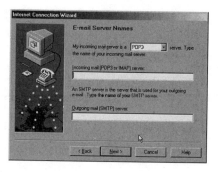

7. The **Internet Mail Logon** screen, shown in Figure M.75, enables you to specify your user name and password, or to specify that Secure Password Authentication (SPA) be used. After you make your selection, click **Next** to continue.

Figure **M.75**

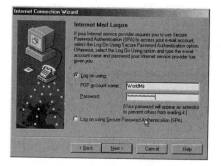

note... When you employ secure password authentication, your logon information is sent in an encrypted state, which means it will be more secure than a standard POP3 mail logon. The standard POP3 method is clear text, so just about anyone can determine what your user ID and password is, provided they have a sniffer somewhere between your machine and your ISP's server.

8. In the **Friendly Name** screen, shown in Figure M.76, type a name for your account that will be easy for you to remember, and then click **Next** to continue.

9. In the **Choose Connection Type** screen, shown in Figure M.77, select the method that best describes how you plan to connect to the Internet (in this example, I have chosen the **Connect Using My Local Area**

Network (LAN) option because I use a cable modem connection, which means that I have a high-speed LAN connection directly to my ISP via the fiber optic cable TV lines in my area). Click **Next** to continue.

Figure **M.76**

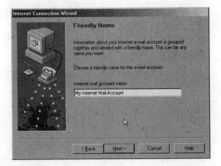

note... If you connect to your ISP via a Windows 98 Dial-Up Networking connection at the beginning of a Windows 98 session and would like to start your email connection at will, you should select the **Connect Using My Local Area Network (LAN)** option. If you select **Connect Using My Phone Line**, your Outlook email software automatically tries to dial your connection to the Internet, even if you are already connected.

Figure **M.77**

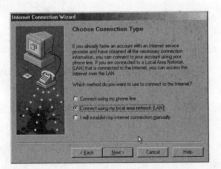

10. To save your settings, click **Finish**, as shown in Figure M.78. You are then returned to the **Internet Accounts** screen, where the new account appears, as shown in Figure M.79.

11. Click the **Close** button to exit the **Internet Accounts** screen and return to the main **Outlook Express** window.

A
B
C
D
E
F
G
H
I
J
K
L
M
N
O
P
Q
R
S
T
U
V
W
X
Y
Z

A
B
C
D
E
F
G
H
I
J
K
L
M
N
O
P
Q
R
S
T
U
V
W
X
Y
Z

Figure **M.78**

Figure **M.79**

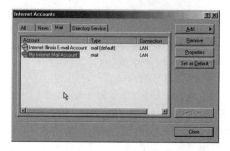

Microsoft Plus! 98

Just as with Windows 95, there is a Plus! Package for the Windows 98 operating system. When fully installed, the Microsoft Plus! 98 package consumes 188.8MB of hard disk drive space. Microsoft Plus! 98 comes with numerous utilities, including the following:

- Compressed Folders   This compression utility is much like WinZip.

- Deluxe CD Player   This CD player far surpasses the one that ships with Windows 98.

- Desktop Themes   This utility offers more than 95 MB of desktop themes.

- Disk Cleanup Add-ons   This utility provides a few extra features for the Windows 98 Disk Cleanup utility.

- Golf 1998 Lite   This is a scaled-down version of Microsoft Golf 1998.

- Lose Your Marbles   This game is quickly becoming my favorite!

- Maintenance Wizard   This utility provides a few extra features for the Windows 98 Maintenance Wizard.

- Organic Art Screensaver   This is just like it sounds!

- Picture It! Express   This utility is a scaled-down version of Picture It!, a very good graphics tool.
- Spider Solitaire   This is yet another very addictive Windows solitaire game.
- Virus Scan   This utility is the McAfee Anti-virus software package.

Microsoft VRML 2.0

Support for the Virtual Reality Modeling Language 2.0 (*VRML*) is built into the Internet Explorer 4 web browser. The contents of a VRML file are better known as a *world*. A VRML file resides on a web site just like an HTML file does and VRML files come in the format of a text file, usually with a **.wrl** extension.

Microsoft Wallet

Microsoft Wallet is an Internet Explorer web browser feature that permits you to store personal information about yourself in electronic format that you might otherwise keep in a wallet (such as your name, address, home and work telephone numbers, ship-to address, bill-to address, and credit card numbers with expiration dates). When you want to purchase something from a web site that supports Microsoft Wallet (not too many do as of yet), you can securely transmit your information from your electronic wallet directly to that web site's purchasing information page. That way, you don't have to type in all that information! To use Wallet, do the following:

1. Right-click the **Internet Explorer** icon on the Windows 98 desktop, and choose **Properties** from the ensuing shortcut menu, as shown in Figure M.80.

Figure **M.80**

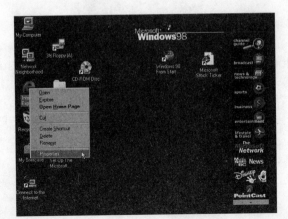

2. Click the **Content** tab in the **Internet Properties** dialog box to view the screen shown in Figure M.81. Click the **Addresses** button near the bottom of the screen.

Figure **M.81**

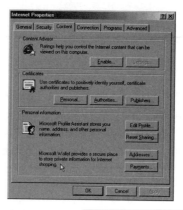

3. The information you enter in the **Address Options** screen, shown in Figure M.82, is what is sent whenever you initiate commerce over the Web. Keep in mind that these are street addresses and not email addresses. Address files can be added, edited, or deleted from the **Address Options** screen. When you are finished entering information in this screen, click the **Close** button to return to the **Internet Properties** screen.

Figure **M.82**

4. Click the **Payments** button below the **Addresses** button to view the **Payment Options** screen, shown in Figure M.83. The information you enter in the **Payment Options** screen is what is sent whenever you initiate commerce over the Web. Credit card files can be added, edited, or deleted from the **Payment Options** screen.

Figure **M.83**

5. Click the **Add** button; you will be prompted for the type of credit card you want to add (MasterCard, Visa, American Express, or Discover Card).

6. After you select the credit-card type, a data-entry screen appears for that type of card. Enter the card number, expiration date, and cardholder's name in the appropriate fields.

7. Click the **OK** button to return to the **Payment Options** screen; click **Close** to return to the **Internet Properties** dialog box, and click **OK** again to complete the modification process.

To view and edit your Microsoft Wallet user profile, do the following:

1. Click the **Edit Profile** button that appears just above the Microsoft Wallet area of the **Internet Properties** dialog box.

2. Update or enter any pertinent information in the **Properties** dialog box, shown in Figure M.84.

Figure **M.84**

A

B

C

D

E

F

G

H

I

J

K

L

M

N

O

P

Q

R

S

T

U

V

W

X

Y

Z

> **note...** Most of the information that can be entered into this screen will save you time when you make electronic purchases from your browser.

3. Click **OK** to return to the **Internet Properties** dialog box, and click **OK** again to complete the modification process.

Microsoft Windows 98 DOS and MS-DOS Prompt

Despite the fact that Windows 98 is a GUI environment, DOS is still an important aspect of the operating system. To access and use the MS-DOS Prompt, do the following:

1. Click the **Start** button, choose **Programs**, and then **MS-DOS Prompt**, as shown in Figure M.85.

Figure **M.85**

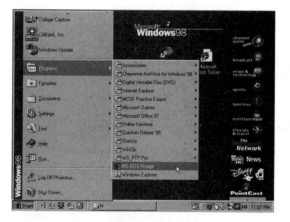

2. The **MS-DOS Prompt** window, shown in Figure M.86, opens. Simply type the command you want to execute and press **Enter**.

Figure **M.86**

There are literally dozens of documented and undocumented DOS commands. However, there are a few commands that you should avoid unless you know how to use them properly:

- **Fdisk**
- **Format**
- **Debug**
- **Sys**
- **Command**
- **Deltree**

note... A few DOS commands, such as **Fdisk**, **Format**, and **Debug**, should be used with extreme care. You should never play with these commands to figure out what they do or how to use them properly. For example, **Fdisk** and **Debug** both enable you to quickly and irrevocably destroy the contents of your entire hard drive.

Countless books and magazines cover the subject of disk operating systems such as MS-DOS, and you would be wise to invest in one before reconfiguring portions of Windows 98 through the DOS prompt.

Modems

The term modem literally means *modulator-demodulator*. In English, a modem is a hardware device that translates the bits of information from your computer into bits of data that an analog telephone line (such as the one you call your mom on every week) can understand enough to transport it to another computer's modem (where the process is reversed).

To see what modems you have installed in your computer, and for a quick lesson in determining whether a modem is working, do the following:

1. Click the **Start** button, choose **Settings**, and then **Control Panel**, as shown in Figure M.87.
2. Double-click the **Modems** icon in the **Control Panel** window, shown in Figure M.88.
3. The modem(s) listed in the **General** tab of the **Modems Properties** dialog box is installed in your computer (see Figure M.89). To determine whether that modem is properly communicating with Windows 98, click the **Diagnostics** tab.

A
B
C
D
E
F
G
H
I
J
K
L
M
N
O
P
Q
R
S
T
U
V
W
X
Y
Z

Figure **M.87**

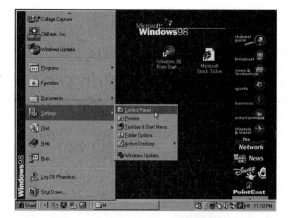

Figure **M.88**

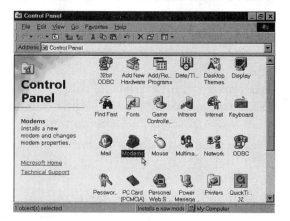

Figure **M.89**

note... If the top box in the **General** tab of the **Modems Properties** dialog box is empty, this means no dial-up modems are properly installed in your computer. However, it is also possible to see a cable modem installed and working properly appear in the box; but this is not the norm.

4. All the available communications ports are listed in the **Diagnostics** tab (shown in Figure M.90), as is the name of the modem installed on each port (in the event you have more than one modem connected to your PC). Select a modem by clicking its port and then click the **More Info** button to check the communications capabilities of that modem.

Figure **M.90**

5. The **More Info** screen, shown in Figure M.91, appears. If the modem is working properly, as is the case in this example, then this screen contains useful information. For instance, you can determine which communications port and interrupt your modem uses. Click the **OK** button to return to the previous screen.

Figure **M.91**

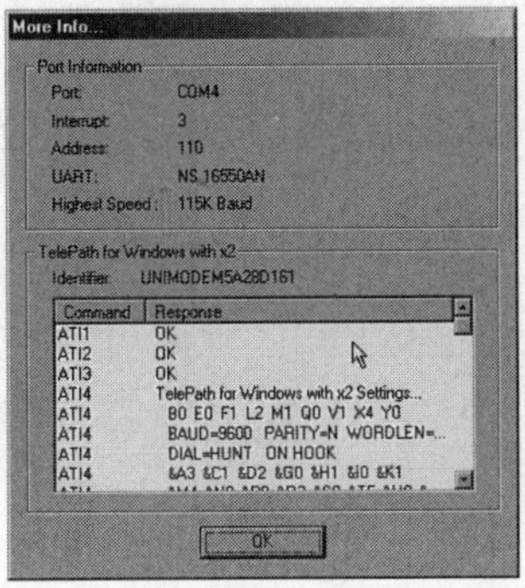

A
B
C
D
E
F
G
H
I
J
K
L
M
N
O
P
Q
R
S
T
U
V
W
X
Y
Z

note...   If no responses are indicated in the box at the bottom, it is likely that the connection between your PC and the modem has failed, or that your modem is not working properly (perhaps because the wrong software drivers are loaded, or because the modem is broken).

6. Click the **General** tab in the **Modems Properties** dialog, and then click the **Properties** button to review and configure the highlighted modem in the *Modem Name* **Properties** dialog box (the **General** tab of this dialog is shown in Figure M.92).

Figure **M.92**

7. The **General** tab enables you to set the maximum speed at which the modem should attempt to connect, and how loud your modem is when it connects.

note...   If you have a 19.2Kbps modem, setting it at 57.6Kbps does not make your modem work faster; it only tells Windows 98 that maybe your modem can transmit information faster than it actually does.

8. Click the **Connection** tab to view information about how the parity data bits are set, how your call preferences are set, how well the port settings are configured, and how well your advanced settings are configured (see Figure M.93).

note...   Windows 98 does an excellent job of configuring the settings in the **Connection** tab whenever a new modem is installed, so if you do not understand these complex terms, you can safely leave them alone.

Figure **M.93**

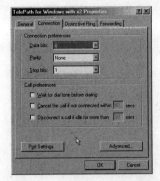

note... To access either port settings or advanced settings, click the **Port Settings** or **Advanced** button, respectively.

9. Click the **Distinctive Ring** tab to view the screen shown in Figure M.94. This screen enables you to configure how the modem will sound if you are using it for inbound telephone calls.

Figure **M.94**

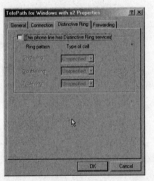

note... In order for you to be able to configure how your modem sounds, your telephone line must support distinctive ring services. Check with your local telephone company for more information.

note... If no Distinctive Ring tab appears on your *Modem Name* **Properties** dialog box, it indicates that your modem device is incapable of supporting this option.

A
B
C
D
E
F
G
H
I
J
K
L
M
N
O
P
Q
R
S
T
U
V
W
X
Y
Z

10. Click the **Forwarding** tab to view the screen shown in Figure M.95. If applicable, click the **This Phone Line Has Call Forwarding** check box, and type the proper activation and deactivation codes for your line (your local telephone company should provide these codes to you).

Figure **M.95**

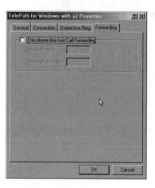

note... In order for you to be able to enter information in the **Forwarding** tab, your telephone line must support forwarding. Check with your local telephone company for more information.

note... If no **Forwarding** tab appears on your *Modem Name* **Properties** dialog box, it indicates that your modem device is incapable of supporting this option.

11. Click the **OK** button to accept any changes. You are returned to the **General** tab of the **Modems Properties** dialog box.

12. Click the **Dialing Properties** button to open the screen shown in Figure M.96. Here you set the location(s) from which you are dialing, as well as any special codes that must first be dialed to reach an outside line, in order to disable call waiting or caller ID, or to use a calling card. When you are satisfied with your selections, click **OK** to return to the **Modems Properties** dialog, and click **OK** again to accept your changes.

Figure **M.96**

Mouse

The mouse is one of the most important pieces of hardware on your computer system. Without one, it is virtually impossible to be productive on a Windows 98 PC.

Most mice have two buttons: a primary one (usually the left button) and a secondary one (usually the right button). Some mice have a third button or a rolling ball or wheel (as is the case with the Microsoft IntelliPoint mouse) in the middle.

To configure your mouse to best suit your needs, do the following:

1. Install it according to your mouse manufacturer's specifications.

note... **Your mouse most likely has a tiny attachment on the end of the cable that plugs into a specific port on the back of your PC. (If your mouse's connection looks like the one for the keyboard, refer to your computer's documentation to figure out where your keyboard and mouse connections belong).**

2. Install the software drivers that came with the mouse that you purchased (if this is a new computer with pre-installed software, chances are that your mouse software has already been installed for you).

3. Click the **Start** button, choose **Settings**, and then click **Control Panel**, as shown in Figure M.97.

4. Double-click the **Mouse** icon in the **Control Panel** window shown in Figure M.98.

A
B
C
D
E
F
G
H
I
J
K
L
M
N
O
P
Q
R
S
T
U
V
W
X
Y
Z

A
B
C
D
E
F
G
H
I
J
K
L
M
N
O
P
Q
R
S
T
U
V
W
X
Y
Z

Figure **M.97**

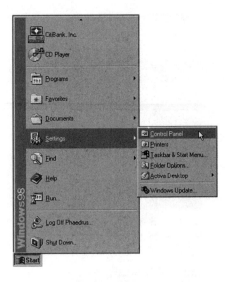

Figure **M.98**

note...   The next several screens are for the Microsoft IntelliPoint mouse, which has a rolling wheel in addition to primary and secondary buttons. If you do not have this type of mouse, many of these screens will vary. In those cases, consult the documentation that came with your mouse so that you can configure it for Windows 98.

5. The **StepSavers** tab of the **Mouse Properties** dialog, shown in Figure M.99, has four timesaving options: SnapTo, Focus, ClickSaver, and SmartSpeed. These features give you the ability to make things happen

faster with fewer mouse clicks or movements. Carefully read each option before making your choices.

Figure **M.99**

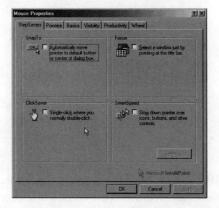

6. Click the **Pointers** tab to view the screen shown in Figure M.100. This tab enables you to change how your mouse pointer appears onscreen. To change your mouse pointer, click the down-arrow button next to the **Scheme** text box to view a drop-down list of available pointer schemes (in this example, the **Mouse** scheme has been selected).

Figure **M.100**

7. Click the **Apply** button to accept the scheme you've selected.

8. Click the **Basics** tab to view the screen shown in Figure M.101. Here you can specify how quickly your pointer moves, which button is the primary, which is the secondary (this is useful if you are left-handed), and the double-click speed.

A
B
C
D
E
F
G
H
I
J
K
L
M
N
O
P
Q
R
S
T
U
V
W
X
Y
Z

A
B
C
D
E
F
G
H
I
J
K
L
M
N
O
P
Q
R
S
T
U
V
W
X
Y
Z

Figure **M.101**

9. Click the **Visibility** tab to view the screen shown in Figure M.102. Click these options to specify whether you want your pointer to vanish while you type, to display pointer trails, or to automatically wrap to the opposite edge of the screen when you start a new line. You can also select the **Sonar** option, which displays a target around your mouse pointer whenever you press the **Ctrl** key on your keyboard.

Figure **M.102**

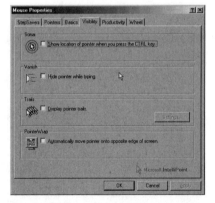

10. Click the **Productivity** tab to view the screen shown in Figure M.103. My personal favorite, the **Odometer** section, lets you see how far your mouse pointer has traveled across your monitor since the day you installed it.

Figure **M.103**

11. Click the **Wheel** tab to view the screen shown in Figure M.104. In addition to enabling you to scroll up and down screens by simply rolling the wheel forward or backward, the wheel can also act as a button when you press it. To change the button features of the wheel, click the down-arrow button to the right of the **Button Assignment** text box. Then you can select from the list of tasks the wheel can perform: double-click, get help (F1), start Windows Explorer, or open the **Start** menu. Press the wheel, and the action you assigned should occur instantly.

Figure **M.104**

12. Click the **Apply** button to accept changes to the mouse wheel.
13. Click the **OK** button to exit the **Mouse Properties** screen.

A
B
C
D
E
F
G
H
I
J
K
L
M
N
O
P
Q
R
S
T
U
V
W
X
Y
Z

Multilanguage Support

Microsoft Windows 98 provides a series of options that permit the support of other languages within the operating system. To install any of the language options, do the following:

1. Click the **Start** button, choose **Settings**, and then click **Control Panel**, as shown in Figure M.105.

Figure **M.105**

2. Click the **Add/Remove Programs** icon in the **Control Panel** Window, shown in Figure M.106.

Figure **M.106**

note... **For more information about the Add/Remove Programs feature, refer to the section titled "Add/Remove Programs."**

3. Click the **Windows Setup** tab in the **Add/Remove Programs** screen.
4. Highlight the **Multilanguage Support** option in the **Components** list. A description of the component appears in the **Description** box, informing you of the available languages, as shown in Figure M.107.

Figure **M.107**

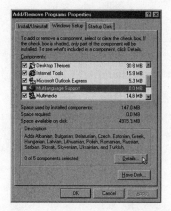

5. Place a check mark next to the **Multilanguage Support** option and then click the **Details** button to view the screen shown in Figure M.108. This screen enables you to install only a portion of the multilanguage support (that is, you can install a single language instead of installing all of them).

Figure **M.108**

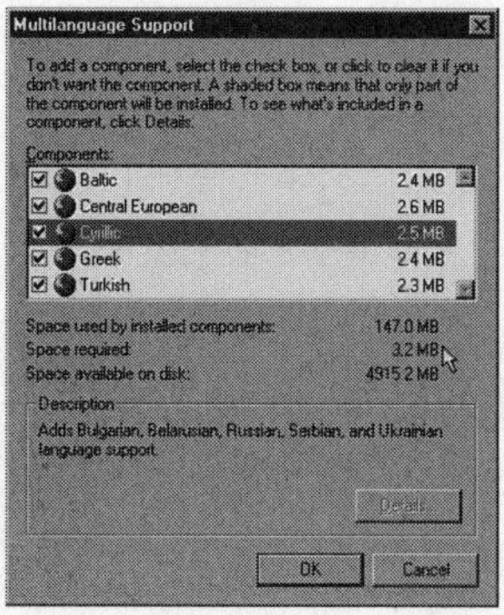

A B C D E F G H I J K L M N O P Q R S T U V W X Y Z

6. Select the language you want to install and then click **OK**. The necessary files are installed.

7. Click **OK** in the **Windows Setup** tab to exit the **Add/Remove Programs** dialog box.

8. If prompted, insert the Windows 98 CD-ROM.

9. Reboot your computer.

Multimedia

The multimedia features of Windows 98 allow a computer to handle audio and video content in a more pleasing manner, as well as to provide you with a more user-friendly way in which to learn new things and perform tasks.

To view multimedia content in Windows 98, you can use the **ActiveMovie** control. For information on using **ActiveMovie**, refer to the section titled "ActiveMovie Control."

My Computer

The **My Computer** icon found on the Windows 98 desktop provides you with a quick means to explore your computer. Double-click it to open an Explorer-type window that enables you to peruse your hard drive just as you do with the Windows Explorer utility.

N

A
B
C
D
E
F
G
H
I
J
K
L
M
N
O
P
Q
R
S
T
U
V
W
X
Y
Z

Net Watcher

Net Watcher enables you to monitor other computer users who are accessing resources on your network. Additionally, Net Watcher permits you to see which resources, such as folders, that you have shared with (or made available to) the rest of the network. This feature applies only to users who are connected to a network, so if you do not have a network connection, then this feature is not for you.

Prior to running the Net Watcher utility, you must have the Client for Microsoft Networks installed with the File and Print Sharing options enabled. To run Net Watcher, do the following:

1. Click the **Start** button, then choose **Programs**, **Accessories**, **System Tools**, and then **Net Watcher**, as shown in Figure N.1.

Figure **N.1**

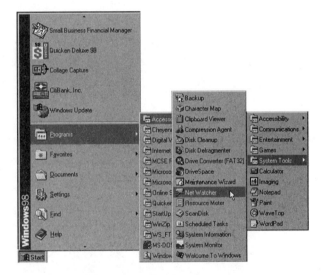

2. The main Net Watcher screen, shown in Figure N.2, appears. To choose which computer to monitor (for example, a file server), click the **Administer** menu option and then choose **Select Server**.

3. The Select Server window, shown in Figure N.3, appears. Here you can type the name of the computer that you want to administer or obtain that computer's name by using the **Browse** button.

Figure **N.2**

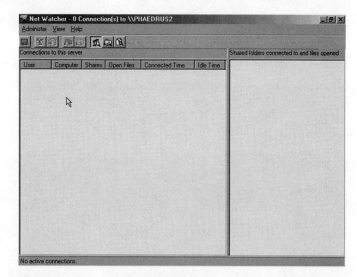

Figure **N.3**

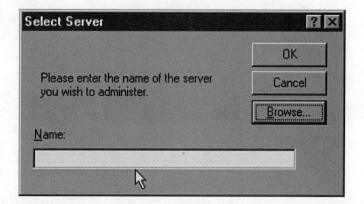

4. If you clicked the **Browse** button in the Select Server window, you see the Browse for Computer screen, shown in Figure N.4. Navigate to the server you want to administer, and select it. In this example, the computer I want to administer is PHAEDRUS2, which is located in the Network Neighborhood (for more information, see the section titled "Network Neighborhood").

5. Click **OK** to return to the Select Server window, shown in Figure N.5, where the server you selected now appears in the **Name** text box. Click **OK** again to confirm your selection.

A
B
C
D
E
F
G
H
I
J
K
L
M
N
O
P
Q
R
S
T
U
V
W
X
Y
Z

Figure **N.4**

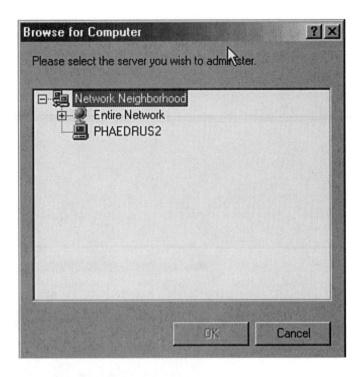

Figure **N.5**

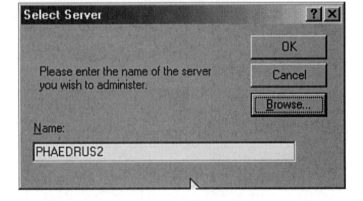

6. You are returned to the main Net Watcher screen. Clicking the toolbar buttons along the top of the screen presents you with different views of the shared resources, and shows you who is accessing those resources at any given time. As shown in Figure N.6, clicking the **Show Shared Folders** button enables you to determine which folders are shared with users who connect to your computer (in this example, **PHAEDRUS2**'s fax and printing capabilities are shared).

Figure **N.6**

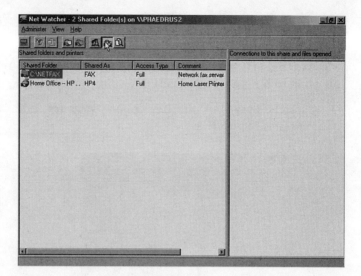

7. The button to the right of the **Show Shared Folders** button is known as the **Show Files** button (see Figure N.7). Clicking this button is a quick way to view which files are opened on your system, from which folder they are shared, and who presently is accessing them.

Figure **N.7**

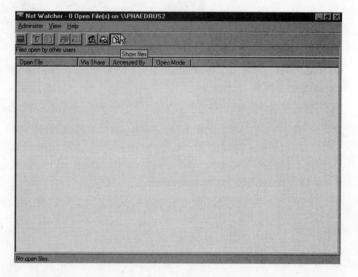

A
B
C
D
E
F
G
H
I
J
K
L
M
N
O
P
Q
R
S
T
U
V
W
X
Y
Z

Network

The Control Panel's Network feature enables you to install and modify the necessary networking client and protocol software required to make a computer talk to a network. To open the Network dialog box, do the following:

1. Click the **Start** button, then choose **Settings**, and **Control Panel**, as shown in Figure N.8.

Figure **N.8**

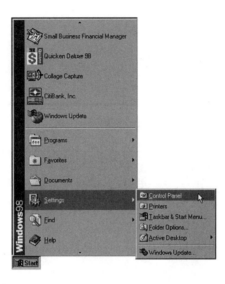

2. Double-click the **Network** icon in the Control Panel window, shown in Figure N.9.

   The **Network** dialog box that appears contains three tabs:

   - The Configuration tab, shown in Figure N.10, enables you to view which network components are currently installed on your computer, to add or remove components, and to modify the properties of installed components.

   - The Identification tab, shown in Figure N.11, enables you to specify the name of your computer, the workgroup in which it appears, and a short description of the computer.

note... The name of the computer must be unique, must not exceed 15 characters (numbers and letters are acceptable), and should be descriptive.

Figure **N.9**

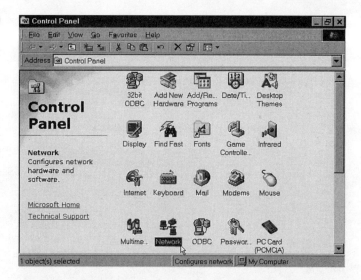

Figure **N.10**

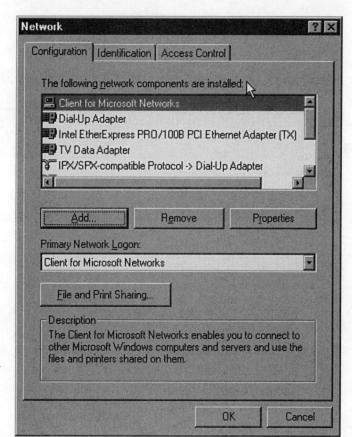

A
B
C
D
E
F
G
H
I
J
K
L
M
N
O
P
Q
R
S
T
U
V
W
X
Y
Z

A

B

C

D

E

F

G

H

I

J

K

L

M

N

O

P

Q

R

S

T

U

V

W

X

Y

Z

Figure **N.11**

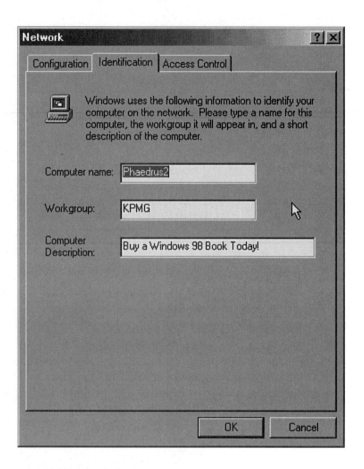

note...　The name of the workgroup should be the same as the networking domain to which you most often connect, or it should be the same as the domain of the server that authenticates you to the network. As with the computer name, it cannot exceed 15 characters (numbers and letters are acceptable).

note...　The computer name and workgroup name must be different. Windows 98 will not permit these two fields to contain the same name!

The Access Control tab, shown in Figure N.12, enables you to define how access to your PC can occur. If you select the **Share-Level Access Control** button, you can password-protect each available resource on your computer. If you select the **User-Level Access Control** button, you control access by specifying which users and groups have access to each shared resource.

Figure **N.12**

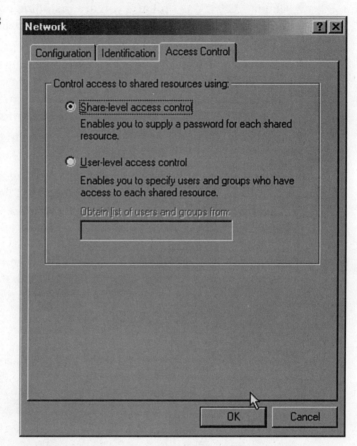

note...   User-level access control is possible only if your network administrator permits it and has preconfigured the network to support it.

Adding a Network Component

To add a network component, do the following:

1. Click the **Add** button in the **Configuration** tab of the **Network** dialog box.

A
B
C
D
E
F
G
H
I
J
K
L
M
N
O
P
Q
R
S
T
U
V
W
X
Y
Z

2. In the Select Network Component Type dialog box that appears, click the type of network component you want to install (see Figure N.13). Your options are as follows:

- Client   Click this option if you are installing client software, such as Novell Directory Services or the Microsoft Client for Microsoft Networks.

- Adapter   Click this option if you are installing network interface card (NIC) software for vendors such as 3Com or Compaq, ISDN network software for EICON NICs, or the Microsoft-specific software for TV Data adapters or virtual private networking (VPN) devices.

- Protocol   Click this option if you are installing a protocol such as TCP/IP, NetBEUI, the Novell IPX ODI protocol, or an ATM protocol.

- Service   Click this option if you are installing a service such as File and Printer Sharing for Microsoft Networks, File and Printer Sharing for Novell Networks, or the Backup Exec Agent for Seagate Software.

note...   If you have a disk containing a client, adapter, protocol, or service that does not appear in the list, add it by clicking the **Have Disk** button (this button appears after you have selected the type of network component you want to install).

Figure **N.13**

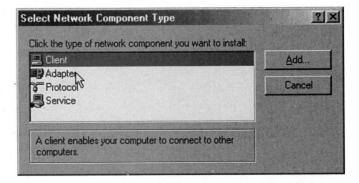

3. Click the **Add** button. Carefully follow all the prompts, and reboot your computer if prompted.

Configuring Resource Sharing

Resource sharing is essentially the act of making your local computer's files and printers available to others across the network. An important fact to keep in mind is that when you use Dial-Up Networking to connect to another computer system (such as the Internet, an Online Service Provider, or your corporate networks), other people on those systems may have the ability to access your computer. Therefore, it is very important that if you do establish a share for one of your system's resources, you should do so carefully. Always assign a password to anything that you should share.

To configure resource sharing, do the following:

1. Click the **File and Print Sharing** button in the **Configuration** tab of the **Network** dialog box.

2. Click the appropriate check boxes in the **File and Print Sharing** dialog box, shown in Figure N.14.

Figure **N.14**

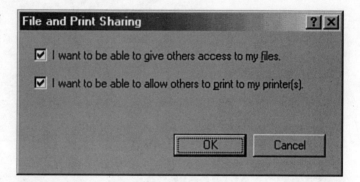

3. Click the **OK** button to return to the Network dialog box. Click **OK** again to return to the Control Panel window (you might be prompted to install additional Windows 98 software).

Removing Unused Network Software

If your computer is not connected to a network, it is wise to remove the network software that is built into Windows 98 from your computer because this software consumes hard disk space and memory as well as system resources. To remove the network software, simply highlight the option you want to remove in the **Configuration** tab of the **Network** dialog box (see Figure N.15), and then click the **Remove** button.

A
B
C
D
E
F
G
H
I
J
K
L
M
N
O
P
Q
R
S
T
U
V
W
X
Y
Z

Figure **N.15**

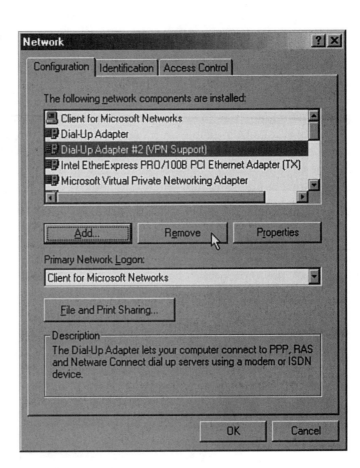

Network Neighborhood

The Windows 98 Network Neighborhood displays all computers presently connected to your network (some Windows NT computers might not appear, as well as most PCs that do not run Microsoft operating systems). If you do not have any network drivers installed on your PC, the **Network Neighborhood** icon is not displayed on your Windows 98 desktop. This section quickly demonstrates how to access a computer's resources that have been shared on your network:

1. Double-click the **Network Neighborhood** icon on your Windows 98 desktop, as shown in Figure N.16.

Figure **N.16**

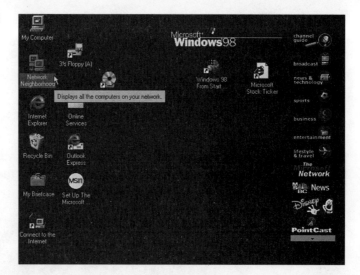

2. The Network Neighborhood window shows which computers and servers are available on your network. Click a PC icon along the left side of the window to view a description of that computer, as shown in Figure N.17. (You might remember that this was the description I entered in the Identification tab of the Network dialog box in the "Network" section.)

Figure **N.17**

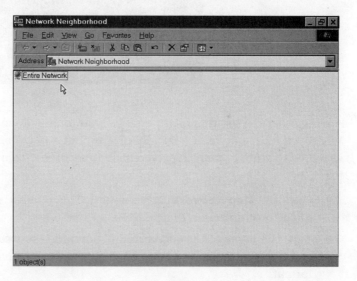

note... Because it is possible to hide a computer from the Windows 98 browser window, you might not be able to view all the computers on the network in the Network Neighborhood window. (This is the exception, however—not the norm.)

3. To close this window, click the × button in the upper-right corner of the window.

To explore Network Neighborhood's other options, right-click the Network Neighborhood icon on the desktop to view the shortcut menu shown in Figure N.18.

Figure **N.18**

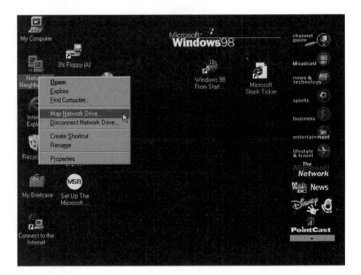

Among other things, this menu enables you to quickly map a network drive. When you map a drive, it basically means that a new "logical" drive letter is assigned to a direct path to server-based resources. To map a drive, do the following:

1. Click the **Map Network Drive** option. This opens the Map Network Drive dialog box, shown in Figure N.19.

2. Type the name of the server and its shared resource (whether it is another folder or a network device such as a fax or printer) in the following format:

*server name**resource name*

Figure **N.19**

3. Click **OK** to map the drive.

Network Printer

A network printer is nothing more than a computer printer that is available to other computers in addition to the one to which the printer has been physically attached. If your computer is not attached to a network, then you do not have access to a network printer. Likewise, you cannot expect your neighbors to be able to connect to one of your locally connected printers unless all of you are on the same network (LAN or WAN).

Newsgroups

Newsgroups are electronically based forums on the Internet where interested parties can exchange information in a text-based manner.

There are literally tens of thousands of Internet newsgroups available to the general public. If there is a topic of any kind that interests you, then there is certain to be an Internet newsgroup that focuses on that topic. The Microsoft Outlook Express client software that is integrated into the Microsoft Internet Explorer web browser is a great tool for perusing these newsgroups.

Notepad

Notepad enables you to create or edit non-formatted text files. These files cannot exceed 64 KB in size, and are saved into the ASCII file format. If you want formatting such as colored text or funky fonts, or if you want to have files that are larger than 64 KB, then you should use WordPad (it, like Notepad, is built into the Windows 98 operating system).

A
B
C
D
E
F
G
H
I
J
K
L
M
N
O
P
Q
R
S
T
U
V
W
X
Y
Z

A
B
C
D
E
F
G
H
I
J
K
L
M
N
O
P
Q
R
S
T
U
V
W
X
Y
Z

To use Notepad, do the following:

1. Click the **Start** button, choose **Programs**, **Accessories**, and then click **Notepad**, as shown in Figure N.20.

Figure **N.20**

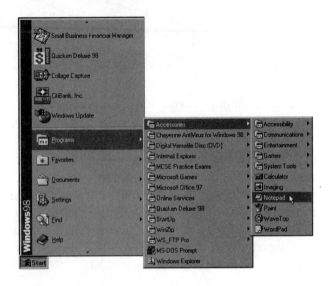

2. To begin using the Notepad application, just start typing as soon as the program begins.

3. Create a new file by clicking the **File** menu option and choosing **New**.

   Or, open an existing file by clicking the **File** menu option and choosing **Open**, as shown in Figure N.21.

Figure **N.21**

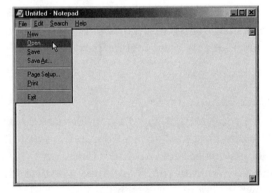

4. In the **Open** dialog box, navigate to the file you want to open, click it, and then click the **Open** button. As shown in Figure N.22, the file you selected opens onto the Notepad screen. Make changes to the text as needed.

Figure **N.22**

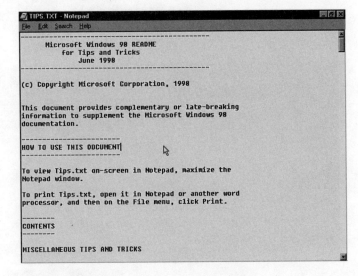

5. To save the file, click the **File** menu option and choose **Save**.
6. To print the file, click the **File** menu option and choose **Print**.
7. To close the file, click the **File** menu option and choose **Close**.

A
B
C
D
E
F
G
H
I
J
K
L
M
N
O
P
Q
R
S
T
U
V
W
X
Y
Z

O

ODBC (Open Database Connectivity)

Online Services

Online User's Guide

A
B
C
D
E
F
G
H
I
J
K
L
M
N
O
P
Q
R
S
T
U
V
W
X
Y
Z

A
B
C
D
E
F
G
H
I
J
K
L
M
N
O
P
Q
R
S
T
U
V
W
X
Y
Z

ODBC (Open Database Connectivity)

ODBC (or Open Database Connectivity) is a programming interface standard used for connecting computer applications to a database (such as Microsoft Access or Microsoft SQL Server) that supports the SQL language. The ODBC standard has been around for several years (almost an eternity in the computing world) and is a commonly accepted way to connect applications with databases as diverse as Oracle, Informix, Sybase SQL Server, Microsoft Access, and Microsoft SQL Server.

To configure ODBC in Windows 98, do the following:

1. Click the **Start** button, click **Settings**, and then click **Control Panel**, as shown in Figure O.1.

Figure **O.1**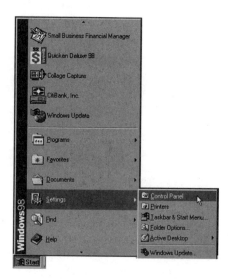

2. Double-click on the **32bit ODBC** icon in the Control Panel window, shown in Figure O.2.

3. The ODBC Data Source Administrator dialog opens. This dialog box contains the following tabs:

   📑 User DSN   This tab, shown in Figure O.3, enables you to add, remove, or configure user data sources.

Figure **O.2**

Figure **O.3**

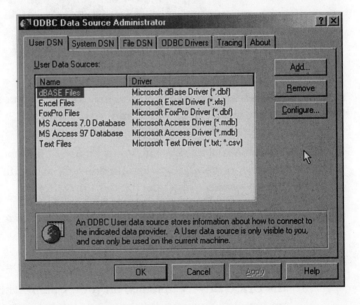

note...   As explained in the User DSN tab, user data sources store information about how you connect to the indicated data provider. Only you can view your user data sources, and they can be used only on your current machine.

A
B
C
D
E
F
G
H
I
J
K
L
M
N
O
P
Q
R
S
T
U
V
W
X
Y
Z

A
B
C
D
E
F
G
H
I
J
K
L
M
N
O
P
Q
R
S
T
U
V
W
X
Y
Z

🖰 System DSN   This tab, shown in Figure O.4, enables you to add, remove, or configure system data sources.

Figure **O.4**

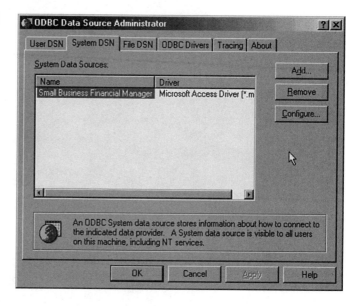

note...   The system data sources work just like user data sources, except that they are visible to all users and services on the PC.

🖰 File DSN   This tab, shown in Figure O.5, enables you to add, remove, or configure file data sources. A file data source enables you to connect to a specific data provider.

note...   Adding and deleting system data sources works much the same as adding and deleting other data sources.

🖰 ODBC Drivers   This tab, shown in Figure O.6, enables you to view the ODBC drivers installed on your system. This screen is for informational purposes only.

note...   To add or remove an ODBC driver, you must use the instructions that came with that driver's installation disk(s).

Figure **O.5**

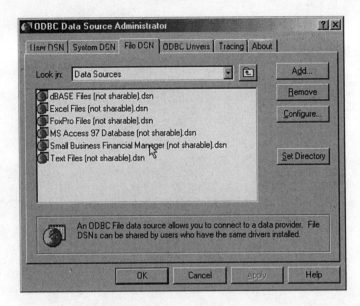

Figure **O.6**

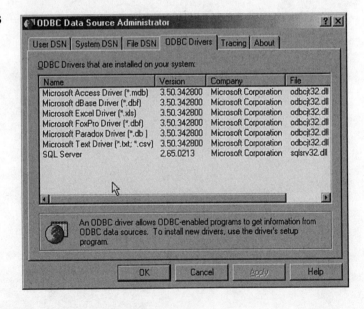

 Tracing   This tab, shown in Figure O.7, enables you to set tracing parameters. An ODBC trace should be used whenever you suspect that a certain ODBC driver has a problem. Selecting the **All the time** radio button in the **When to trace** area is not recommended because this creates extra overhead for the computer.

A
B
C
D
E
F
G
H
I
J
K
L
M
N
O
P
Q
R
S
T
U
V
W
X
Y
Z

Figure **O.7**

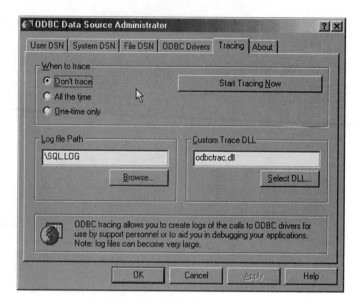

About This tab, shown in Figure O.8, contains information about all the ODBC core components.

Figure **O.8**

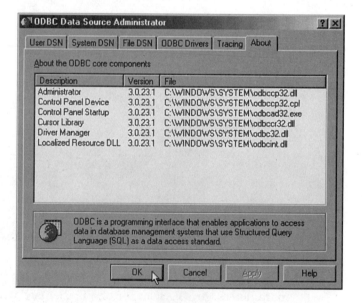

4. To add or remove a data source, click the appropriate tab in the ODBC Data Source Administrator dialog box.

5. Click the data source you want to add or remove to highlight it.

6. Click the **Add** or **Remove** button, depending on what action you want to take, and then carefully follow the prompts.

7. Click **OK** to accept your changes and close the ODBC Data Source Administrator dialog box.

Online Services

The installation software for five online service providers is provided with the Windows 98 operating system (on the Windows 98 CD-ROM):

- America Online (AOL)
- AT&T WorldNet Service
- CompuServe
- Prodigy Internet
- The Microsoft Network (MSN)

All these services can be loaded from the Windows 98 CD, but none are installed by default. To access these services, do the following:

1. Double-click the **Online Services** folder on the Windows 98 desktop, shown in Figure O.9.

Figure **O.9**

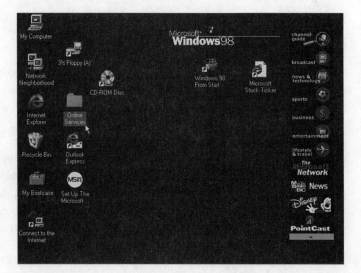

A
B
C
D
E
F
G
H
I
J
K
L
M
N
O
P
Q
R
S
T
U
V
W
X
Y
Z

The Online Services window, shown in Figure O.10, opens.

Figure **O.10**

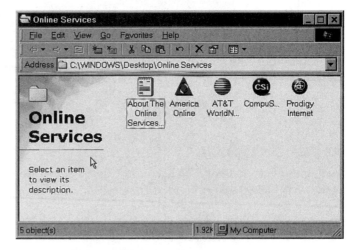

note...   Microsoft does not put its **MSN** icon inside the Online Services folder when you install Windows 98. Instead, Microsoft puts "the other guys" in the folder and its own MSN **Set Up The Microsoft Network** icon directly on the Windows 98 desktop.

2. To install any of these services, double-click the one you want and then follow the prompts.

note...   All these online services require fees that can cost about $20-30 per month.

3. Also found in the **Online Services** folder is a shortcut to a small text file called **About The Online Services**, which covers some of the basics about these online services. To open this file, double-click it. The file's contents open in Notepad, as shown in Figure O.11.

note...   This file contains contact information for these online service providers, including technical support and billing telephone numbers for each service provider listed. Furthermore, basic information about product support and payments, setting up new accounts, and setting up your computer to use an existing account is provided within this text file.

Figure **O.11**

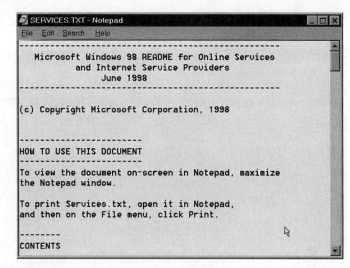

Online User's Guide

Windows 98 comes with an electronic version of its user manual. This electronic version of the user manual is known as the Online User's Guide (not to be confused with the Online Services discussed in the previous topic). To access this user guide, do the following:

1. Click the **Start** button and choose **Help**, as shown in Figure O.12.

Figure **O.12**

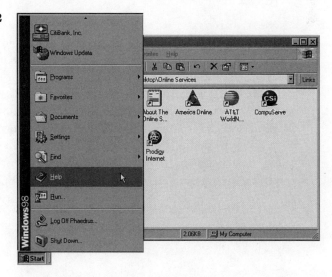

A
B
C
D
E
F
G
H
I
J
K
L
M
N
O
P
Q
R
S
T
U
V
W
X
Y
Z

A
B
C
D
E
F
G
H
I
J
K
L
M
N
O
P
Q
R
S
T
U
V
W
X
Y
Z

2. The Windows Help screen opens. Click the **Getting Started Book:
Online Version** to reveal the **Microsoft Windows 98 Getting Started
Book** hyperlink, as shown in Figure O.13. Double-click this hyperlink to
view the book online.

Figure **O.13**

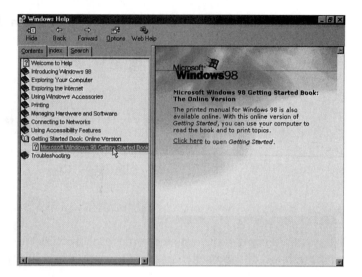

3. After this book is open, you are able to quickly jump around between
topics without any difficulties. Simply double-click on the topic that
interests you, and it opens up automatically.

note... There are three tabs at the top of the window: **Contents**, **Index**, and
Search. To select a tab, click the tab of your choice and it appears for
your use. Entry-level Windows 98 users will probably find the **Contents**
tab most useful; it contains little books on each general topic area
(such as **Using a Mouse**, **Internet Basics**, and **Glossary**). Intermediate
users (those who are former users of either Windows 95 or Windows NT
Workstation), should enjoy the layout of the **Index** tab. This tab permits you to type the specific topic about which you need information,
and it appears in the list below. Advanced users of Windows 98 will find
the **Search** tab the most useful. Here, you can obtain a list of the topics
that relate to a specific "higher-level" topic.

P

A
B
C
D
E
F
G
H
I
J
K
L
M
N
O
P
Q
R
S
T
U
V
W
X
Y
Z

A

B

C

D

E

F

G

H

I

J

K

L

M

N

O

P

Q

R

S

T

U

V

W

X

Y

Z

Paint

The Microsoft Paint program enables you to view and slightly modify graphics files. Please keep in mind, though, that Paint permits you to create or modify just a few of the many different types of graphics files. Only the bitmap (BMP), GIF (GIF), and JPEG (JPG and JPEG) file formats can be opened with Microsoft Paint. However, these three formats plus the monochrome (black-and-white), 16- and 256-color, and 24-bit bitmap file formats (BMP and DIB) are acceptable forms in which to save Microsoft Paint files. To use the Paint application, do the following:

1. Click once on the **Start** button, choose **Programs**, **Accessories**, and then **Paint**, as shown in Figure P.1.

Figure **P.1**

2. This opens the main **Paint** screen. To open an existing graphics file, click the **File** menu option and choose **Open**, as shown in Figure P.2.

note... To create a new picture from scratch, click the **File** menu option and click **New**.

3. In the **Open** dialog, navigate to the file you want to open, click to select it, and then click the **Open** button.

4. The file you selected opens into the **Paint** window, as shown in Figure P.3.

Figure **P.2**

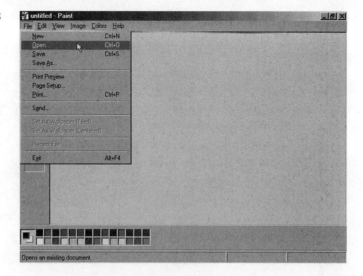

Figure **P.3**

5. Paint provides many tools for modifying graphic files. In this example, I
   have clicked the **Fill** tool, which I can use to fill a selected area with the
   color I select in the palette (along the bottom of the window). The results
   of using the **Fill** tool are shown in Figure P.4.

A
B
C
D
E
F
G
H
I
J
K
L
M
N
O
P
Q
R
S
T
U
V
W
X
Y
Z

Figure **P.4**

note... Notice that some of the white space within the letters of Mr. Caray's name did not get filled in because they were completely surrounded by another color (in this case, the color of the letter itself). These areas must be filled individually.

6. To print a copy of your masterpiece, click the **File** menu option and choose **Print**. This sends a copy of your image to the default printer.

note... My favorite aspect of the Paint application is that it lets you undo your mistakes. This enables you to play with this application until you feel more comfortable with it.

Passwords

Think of a password as an electronic key. This key is a bit of information that is entered into a computer program to gain access to that particular application. There are many different kinds of passwords for Windows 98, and most of them can be altered from a single location. To change your passwords, do the following:

1. Click **Start**, choose **Settings**, and click **Control Panel**, as shown in Figure P.5.

Figure **P.5**

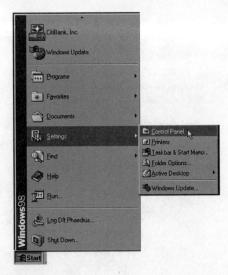

2. Double-click on the **Passwords** icon in the Control Panel screen, shown in Figure P.6.

Figure **P.6**

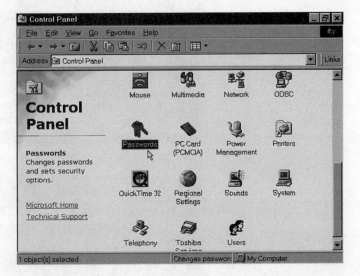

3. In the **Change Passwords** tab of the Passwords Properties dialog box, shown in Figure P.7, click the **Change Windows Password** button.

4. The **Change Windows Password** dialog box, shown in Figure P.8, opens. Type your old password (if this is the first time you're setting a password,

leave this box blank), then type your new password twice: once in the **New password** field, and once in the **Confirm new password** field. Click **OK** to accept the password change.

Figure **P.7**

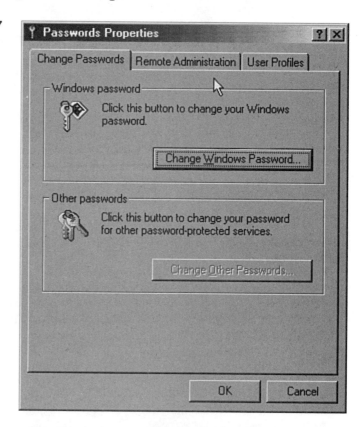

Figure **P.8**

note... You can change passwords such as those needed for the Windows NT network in the Other Passwords dialog box, which you reach by clicking **Change Other Passwords** in the **Change Passwords** tab of the **Passwords Properties** dialog box.

5. Click the **Remote Administration** tab, shown in Figure P.9. If you want to allow others to remotely manage your files and printers, click that check box in this tab, and then type the password that others must know in order to remotely administer your PC.

Figure **P.9**

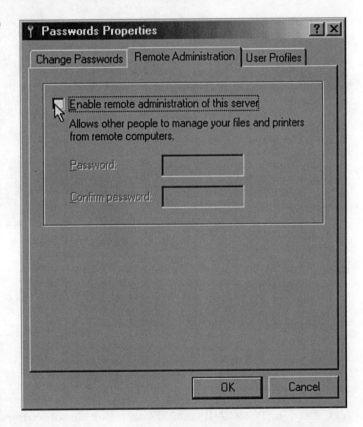

6. Click the **User Profiles** tab, shown in Figure P.10. If you want to configure your computer for use by multiple users, follow the prompts on this screen.

A
B
C
D
E
F
G
H
I
J
K
L
M
N
O
P
Q
R
S
T
U
V
W
X
Y
Z

Figure **P.10**

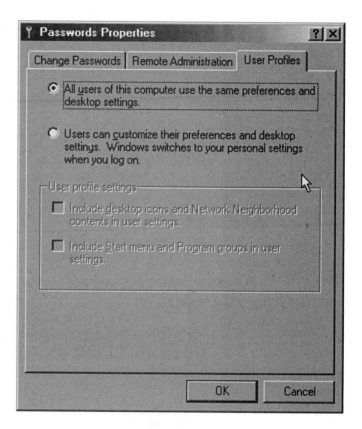

note... This is the same feature as the one discussed in the section titled "User Profile."

7. When you are finished changing the password options, click on the **OK** button.

PC Card (PCMCIA)

A PC Card, or PCMCIA (Personal Computer Manufacturers Cards International Association) device, is a credit card-sized piece of hardware that enables specific functions on computers that support this option. PC Card slots are typically found only on laptop, notebook, and handheld computing devices, but special drives can be installed on desktop PCs so that they are able to handle these types of devices. These devices are usually fax/modem, memory, or hard drive devices that are used to expand the functionality of the computers in which they are installed.

Windows 98 supports the Plug and Play features of countless numbers of these devices out of the box, and many more through add-on software drivers. Double-click the **PCMCIA** icon in the Windows 98 **Control Panel** to verify settings for these devices.

Personal Web Server

The Windows 98 Personal Web Server enables you to quickly create and display web pages and sites on your own computer. A nifty wizard application helps you create your first web site, which can then be copied to another server (maybe your ISP's), where it can be accessed via the Internet. To install Personal Web Server for use, do the following:

1. Insert the Windows 98 CD-ROM into your CD-ROM drive.

2. Click the **Start** button and choose **Run**.

3. As shown in Figure P.11, type the exact path to your Windows 98 CD-ROM, and to the Personal Web Server setup program. Then click **OK** to start the installation process.

Figure **P.11**

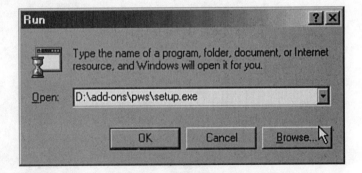

note... Windows 98 provides instructions for installing Personal Web Server. To view them, type **C:\windows\help\pws_main.htm** in the **Run** dialog box shown in Figure P.11.

4. Figure P.12 shows the first installation screen. Click **Next** to continue.

A
B
C
D
E
F
G
H
I
J
K
L
M
N
O
P
Q
R
S
T
U
V
W
X
Y
Z

Figure **P.12**

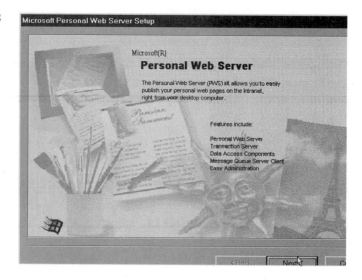

5. The licensing agreement screen, shown in Figure P.13, appears. Failure to accept the agreement results in the termination of the installation process, so it is advised that you click **Accept**. Click **Next** to continue.

Figure **P.13**

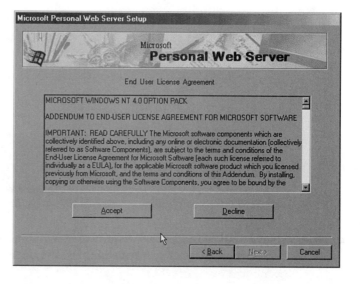

6. In the screen shown in Figure P.14, select the type of installation that best suits your needs. Although the **Typical** installation would probably work for your, click **Custom** so you can pick and choose exactly which components get installed on your computer. Then click **Next** to continue.

Figure **P.14**

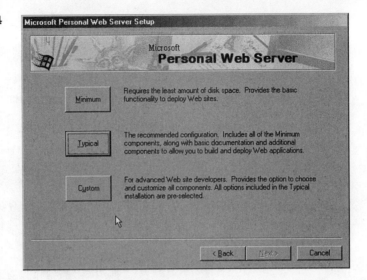

7. The Microsoft Personal Web Server Setup screen, shown in Figure P.15, lists all the components you can select to install (use the scrollbars to view the list in its entirety). Click the check box that corresponds with the components you want to install. Click the **Show Subcomponents** button to view the subcomponents of the highlighted component. After you select all the features you want, click **Next**.

Figure **P.15**

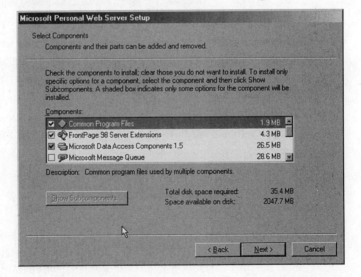

A
B
C
D
E
F
G
H
I
J
K
L
M
N
O
P
Q
R
S
T
U
V
W
X
Y
Z

note...   If a component's corresponding check box is checked but grayed out, it indicates that not all of that component's subcomponents have been installed.

8. The screen shown in Figure P.16 enables you to set or change the default folder destinations for any of the services on the screen. Simply enter the new folder path in the appropriate box. Click **Next** to continue.

Figure **P.16**

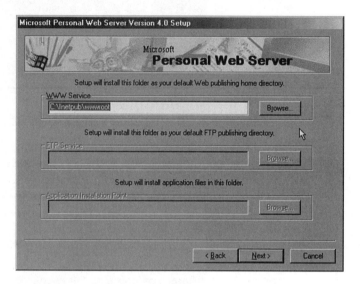

9. The screen shown in Figure P.17 enables you to specify where the Microsoft Transaction Server is to be installed. Either accept the default location or change it to one that better meets your needs, and then click the **Next** button to continue.

10. The progress bar shown in Figure P.18 keeps track of the installation's progress. When installation is complete, click the **Next** button.

11. The Personal Web Server installation process is now complete. Click the **Finish** button in the screen shown in Figure P.19.

12. You are prompted to restart your computer, as shown in Figure P.20. Click **Yes**.

To use the Personal Web Server after it has been installed, do the following:

1. Double-click the **Publish** icon that now appears on your desktop, as shown in Figure P.21.

Figure **P.17**

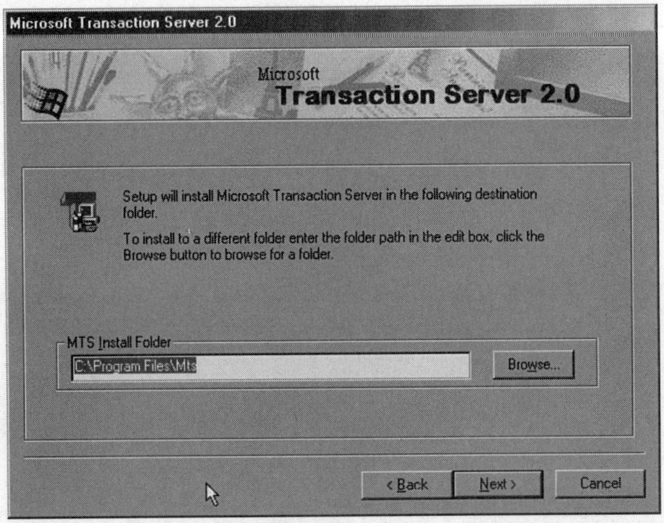

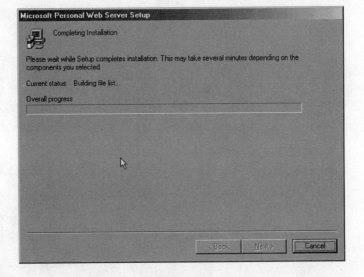

Figure **P.18**

2. The Personal Web Server application starts, first displaying the **Tip of the day** dialog box (see Figure P.22). Either click on the **Next** button to view another tip, or click the **Close** button to exit the **Tip of the day** dialog box.

A
B
C
D
E
F
G
H
I
J
K
L
M
N
O
P
Q
R
S
T
U
V
W
X
Y
Z

Figure **P.19**

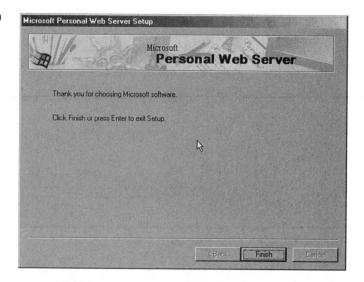

Figure **P.20**

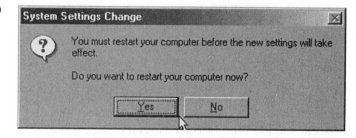

Figure **P.21**

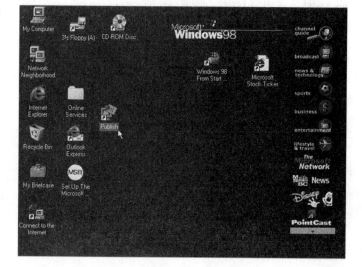

Figure **P.22**

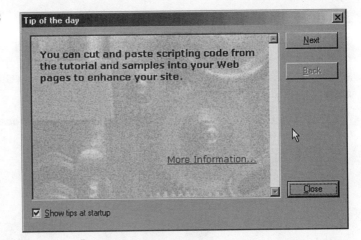

A
B
C
D
E
F
G
H
I
J
K
L
M
N
O
P
Q
R
S
T
U
V
W
X
Y
Z

note... To prevent this dialog box from appearing each time you start the Personal Web Server, uncheck the **Show tips at startup** check box.

3. If you clicked the **Close** button in the previous step, the Personal Web Manager screen appears (see Figure P.23). From here, you can fully manage your web site, including creating new pages through the Publish Wizard. Play with the various options found within this screen to become more familiar with them.

Figure **P.23**

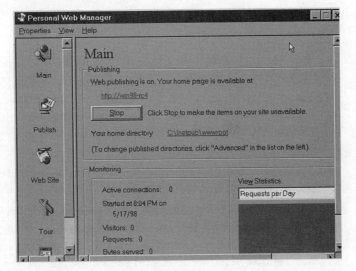

Phone Dialer

The Windows 98 Phone Dialer enables you to make telephone calls from your computer by using your modem or another Windows telephony device (see the section titled "Telephony" for more information). To use the Phone Dialer application, do the following:

1. Click the **Start** button, select **Programs**, choose **Accessories**, click **Communications** and then choose **Phone Dialer**, as shown in Figure P.24.

Figure **P.24**

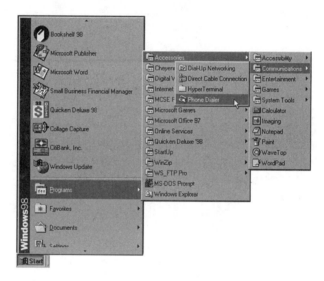

2. The **Phone Dialer** dialog box, shown in Figure P.25, opens. Notice that this screen is laid out just like a touch-tone telephone.

3. You must determine what hardware this application must connect to in order to place calls. To do this, click the **Tools** menu option and select **Connect Using**. This opens the **Connect Using** screen, shown in Figure P.26.

4. Specify the hardware device (such as a modem) to be used in the **Line** drop-down list box.

5. To modify how telephone calls are to be made, click the **Line Properties** button to open the *Modem Name* **Properties** dialog box, shown in Figure P.27. Use this screen to modify the properties of the modem that has been selected for use, and then click the **OK** button to return to the main Phone Dialer screen.

Figure **P.25**

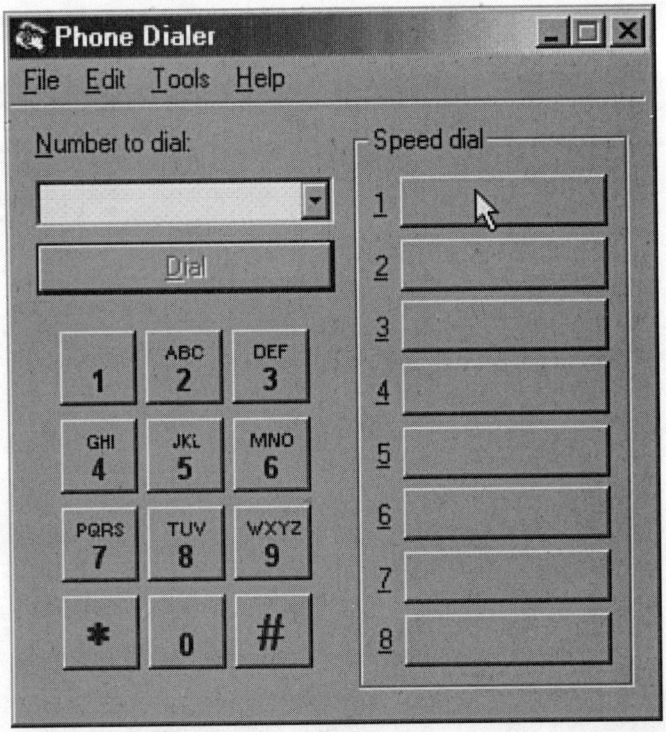

Figure **P.26**

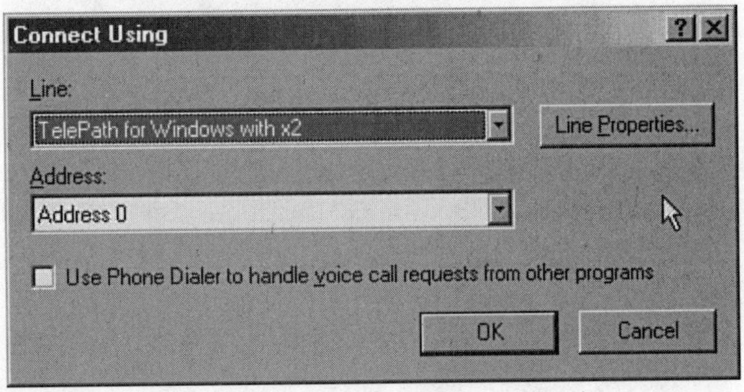

note... For a more detailed description of the options on this dialog box, refer
to the section titled "Modems."

A
B
C
D
E
F
G
H
I
J
K
L
M
N
O
P
Q
R
S
T
U
V
W
X
Y
Z

A
B
C
D
E
F
G
H
I
J
K
L
M
N
O
P
Q
R
S
T
U
V
W
X
Y
Z

Figure **P.27**

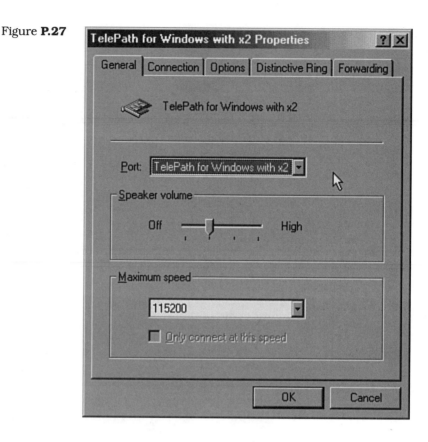

6. Click the **Tools** menu option and choose **Dialing Properties**. This opens the **Dialing Properties** screen, shown in Figure P.28. Use this screen to specify or modify information about the location from which you are dialing, and then click the **OK** button to return to the main Phone Dialer screen.

note... For details on filling in the Dialing Properties screen, refer to the section titled "Modems."

Figure **P.28**

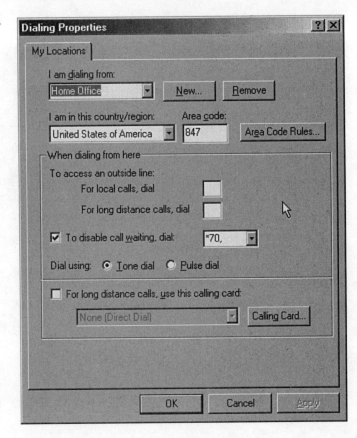

Before you make a telephone call, it's helpful to add the intended recipient to your Speed Dial list (although you don't have to). To add someone to your list, do the following:

1. In the main **Phone Dialer** window, click the **Edit** menu option and then choose **Speed Dial**. This opens the **Edit Speed Dial** screen shown in Figure P.29.

2. Type the name of the person you want to add in the **Name** field.

3. Type the person's phone number in the **Number to dial** field.

4. Repeat these steps for any other people you want to add to speed dial.

5. Click the **Save** button to return to the **Phone Dialer** screen, shown in Figure P.30. Notice that eight new names have been added.

6. To place a call using speed dial, simply click the button labeled with the name of the person you want to call.

Figure **P.29**

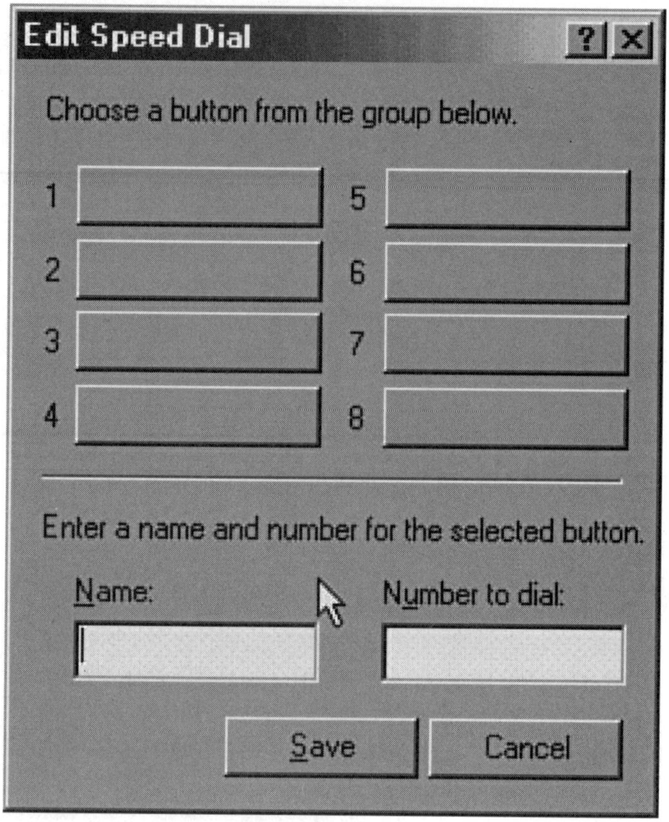

Edit Speed Dial

Choose a button from the group below.

1   5

2   6

3   7

4   8

Enter a name and number for the selected button.

Name: Number to dial:

Save   Cancel

note... To place a call without using the speed-dial feature, use your keypad or click the numbers on the Phone Dialer screen to enter the complete telephone number (with area code, if necessary) in the **Number to dial** box. Click the **Dial** button to start the call.

Plug and Play

Plug and Play refers to the capability to add new hardware devices or take away old ones on-the-fly. Suppose, for example, that you use a laptop computer and want to install a PCMCIA (or PC Card) modem. With Windows 98's plug and play capability, you can simply pop the modem into your laptop. The modem is then automatically recognized and installed.

Figure **P.30**

Power Management

The Windows 98 power management feature helps you conserve energy by reducing the power consumption needs of your computing devices. This feature functions by making you create a power scheme—essentially a series of settings that manages PC power needs. For example, you can configure your PC to save power by automatically turning off the system monitor or stopping the hard drive after a preset period of idle time. To configure power management for your PC (assuming, of course, that your computer system is designed to support this feature), do the following:

1. Click the **Start** button, choose **Settings**, and click **Control Panel**, as shown in Figure P.31.

2. Double-click the **Power Management** icon in the Control Panel window, shown in Figure P.32.

3. The **Power Schemes** tab of the **Power Management Properties** dialog box opens. Click the down-arrow button to the right of the **Power schemes** field to view a drop-down list box containing the three available sample power management schemes, as shown in Figure P.33.

A
B
C
D
E
F
G
H
I
J
K
L
M
N
O
P
Q
R
S
T
U
V
W
X
Y
Z

Figure **P.31**

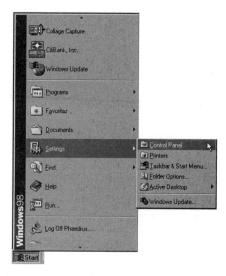

Figure **P.32**

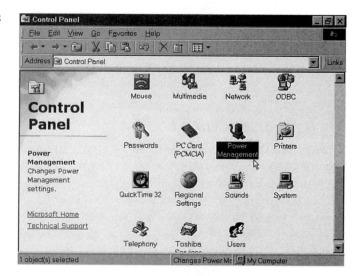

4. Choose the power scheme that best describes your work environment, and set the time limits at the bottom of the screen.

Figure **P.33**

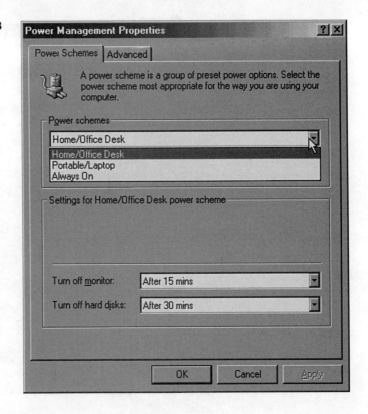

5. Click the **Advanced** tab to view the screen shown in Figure P.34. Here, you can select whether you want to show the power meter on the taskbar and whether you want to be prompted for a password when the computer goes off standby mode.

6. Click the **OK** button.

A
B
C
D
E
F
G
H
I
J
K
L
M
N
O
P
Q
R
S
T
U
V
W
X
Y
Z

A
B
C
D
E
F
G
H
I
J
K
L
M
N
O
P
Q
R
S
T
U
V
W
X
Y
Z

Figure **P.34**

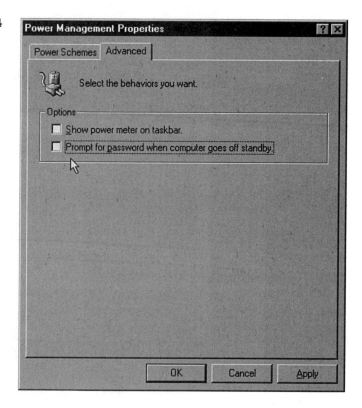

Printers

A basic but important need of any Windows 98 user is the ability to print information from his or her computer. To do this, you must have a physical printer and be able to install the proper software drivers for your locally connected printer (assuming you have one). For instructions about installing a printer, refer to the section titled "Add Printer Wizard."

After your printer is installed, to take a closer look at the printer(s) that are available for use with your computer, do the following:

1. Click the **Start** button, click **Settings**, and then click **Printers**.

2. The **Printers** folder, shown in Figure P.35, opens. The default printer is indicated by a check mark. Whenever you print from a Windows 98 application, such as your word processor, your document automatically goes to this default printer.

Figure **P.35**

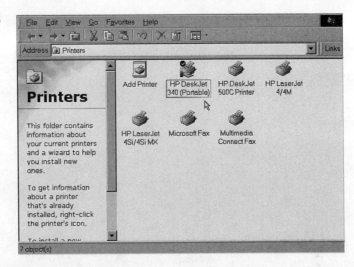

note... When you are getting ready to print something, you are usually presented with an option to preview your document. This enables you to see
exactly what your printed document will look like before you actually
print it.

Programs

In the context of Windows 98, programs are the start of everything. A word
processing application is a program; so are all the Windows 98 accessories,
utilities, and online services. When you examine the Windows 98 **Programs**
menu, you will see the starting points (or *shortcut links*) to all your additional
software applications that you have installed on your computer.

Programs Menu Option

The **Programs** menu option contains all applications folders and shortcuts.
This, of course, can be changed, but does hold true immediately following the
installation of the Windows 98 operating system on a brand new computer. To
view the contents of the **Programs** menu option, click the **Start** button, then
choose **Programs** (see Figure P.36).

A
B
C
D
E
F
G
H
I
J
K
L
M
N
O

P

Q
R
S
T
U
V
W
X
Y
Z

Figure **P.36**

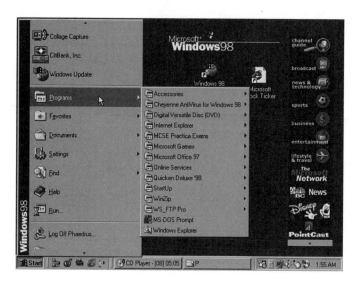

Q

Quick Launch

Quick View

A
B
C
D
E
F
G
H
I
J
K
L
M
N
O
P
Q
R
S
T
U
V
W
X
Y
Z

Quick Launch

Unlike previous versions of Windows, Windows 98 has toolbars all over the place. A good example is the Quick Launch toolbar, which automatically sets up links or shortcuts to key features such as the Windows 98 desktop, Outlook Express, Internet Channels, and the Microsoft Internet Explorer browser, just to name a few. You'll find the Quick Launch area to the right of the Start button on the taskbar, shown in Figure Q.1.

Figure **Q**.1

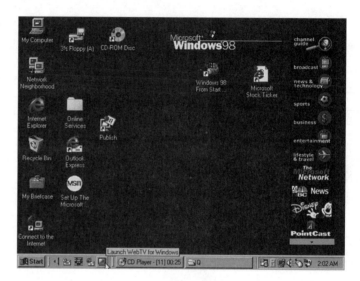

You can place additional shortcut icons on the Quick Launch toolbar simply by clicking the shortcut you want to add, and dragging it to the Quick Launch area (it automatically inserts itself on the toolbar).

Quick View

To quickly view the contents of a file, you can usually use the Windows 98 utility known as Quick View. To use Quick View, first navigate to the file you want to view (for more information on navigation in Windows 98, see the section titled "Windows Explorer"). Once you've found the file, right-click it and select Quick View from the ensuing shortcut menu, as shown in Figure Q.2. The file you selected opens inside the Quick View application, as shown in Figure Q.3.

Figure **9.2**

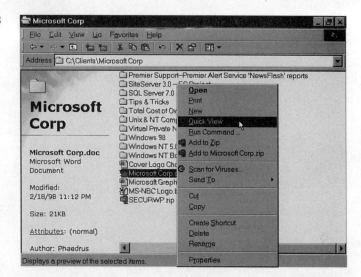

Figure **9.3**

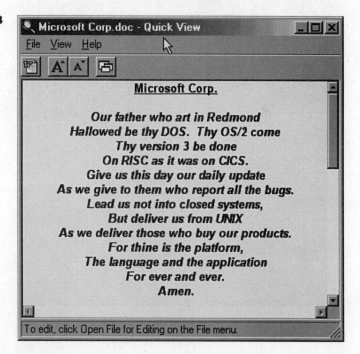

R

A
B
C
D
E
F
G
H
I
J
K
L
M
N
O
P
Q
R
S
T
U
V
W
X
Y
Z

A
B
C
D
E
F
G
H
I
J
K
L
M
N
O
P
Q
R
S
T
U
V
W
X
Y
Z

Rebooting Windows 98

Reboot is just another way of saying *restart*. So when Windows 98 prompts you to reboot your system, it just means that you need to shut it down and restart it. Simply do the following:

1. Click the **Start** button and choose **Shut Down**, as shown in Figure R.1.

Figure **R.1**

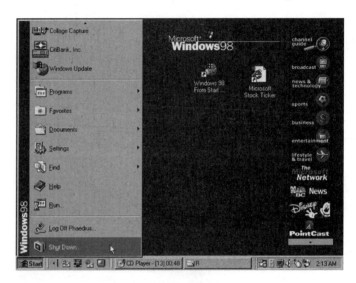

2. The **Shut Down Windows** dialog, shown in Figure R.2, appears. Click the **Restart** radio button and then click the **OK** button to begin the rebooting process.

Figure **R.2**

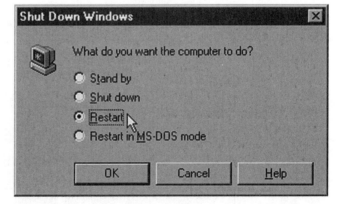

note...   Whichever radio button you selected the last time you shut down is
selected by default (if this is the first time you've used this screen, the
top option is selected).

Recycle Bin

When a file or folder is deleted from your computer, it first goes to the Recycle
Bin, which is found on the Windows 98 desktop (see Figure R.3).

Figure **R.3**

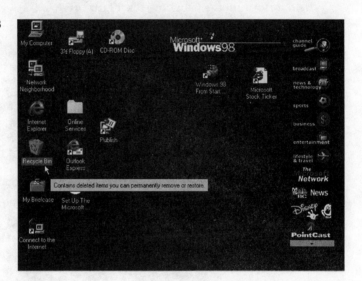

note...   When the Recycle Bin contains no files or folders, the **Recycle Bin** icon
shown on the desktop appears to be empty. When files or folders have
been placed in the Recycle Bin, the **Recycle Bin** icon appears to be
stuffed with paper.

note...   If you do not see the **Recycle Bin** icon on your desktop, it's probably
just hiding behind one of your open folders or applications. Try right-
clicking a blank area of the taskbar and choosing **Minimize All
Windows**; the **Recycle Bin** icon should then be revealed.

A
B
C
D
E
F
G
H
I
J
K
L
M
N
O
P
Q
R
S
T
U
V
W
X
Y
Z

A
B
C
D
E
F
G
H
I
J
K
L
M
N
O
P
Q
R
S
T
U
V
W
X
Y
Z

To view the contents of the Recycle Bin, double-click its icon on the desktop. If you decide that you no longer wish to delete a file or folder you've placed in the Recycle Bin, simply right-click the file in the **Recycle Bin** window and choose **Restore** from the ensuing shortcut menu. This returns the file or folder to the location where it resided before you attempted to delete it.

To empty the Recycle Bin and permanently remove its contents from your computer, do the following:

1. Right-click the **Recycle Bin** icon and choose **Empty Recycle Bin** from the shortcut menu, as shown in Figure R.4.

Figure **R.4**

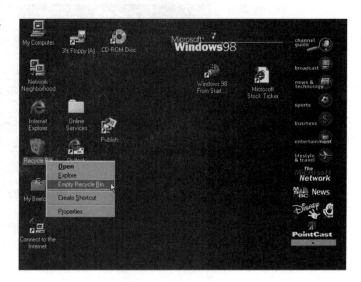

2. The dialog shown in Figure R.5 opens. If you are certain you want to delete the contents of the Recycle Bin, click **Yes**.

Figure **R.5**

note...   If the Recycle Bin contains only one file, the dialog shown in Figure R.5 provides the name of the file to be deleted. If the Recycle Bin contains multiple files, the dialog simply tells you how many files will be deleted.

3. You are returned to the Windows 98 desktop. As shown in Figure R.6, the **Recycle Bin** icon no longer appears to be stuffed with paper.

Figure **R.6**

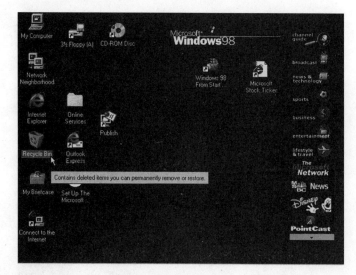

Regional Settings

Windows 98's Regional Settings feature makes it much easier to change the default time, date, currency, and number configurations for your PC. To configure your PC using this feature, do the following:

1. Click the **Start** button, choose **Settings**, and then select **Control Panel**, as shown in Figure R.7.

Figure **R.7**

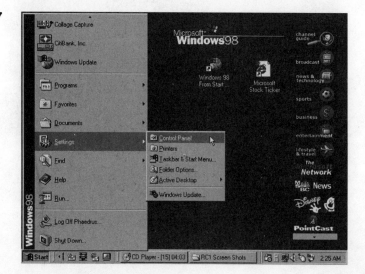

A
B
C
D
E
F
G
H
I
J
K
L
M
N
O
P
Q
R
S
T
U
V
W
X
Y
Z

A
B
C
D
E
F
G
H
I
J
K
L
M
N
O
P
Q
R
S
T
U
V
W
X
Y
Z

2. Double-click the **Regional Settings** icon in the **Control Panel** window, shown in Figure R.8.

Figure **R.8**

3. The **Regional Settings** tab of the **Regional Settings Properties** dialog opens, as shown in Figure R.9. Because I live in Chicago, I've left the default option, **English (United States)**, selected. To select a different language (such as British English, Russian, Slovak, Polish, or Macedonian, to name a few), click the down-arrow button next to the text field and select the language you want to use.

Figure **R.9**

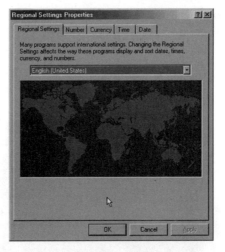

note... You might be prompted to reboot your computer immediately following a language change. Click **Yes** and reboot before changing more regional settings.

4. Click the **Number** tab to view the screen shown in Figure R.10. Here you specify exactly how numbers and decimal points are configured for their local environment. Two sample boxes near the top of the screen display how positive and negative numbers look with the new regional settings.

Figure **R.10**

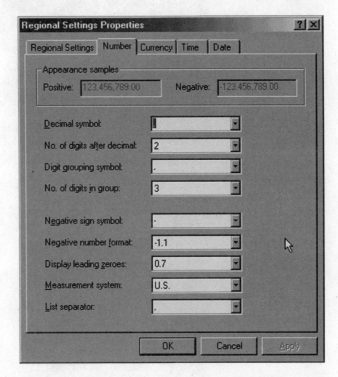

5. Click the **Currency** tab to view the screen shown in Figure R.11. Here you specify how currency figures are to be configured for your local environment. Two sample boxes near the top of the screen display how a positive and negative currency amount appears with the new regional settings.

6. Click the **Time** tab to view the screen shown in Figure R.12. Here you select the format of the system clock.

7. Click the **Date** tab to view the screen shown in Figure R.13. Here you select the format of the local calendar and date type, as well as the Year 2000 system settings.

8. Click the **OK** button to accept your changes and return to the Windows 98 desktop.

A
B
C
D
E
F
G
H
I
J
K
L
M
N
O
P
Q
R
S
T
U
V
W
X
Y
Z

A
B
C
D
E
F
G
H
I
J
K
L
M
N
O
P
Q
R
S
T
U
V
W
X
Y
Z

Figure **R.11**

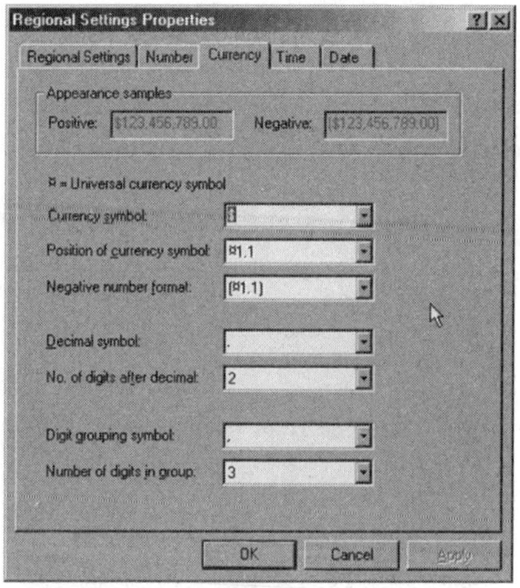

Figure **R.12**

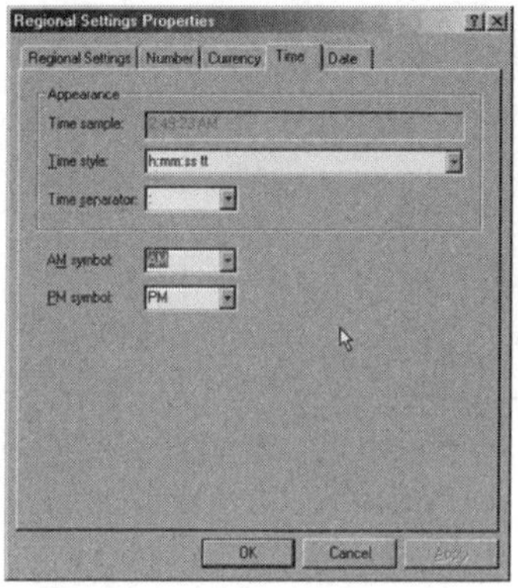

Figure **R.13**

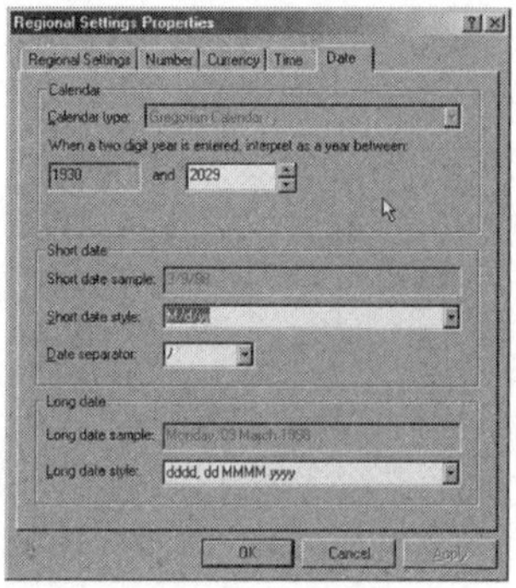

Registering Windows 98

After you have installed Windows 98 (or have set up a PC with Windows 98 pre-installed), you should register the operating system software with Microsoft. If you register Windows 98, you become eligible for product support, and are ensured that you will be updated on future product enhancements. To register, do the following:

1. Connect to the Internet.

2. Click the **Start** button, choose **Programs**, select **Accessories**, click **System Tools**, and then choose **Welcome to Windows**, as shown in Figure R.14.

Figure **R.14**

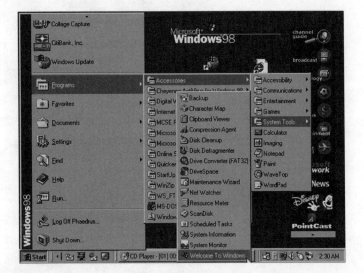

3. Click the **Register Now** entry in the **Contents** menu of the Welcome to Windows 98 screen, shown in Figure R.15.

4. The first screen of the **Registration** wizard, shown in Figure R.16, tells you why you should register. To continue the registration process, click the **Next** button.

5. The wizard's second screen, shown in Figure R.17, informs you that the **Registration** wizard is about to inventory your system's hardware. Click the **Next** button to continue.

A
B
C
D
E
F
G
H
I
J
K
L
M
N
O
P
Q
R
S
T
U
V
W
X
Y
Z

Figure **R.15**

Figure **R.16**

Figure **R.17**

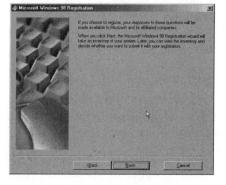

note...   Don't panic! Microsoft is not stealing information from your PC, nor is it gathering bits of information about competitive products you may be using. This is simply a harmless information-gathering procedure to help Microsoft customer support, should you require assistance somewhere down the road.

6. In the wizard's third screen, shown in Figure R.18, you type your first name, last name, and company name (type your company name only if your employer—not you—purchased this version of Windows 98). Click the **Next** button to continue.

Figure **R.18**

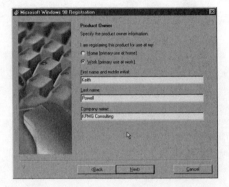

7. In the screen shown in Figure R.19, enter your address information, including country. If you provide an email address, Microsoft will occasionally send you electronic messages informing you of changes to the product. Click the **Next** button to continue.

Figure **R.19**

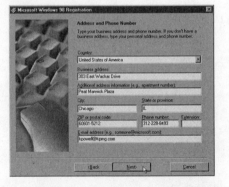

8. The screen shown in Figure R.20 enables you to specify where you bought your copy of Windows 98, and whether you want to be included in various offers of non-Microsoft products and services. Click the **Next** button to continue.

A
B
C
D
E
F
G
H
I
J
K
L
M
N
O
P
Q
R
S
T
U
V
W
X
Y
Z

A
B
C
D
E
F
G
H
I
J
K
L
M
N
O
P
Q
R
S
T
U
V
W
X
Y
Z

Figure **R.20**

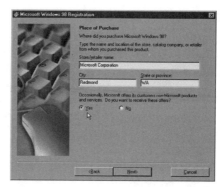

note... Entering information in the screen shown in Figure R.20 is not required.

9. The screen shown in Figure R.21 contains the information the **Registration** wizard was able to glean from your computer system while you were filling in information on previous screens (sneaky, huh?). If you decide to forward this information to Microsoft by clicking the **Yes** radio button, you will receive more efficient product support. Click the **Next** button to continue.

Figure **R.21**

10. The final informational screen, shown in Figure R.22, appears. Write down the Windows 98 product ID number that appears in the middle of the screen (this number is unique to your computer and will be required should you ever need product support from Microsoft). Click the **Register** button.

11. You'll see a message box informing you that your registration information is being sent to Microsoft. Once the registration process is complete, you'll see a confirmation dialog like the one shown in Figure R.23. Click **Finish**.

Figure **R.22**

Figure **R.23**

12. You are returned to the Welcome to Windows 98 screen, shown in Figure R.24. The Register Now entry now has a check mark to the right of it, which indicates that you have successfully completed the Windows 98 registration process. Click the × button in the upper-right corner of the screen to close this window.

Figure **R.24**

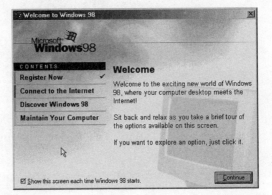

A
B
C
D
E
F
G
H
I
J
K
L
M
N
O
P
Q
R
S
T
U
V
W
X
Y
Z

A
B
C
D
E
F
G
H
I
J
K
L
M
N
O
P
Q
R
S
T
U
V
W
X
Y
Z

Resource Kit Sampler

The Windows 98 CD-ROM contains a set of programs known as the Windows 98 Resource Kit Sampler. This is a scaled-down version of the actual resource kit applications, which include the following component categories:

- Configuration tools
- Deployment tools
- Desktop tools
- Diagnostics and troubleshooting tools
- File tools
- Network automation tools
- Scripting tools

Unless you are intent on purchasing the full Windows 98 Resource Kit or are unless you are inherently curious, it is not recommended that the beginning user work with any of these tools. If any of these tools are misused, even in their limited forms, it can destroy your existing Windows 98 operating environment (requiring you to re-install Windows 98 on your PC). That said, you can install the kit by doing the following:

1. Click the **Start** button and choose **Run**.

2. In the Run dialog, shown in Figure R.25, type
   D:\tools\reskit\setup.exe

Figure **R.25**

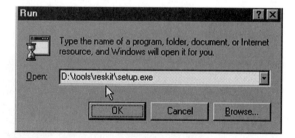

3. Follow all the prompts to complete the installation of the kit. The kit, by default, is placed in the C:\Win98RK folder, but you can put these files anywhere you want.

4. When the installation is complete, click the **OK** button.

5. To use the various tools of the kit, click the **Start** button, select **Programs**, and choose **Windows 98 Resource Kit**, as shown in Figure R.26.

Figure **R.26**

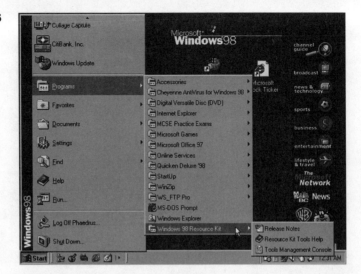

6. The **Tools Management Console** is the starting point for the use of each of the Resource Kit's tools.

note... Remember that these are not full versions of each tool (that is, their functionality is limited), so don't be surprised if something doesn't quite work the way you thought it would.

Resource Meter

You can use the Windows 98 Resource Meter to monitor the health of your computer system by displaying how much of your system's resources are available. To run the Resource Meter, do the following:

1. Click the **Start** button, choose **Programs**, select **Accessories**, click **System Tools**, and then choose **Resource Meter**, as shown in Figure R.27.

2. Read the informational box in Figure R.28 and then click **OK** to continue.

note... Click the **Don't display this message again** check box if you don't want to be bothered with this dialog again.

A
B
C
D
E
F
G
H
I
J
K
L
M
N
O
P
Q
R
S
T
U
V
W
X
Y
Z

Figure **R.27**

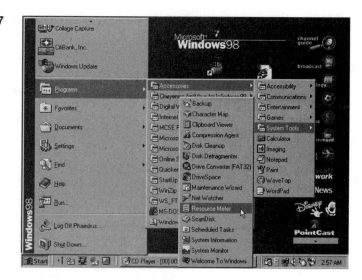

Figure **R.28**

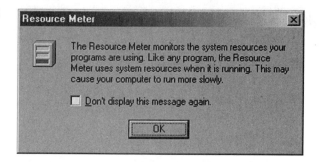

note...   To avoid draining system resources unnecessarily, run the Resource Meter only when you need to know how many of your system's resources are available.

3. You are now returned to the Windows 98 desktop. In the far-right portion of the taskbar, you'll find an icon that represents the Resource Meter. If you hover your mouse pointer over this icon (as shown in Figure R.29), you can view what percentage of the following resources are free:

● **System**   A System resource is required by Windows 98 and will almost always be present. There is not much tuning or tweaking you can do to lower this number, other than to eliminate some Windows 98 features and functions.

Figure **R.29**

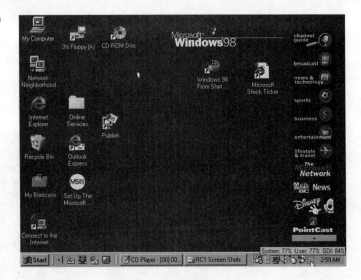

- 📌 **User**   User resources are those that are consumed by the use of backgrounds, the addition of icons and HTML files to the desktop, the simultaneous opening of several programs, and so on.

- 📌 **GDI**   GDI resources are consumed by the graphics capabilities of your PC. To decrease the consumption of GDI resources, you might reduce the number of colors your monitor shows from High (either 24-bit, which equates to 16.7 million colors, or 16-bit, which equates to 65,000 colors) to 256.

If you have trouble seeing the percentages on the desktop, right-click the **Resource Meter** icon and click **Details** in the ensuing shortcut menu. This opens the screen shown in Figure R.30; click **OK** to close it.

Figure **R.30**

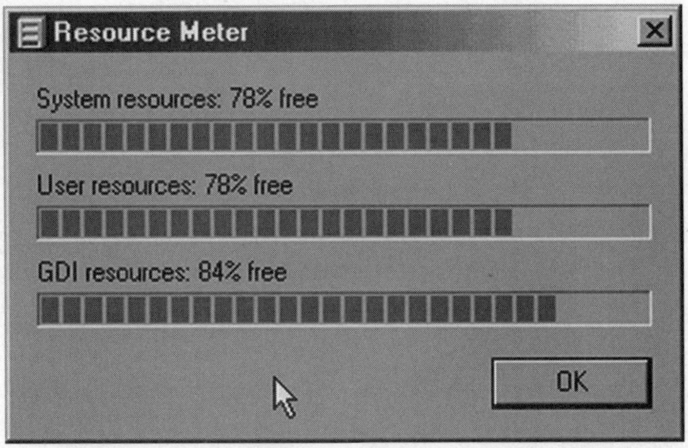

Run

The **Windows 98 Run** window enables you to execute **Run** commands to start programs or open folders, documents, or Internet resources. To use this window, do the following:

1. Click the **Start** button and choose **Run**, as shown in Figure R.31.

Figure **R.31**

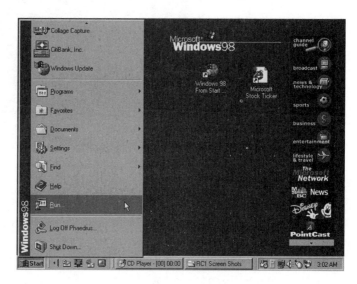

2. In the **Run** window, shown in Figure R.32, type the full path to the program you want to run, including the name of the executable file (if you don't know the full path, click the **Browse** button to find the file). In this example, I've typed the path to setup file of the Windows 98 Personal Web Server add-on product, which is located in my CD-ROM drive.

Figure **R.32**

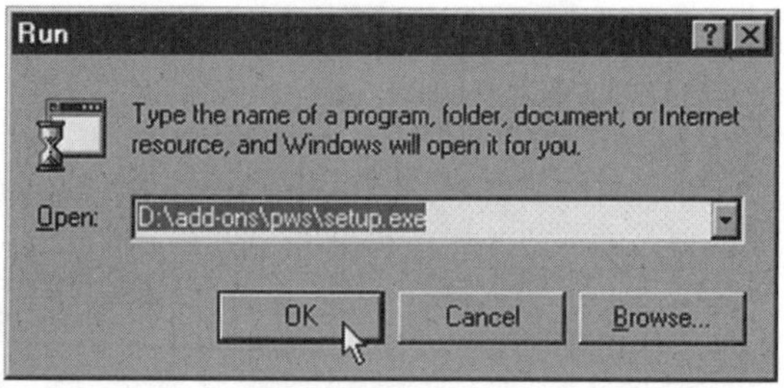

S

A
B
C
D
E
F
G
H
I
J
K
L
M
N
O
P
Q
R
S
T
U
V
W
X
Y
Z

ScanDisk

ScanDisk is used for examining and repairing problems on your hard drive. To use ScanDisk, do the following:

1. Click the **Start** button, choose **Programs**, select **Accessories**, click **System Tools**, and then choose **ScanDisk**, as shown in Figure S.1.

Figure **S.1**

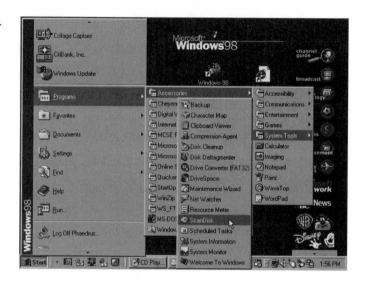

2. Click the **Advanced** button in the ScanDisk window (see Figure S.2).

Figure **S.2**

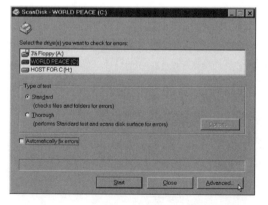

3. The ScanDisk Advanced Options dialog box, shown in Figure S.3, enables you to specify various advanced options, such as whether to use

log files and how to deal with lost file fragments and cross-linked files. Select the check boxes and radio buttons as needed, and then click the **OK** button to return to the main screen.

Figure **S.3**

A
B
C
D
E
F
G
H
I
J
K
L
M
N
O
P
Q
R
S
T
U
V
W
X
Y
Z

note... It's recommended that you select the **Append to Log** option instead of the default Replace log option in the **Log File** area. That way, you will have a running history of ScanDisk usage on your PC. In addition, it is useful to configure ScanDisk to check for invalid dates and times because such files tend to result in cross-linking of files down the road.

A cross-linked file is a file that contains pointers to multiple locations. For example, suppose you own two identical cars (one is yours and one is your spouse's). You tell your kid to wash your spouse's car, but because they are identical, he has no way of figuring out which one to clean. Cross-linked files are like your identical cars; your computer may not know which one to open (or may open the two at once as a single file).

4. Click the **Start** button in the main ScanDisk window to run the ScanDisk application for the highlighted hard drive (you can select a different drive by clicking it). You will be notified when the program finishes.

A
B
C
D
E
F
G
H
I
J
K
L
M
N
O
P
Q
R
S
T
U
V
W
X
Y
Z

Screen Saver

Screen savers provide a series of graphics that hide the application that's open on your computer. The original purpose of a screen saver was to help prevent screen *burn-in*, in which a faint image of your screen's former contents remained visible even after you turned off your monitor or moved to new contents. Although some people still use screen savers for this purpose, they are used mostly for their entertainment value only.

To designate one of Windows 98's built-in screen savers for use, do the following:

1. Right-click a blank portion of the desktop and choose **Properties**, as shown in Figure S.4.

Figure **S.4**

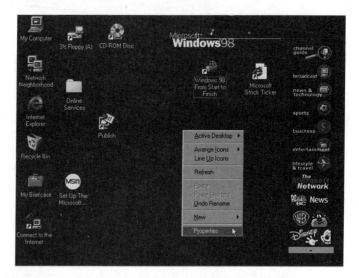

2. Click the **Screen Saver** tab in the Display Properties dialog box to view the screen shown in Figure S.5.

3. Click the down-arrow button to the right of the Screen Saver field and select a screen saver from the drop-down list. To set the options for a specific screen saver, click the **Settings** button to view that screen saver's Options dialog box. (The one shown in Figure S.6 shows the options for the Curves and Colors screen saver.)

Figure **S.5**

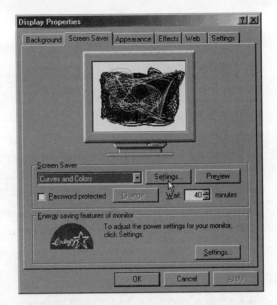

Figure **S.6**

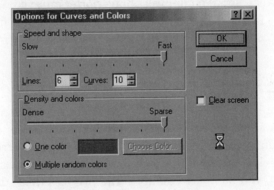

4. After you set your screen saver's options, click **OK** to return to the Screen Saver tab of the Display Properties dialog box. Click the **Preview** button to view a full-screen preview of the screen saver; click or move the mouse to end the preview session.

5. To password-protect the screen saver, check the **Password Protected** check box and click the **Change** button. This opens the Change Password dialog box, shown in Figure S.7.

A
B
C
D
E
F
G
H
I
J
K
L
M
N
O
P
Q
R
S
T
U
V
W
X
Y
Z

Figure **S.7**

6. If you have never added a password to a screen saver, you will be prompted to enter and confirm the new password (as is the case in Figure S.7). Otherwise, you will need to know the original password before you can change it to a new one. Fill in the text fields as necessary.

7. Click the **OK** button to return to the Display Properties dialog box, and then click **OK** again to accept all changes and return to the desktop.

Serial Mouse

A serial mouse is simply a pointing device that is connected directly to one of your computer's serial communications ports, more commonly referred to as COM:x ports (where the x equals the port number). For more information on mouse devices, refer to the section titled "Mouse."

Serial Printer

A serial printer is one that is connected to your computer's serial communications port. A *serial communications port* is better known as a COMx port (where x equals a number, usually 1 or 2). Because a serial printer tends to operate at a slower rate (9,600bps) than a parallel printer (roughly 232,000bps), you do not see many serial printers these days.

Shortcuts

A Windows 98 shortcut is also known as a *link*. It permits you to access a file or application without having to navigate to it on your hard drive. Shortcuts on your Windows 98 desktop are represented by icons containing a small curved arrow in the lower-left corner (see Figure S.8).

Figure **S.8**

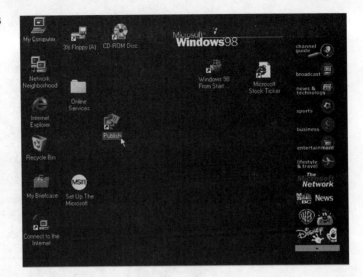

To view information about a shortcut on your desktop, do the following:

1. Right-click a shortcut and choose **Properties** from the shortcut menu, as shown in Figure S.9.

Figure **S.9**

2. The Properties dialog box for the shortcut you've selected opens (in this case, it's the Publish Properties dialog box, shown in Figure S.10). The Target text field on the Shortcut tab contains the shortcut's path and

A
B
C
D
E
F
G
H
I
J
K
L
M
N
O
P
Q
R
S
T
U
V
W
X
Y
Z

executable file. (If the shortcut is to a folder and not a program, there is no executable file at the end of the target statement.)

Figure **S.10**

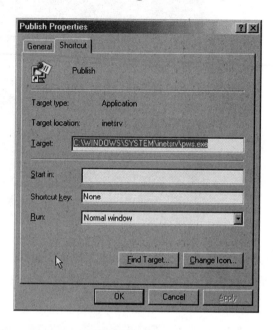

3. Click the **Find Target** button to go to the folder containing the shortcut. Figure S.11 shows the target folder for the Publish shortcut.

Figure **S.11**

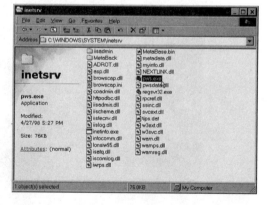

4. Close this window to return to the Shortcut tab of the Properties dialog box, and then click the **Change Icon** button to alter the shortcut's icon. This opens the dialog shown in Figure S.12.

Figure **S.12**

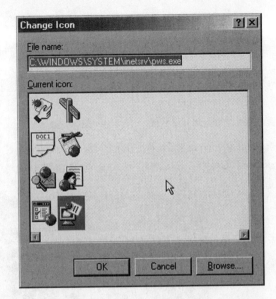

5. Select the icon you want to use, or click the **Browse** button to find other icons. After you have selected the icon you want, click the **OK** button.

6. Click on the **General** tab to view the screen shown in Figure S.13. Here you can determine the shortcut's MS-DOS name and other specific properties (such as the dates it was created, modified, and last accessed).

Figure **S.13**

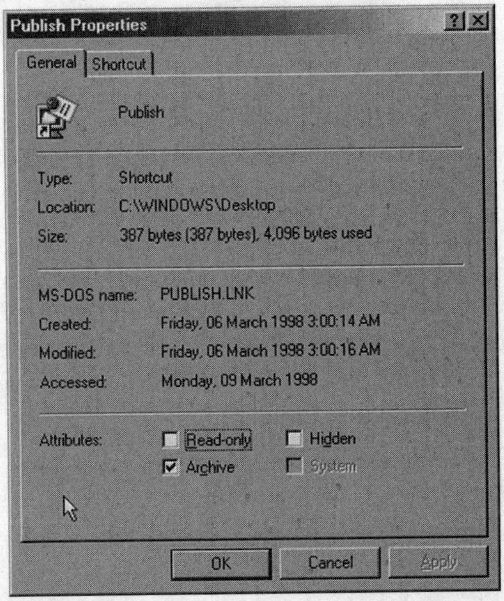

note... You can make a shortcut hidden or read-only by clicking the applicable check box in the Attributes section at the bottom of the General tab.

7. To accept changes and exit, click the **OK** button in the Properties dialog box.

To create a shortcut from scratch, do the following:

1. Right-click any blank spot on the desktop and, in the ensuing shortcut menu, choose **New** and then **Shortcut**, as shown in Figure S.14.

Figure **S.14**

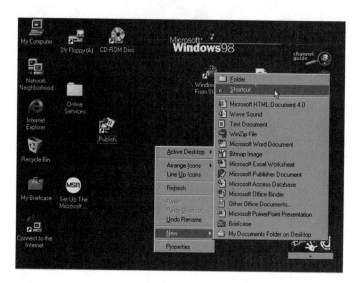

2. The Create Shortcut Wizard starts. In the first screen (shown in Figure S.15), either type the full path including the target file for your shortcut, or click the **Browse** button to find the file on your computer. Click **Next** to continue.

3. In the wizard's second screen, shown in Figure S.16, type a descriptive name for your shortcut (this is the name you will see on the desktop).

4. In most cases, the shortcut will be assigned a default icon, which appears on the Windows 98 desktop. In other cases, the **Select an Icon** screen may appear (see Figure S.17). To select an icon, click the one of your choice.

Figure **S.15**

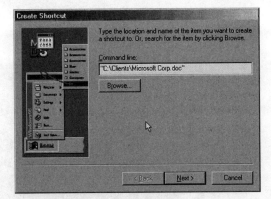

Figure **S.16**

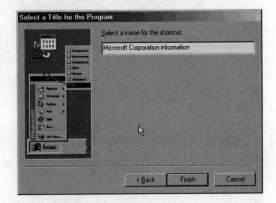

Figure **S.17**

A
B
C
D
E
F
G
H
I
J
K
L
M
N
O
P
Q
R
S
T
U
V
W
X
Y
Z

5. Click the Finish button to complete the wizard and return to the desktop. As you can see in Figure S.18, the newly created shortcut appears.

Figure **S.18**

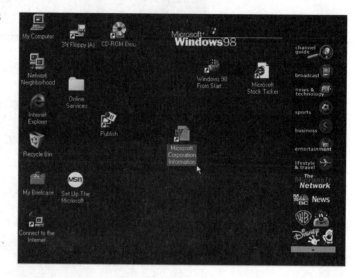

Shutting Down Windows 98

Because Windows 98 performs so many tasks in the background (including caching memory prior to saving it), it is imperative that you turn off your PC in a structured manner. If you were to simply cut the power to your PC, you might lose data that you thought you had already saved to the hard drive. To properly shut down Windows 98, do the following:

1. Click the **Start** button and choose **Shut Down**, as shown in Figure S.19.

2. Select the **Shut Down** option button in the Shut Down Windows dialog box. Then click **OK**. Your computer will automatically shut itself down and, in some cases, power itself off (if your computer's internal BIOS supports such a function, which most laptop and newer desktop PCs do).

Figure **S.19**

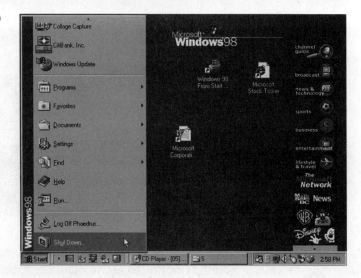

Sound Recorder

The Windows 98 Sound Recorder enables you to play, record, and edit sound (WAV) files.

note... If you do not have a sound card with speakers, this feature will not work on your PC.

note... A microphone, which usually plugs into the back of the sound card, is necessary for recording live sound.

To use Sound Recorder, do the following:

1. Click the **Start** button, choose **Programs**, select **Accessories**, click **Entertainment**, and then choose **Sound Recorder**, as shown in Figure S.20.

A
B
C
D
E
F
G
H
I
J
K
L
M
N
O
P
Q
R
S
T
U
V
W
X
Y
Z

A
B
C
D
E
F
G
H
I
J
K
L
M
N
O
P
Q
R
S
T
U
V
W
X
Y
Z

Figure **S.20**

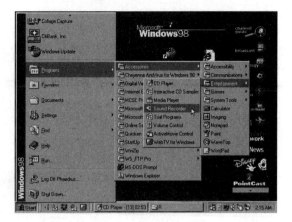

2. This opens the Sound Recorder window, shown in Figure S.21. To configure your version of Sound Recorder, click the **Edit** menu and choose **Audio Properties**.

Figure **S.21**

3. Make any necessary changes in the Audio Properties dialog box, and then click **OK** to return to the Sound Recorder screen.

note... Most computers have only a single configurable option on the Audio Properties screen.

4. Open the **Effects** menu to view your choices for editing existing WAV files (see Figure S.22).

5. To record using the microphone, click the **Record** button (the one with a circle on it). The status bar in the center of the screen begins to move (see Figure S.23), indicating that recording has begun. Start talking, singing, or making whatever sounds you want to record.

Figure **S.22**

Figure **S.23**

6. Click the **Stop** button (the one with a rectangle on it) to stop the recording process.

note...   No matter what you record, Sound Recorder will limit your time to
          roughly 50 seconds.

7. To listen to what you just recorded, click the **Rewind** button (the left-
   most button), and then click the **Play** button (the one in the middle).

Start Menu

The Windows 98 Start menu consists of all those menu options that appear
above the Start button when you click it. They include Run, Help, Find,
Settings, Documents, Favorites, Programs, and any shortcuts you may have
added. To examine and manipulate the contents of the Start menu, do the following:

1. Start Windows Explorer and navigate to the **C:\Windows\Start Menu**
   folder, as shown in Figure S.24. (For more information about navigating
   in Explorer, refer to the section titled "Windows Explorer.")

2. Click the Start Menu folder in the left pane, and its contents will appear
   in the right pane. Using standard Explorer techniques, you can delete,
   move, or add any of the Start menu's contents.

A
B
C
D
E
F
G
H
I
J
K
L
M
N
O
P
Q
R
S
T
U
V
W
X
Y
Z

Figure **S.24**

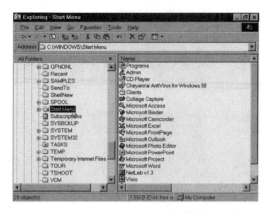

Starting Windows 98

Starting the Windows 98 operating system is simple: Just turn on your PC and let it boot directly into the Windows 98 graphical user interface (GUI). If you are unable to get in, try using your Windows 98 startup disk.

If you ever wind up at a DOS prompt and cannot get back into the Windows 98 GUI, try typing the command **win** and pressing the **Enter** key. If that doesn't work, try turning your PC off and then turning it back on.

Startup Disk

The purpose of the Windows 98 startup disk is to enable you to recover in the event that something dreadful happens to your PC (for example, if you turn on your computer one morning and get the error message `No operating system found`, you are in deep trouble). If you have a startup disk (think of it as an emergency repair disk), you can pop it into the A: drive and reboot the system.

To create a startup disk, sometimes called a *boot disk*, do the following:

1. Click the **Start** button, choose **Settings**, and then select **Control Panel**, as shown in Figure S.25.

2. Double-click the **Add/Remove Programs** icon in the Control Panel window, as shown in Figure S.26.

3. In the Add/Remove Programs Properties dialog box, click the **Startup Disk** tab to view the screen shown in Figure S.27.

Figurc **S.25**

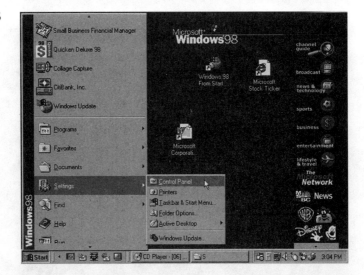

Figure **S.26**

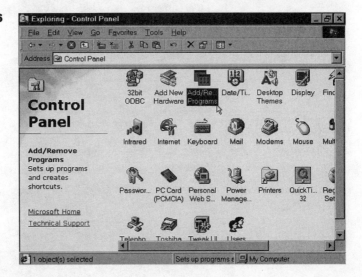

note... Note that you must have a formatted 3 1/2-inch high-density (1.44MB) floppy disk available in order to complete this process.

4. Click the **Create Disk** button, and the system begins to prepare startup disk files. (The Startup Disk tab changes to display a status bar, as shown in Figure S.28.)

note... You may be prompted to put the Windows 98 CD-ROM into an available CD-ROM drive bay. Simply follow the prompts.

Figure **S.27**

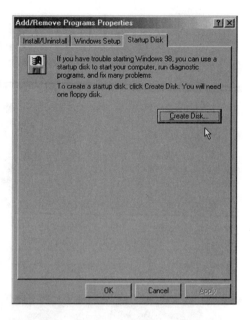

Figure **S.28**

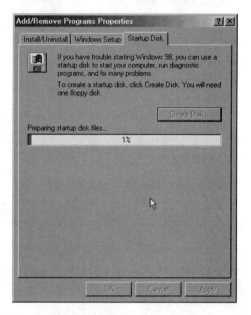

5. You will be prompted to insert a floppy disk into the A: drive (see Figure S.29). Insert the disk and click **OK**.

6. The process will continue and will probably take several minutes. When it is complete, you will be returned to the Startup Disk tab of the Add/Remove Properties dialog box. The disk is now complete and ready for use. Close the dialog box.

Figure **S.29**

Suspending a Windows 98 Session

Suspending a Windows 98 session is like putting the machine into hibernation. Your computer is not turned off; rather, it is suspended exactly where you left off, waiting for you to begin using it again. (Of course, your PC must be able to support this feature in order for you to use it.)

To place your Windows 98 PC into suspend mode, simply click the **Start** button and click **Suspend** (if this menu selection does not appear, you cannot suspend your computer session).

System Information

The System Information utility for Windows 98 does exactly what its name implies: It provides you with information about your computer. To use this utility, do the following:

1. Click the **Start** button, choose **Programs**, select **Accessories**, click **System Tools**, and then choose **System Information**, as shown in Figure S.30.

A
B
C
D
E
F
G
H
I
J
K
L
M
N
O
P
Q
R
S
T
U
V
W
X
Y
Z

A
B
C
D
E
F
G
H
I
J
K
L
M
N
O
P
Q
R
S
T
U
V
W
X
Y
Z

Figure **S.30**

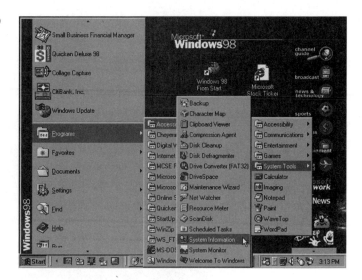

2. The Microsoft System Information screen, shown in Figure S.31, opens. The pane on the right contains basic information regarding your PC's its resources. The left pane breaks the system information into three categories: hardware resources, components, and software environment.

Figure **S.31**

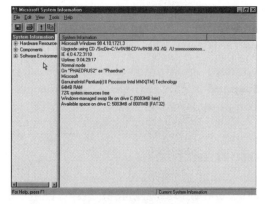

3. Click the plus symbol next to any of these categories to reveal even more data. Figure S.32 shows the details of the Hardware Resources category.

Figure **S.32**

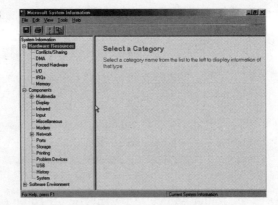

4. Click any option within a specific category to reveal detailed information about that topic.

5. Open the **Tools** menu to access these other Windows 98 utilities:

- The Update Wizard Uninstall Tool
- The Signature Verification Tool
- The System File Checker
- The Registry Checker
- The Automatic Skip Driver Agent
- Dr. Watson
- The System Configuration Utility
- ScanDisk
- The Version Conflict Manager

note... Although these tools will certainly aid any information systems professional, they will probably cause information overload for the basic Windows 98 user.

6. To save your system information data to a separate file, click the **File** menu option and choose **Export**. This opens the Save As dialog box, shown in Figure S.33.

A
B
C
D
E
F
G
H
I
J
K
L
M
N
O
P
Q
R
S
T
U
V
W
X
Y
Z

A
B
C
D
E
F
G
H
I
J
K
L
M
N
O
P
Q
R
S
T
U
V
W
X
Y
Z

Figure **S.33**

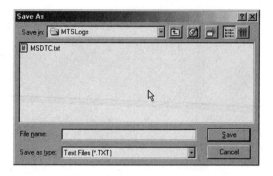

7. Navigate to the folder where you want the file to be saved, type a name for the file you're exporting (it will be saved in a text format), and click **Save**. Even on fast computer systems, this process takes several minutes to complete.

System Monitor

The Windows 98 System Monitor enables you to more closely track how specific resources are being used within your PC.

note...   Probably 90% of the System Monitor's available options will soar directly over your head if you are a general user; this tool was designed for information systems professionals.

To use this utility, do the following:

1. Click the **Start** button, choose **Programs**, select **Accessories**, click **System Tools**, and then choose **System Monitor**, as shown in Figure S.34.

2. The System Monitor window, shown in Figure S.35, appears. Click the **File** menu and choose **Start Logging**. This starts the System Monitor utility.

3. To add a system process to be monitored, click **File** and then **Add**. This opens the Add Item dialog box, shown in Figure S.36. Select a category from the **Category** list, and then click an item in the **Item** list. Click **OK** to confirm your choices.

Figure **S.34**

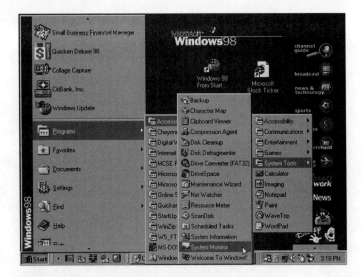

Figure **S.35**

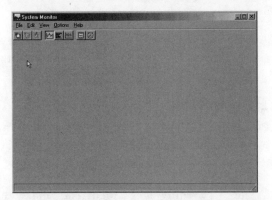

Figure **S.36**

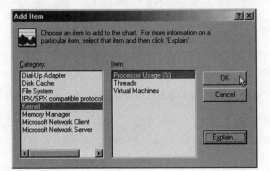

A
B
C
D
E
F
G
H
I
J
K
L
M
N
O
P
Q
R
S
T
U
V
W
X
Y
Z

A
B
C
D
E
F
G
H
I
J
K
L
M
N
O
P
Q
R
S
T
U
V
W
X
Y
Z

4. You are returned to the System Monitor window, where the item you selected in the previous step is visible. Open the **View** menu to change the manner in which the monitors are graphically presented (see Figure S.37).

Figure **S.37**

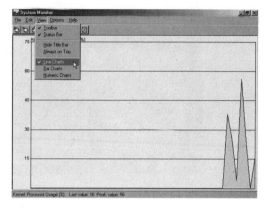

5. To add, remove, or edit items, click the **Edit** menu option, click the appropriate command, and then follow the prompts.

System Properties

The System Properties screens of Windows 98 provide raw information about the hardware installed on your computer system, as well as a starting point for troubleshooting hardware configurations gone wrong.

warning... A word of warning: If you incorrectly make changes on any of these screens, you can mess things up so badly that reinstalling the Windows 98 operating system is your only hope for recovery.

To use the System Properties screens, right-click the **My Computer** icon on the desktop and choose **Properties** from the shortcut menu (see Figure S.38).

The System Properties dialog box contains several tabs:

- *General.* This informational tab, shown in Figure S.39, contains information about your system, including how much memory you have installed in your PC.

Figure **S.38**

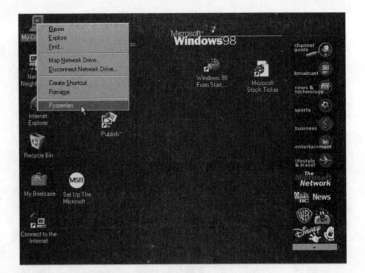

Figure **S.39**

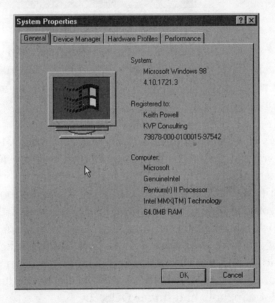

📖 *Device Manager*. This tab, shown in Figure S.40, lists all your hardware devices and their connection points.

A
B
C
D
E
F
G
H
I
J
K
L
M
N
O
P
Q
R
S
T
U
V
W
X
Y
Z

A
B
C
D
E
F
G
H
I
J
K
L
M
N
O
P
Q
R
S
T
U
V
W
X
Y
Z

Figure **S.40**

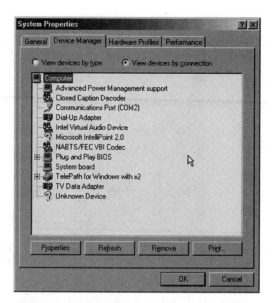

note... If an icon is overlapped with a black exclamation point in a yellow circle, the hardware device represented by the overlapped icon may or may not work properly. Whether this indication is accurate, however, varies from system to system.

- *Hardware Profiles.* This screen, shown in Figure S.41, enables you to create separate boot profiles for your hardware devices. For example, suppose you use a notebook computer. When you are using it at work, it plugs into a docking station with network cards, modems, and the like. When you are using it at home, it sits on a table with a separate monitor, keyboard, mouse, and Yamaha sound system connected to it. Keeping track of all these hardware devices in a single configuration would drive you mad. Using the Hardware Profiles tab, you can create separate hardware configuration schemes; this is similar to the multiple boot options that a lot of people had under DOS 6.*x*.

- *Performance.* The top area of this tab, shown in Figure S.42, is for informational purposes. The three buttons along the bottom—File System, Graphics, and Virtual Memory—enable you to modify key elements of your computer system.

Figure **S.41**

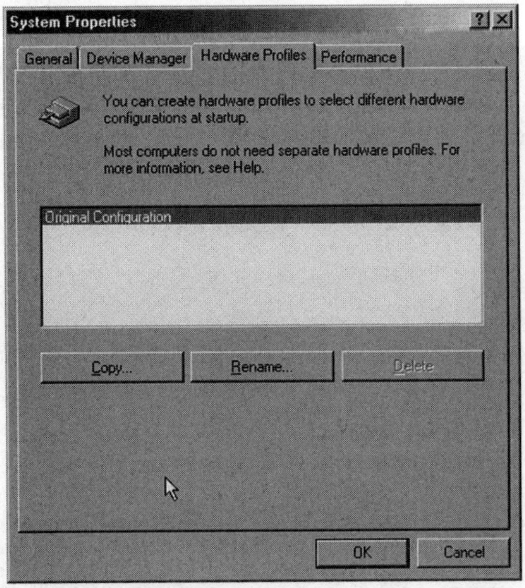

Figure **S.42**

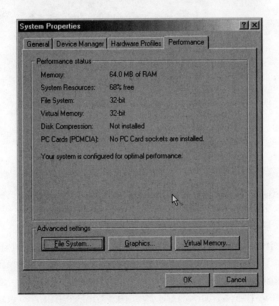

A
B
C
D
E
F
G
H
I
J
K
L
M
N
O
P
Q
R
S
T
U
V
W
X
Y
Z

A

B

C

D

E

F

G

H

I

J

K

L

M

N

O

P

Q

R

S

T

U

V

W

X

Y

Z

note...   If you do not completely understand what you are doing in the File System, Graphics, and Virtual Memory areas, stay with the settings that the Windows 98 operating system installed for you (they are probably adequate). Failure to make the correct selections—which will vary from PC to PC—can cause intermittent computer system deficiencies.

System Tools

The System Tools folder contains many applications that are necessary for tuning and maintaining the Windows 98 operating system. To access this folder, click the **Start** button, choose **Programs**, and then select **System Tools**, as shown in Figure S.43.

Figure **S.43**

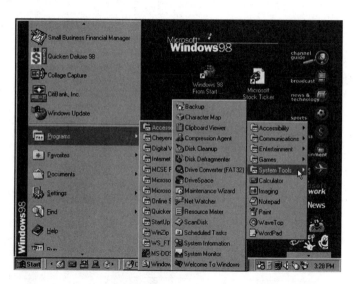

Many of the items in the Systems Tools folder are covered in detail elsewhere in this book. If you can use only one of these tools on your computer, make it Backup, which provides everything you need to avoid system failure and data loss. If you use the Windows 98 Backup tool regularly, you will always have a copy of your vital files and applications in case of system loss.

T

A
B
C
D
E
F
G
H
I
J
K
L
M
N
O
P
Q
R
S
T
U
V
W
X
Y
Z

Taskbar Properties

The Windows 98 taskbar is the long, rectangular box that contains the **Start** button, the clock, the system tray icons, and the **Quick Launch** icons. Whenever a Windows application is running, a button representing that application also appears in the taskbar. Although the taskbar appears along the bottom of the desktop by default, it can be moved to either side or to the top.

The Windows 98 taskbar serves many purposes, including providing easy access to applications and folders, as well as to the Internet. A new feature in Windows 98 is the ability for users to create as many new taskbars as they want (it's not a great idea to create too many, but this is a nice feature nonetheless). To configure your taskbar to your liking, do the following:

1. Right-click an empty area of the taskbar and choose **Properties**, as shown in Figure T.1.

   Figure **T.1**

2. The **Taskbar Options** tab of the **Taskbar Properties** dialog, shown in Figure T.2, opens. The top two check boxes control the visibility of the taskbar; if the taskbar is always on top, then it never gets hidden (of course, this consumes precious real estate on smaller monitors). Click the **Show small icons in Start menu** check box if you want your monitor to display smaller than normal icons. Leave the **Show clock** check box checked so you can view the time on the taskbar.

3. Click the **Start Menu Programs** tab to view the screen shown in Figure T.3. Here you can add items to or remove items from your **Start** menu, and you can clear the contents of the **Documents** menu (review the sections titled "Start Menu" and "Documents Menu" for more information).

4. To add an item to the **Start** menu, click the **Add** button. This starts the **Create Shortcut** wizard, as shown in Figure T.4.

Figure **T.2**

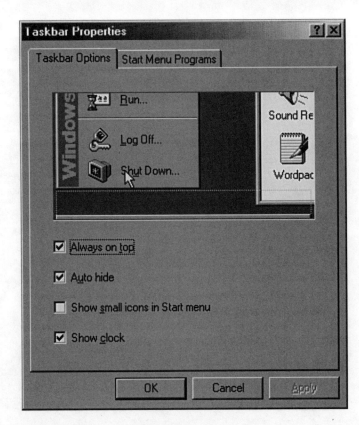

note... This wizard is slightly different from the one discussed in the "Shortcut" section.

5. If you know the full path for the shortcut you want to add, type it in the **Command line** text field. If not, click **Browse** to open the **Browse** window, shown in Figure T.5.

6. Navigate to the folder that contains the file for the shortcut you want to add. Click the file and then click **Open** to continue to the screen shown in Figure T.6. Notice that the path and filename are automatically entered in the **Command line** field.

7. Click the **Next** button to continue to the Select Program Folder screen, shown in Figure T.7. If you want to create a new area in your **Start** menu for the shortcut you want to add, click the **New Folder** button. Otherwise, simply locate the folder in which you want to house the shortcut and then click Next.

Figure **T.3**

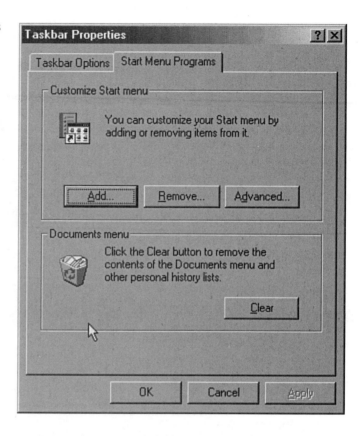

Figure **T.4**

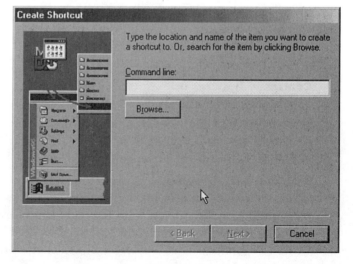

Figure **T.5**

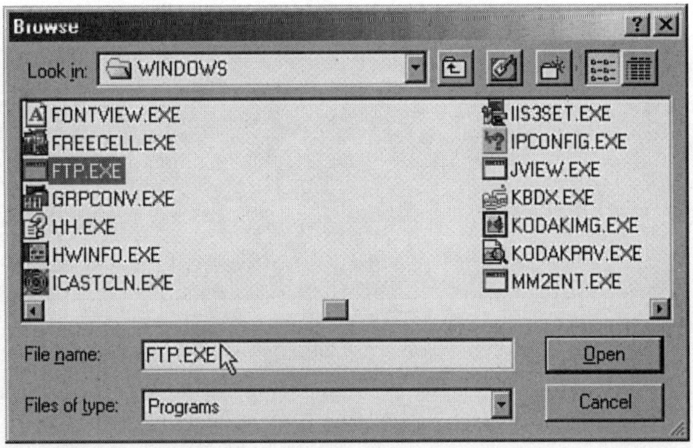

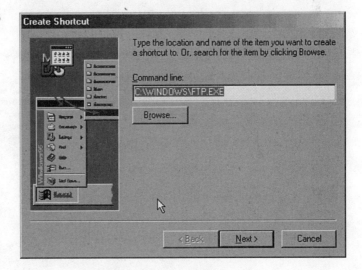

Figure **T.6**

8. In the Select a Title for the Program screen, shown in Figure T.8, type a descriptive name for your shortcut (this is the name that appears in the **Start** menu), and then click the **Finish** button.

As shown in Figure T.9, the newly created shortcut is now part of the **Start Menu** structure.

A
B
C
D
E
F
G
H
I
J
K
L
M
N
O
P
Q
R
S
T
U
V
W
X
Y
Z

A
B
C
D
E
F
G
H
I
J
K
L
M
N
O
P
Q
R
S
T
U
V
W
X
Y
Z

Figure **T.7**

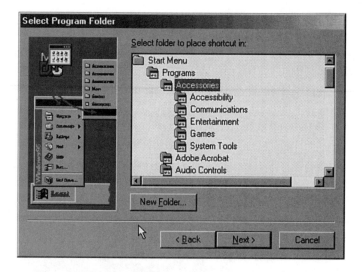

Figure **T.8**

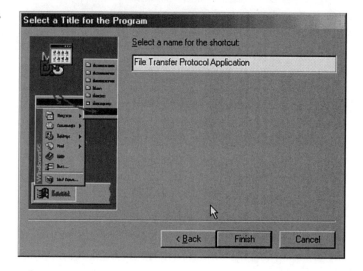

Figure **T.9**

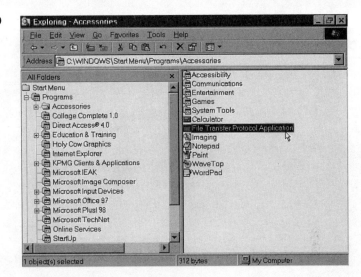

Adding a New Toolbar to the Taskbar

To add a new toolbar to the taskbar, do the following:

1. Right-click a blank area of the taskbar, click the **Toolbars** menu option and then choose **New Toolbar** (see Figure T.10).

Figure **T.10**

2. In the **New Toolbar** dialog, shown in Figure T.11, either type the location on the hard drive where the new toolbar should point, click one of the folders, or type an Internet address (such as http://www.microsoft.com/exchange/default.asp), and then click **OK**.

3. As shown in Figure T.12, the new toolbar appears on your taskbar.

A
B
C
D
E
F
G
H
I
J
K
L
M
N
O
P
Q
R
S
T
U
V
W
X
Y
Z

Figure **T.11**

New Toolbar

Figure **T.12**

Task Scheduler

The Windows 98 Task Scheduler enables you to schedule tasks, such as ScanDisk, at the time you specify. Task Scheduler starts every time Windows 98 starts and is present in the background system memory as a TSR (terminate-and-stay resident). When Task Scheduler is operational, its icon appears on the taskbar next to the clock, as shown in Figure T.13.

Figure **T.13**

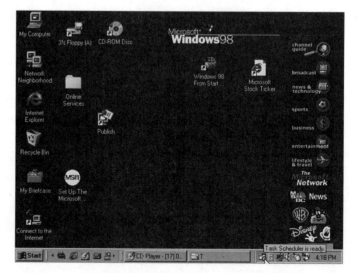

note... If you hover the mouse pointer over the **Task Scheduler** icon, a tiny message box appears, showing the status of the Task Scheduler application.

To add a task to Task Scheduler, do the following:

1. Double-click the taskbar icon to open the **Scheduled Tasks** window, shown in Figure T.14. This screen shows all the presently scheduled tasks and provides the entry point into the **Add Scheduled Task** wizard.

Figure **T.14**

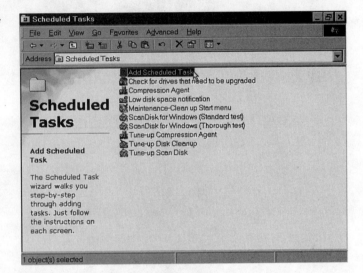

2. Double-click the **Add Scheduled Task** icon to start the wizard. Its first screen, shown in Figure T.15, contains information about adding tasks. Click **Next** to continue.

3. The next screen, shown in Figure T.16, lists all applications that have been registered with the Windows 98 operating system, but you can always click the **Browse** button to locate applications that are not present in the list. After you select the item you want Windows to run, click **Next**.

4. In the screen shown in Figure T.17, type a descriptive name for the task (this name will be shown in the main **Task Scheduler** window). Click the appropriate radio button to specify how often you want this task performed, and then click **Next** to continue.

A
B
C
D
E
F
G
H
I
J
K
L
M
N
O
P
Q
R
S
T
U
V
W
X
Y
Z

A
B
C
D
E
F
G
H
I
J
K
L
M
N
O
P
Q
R
S
T
U
V
W
X
Y
Z

Figure **T.15**

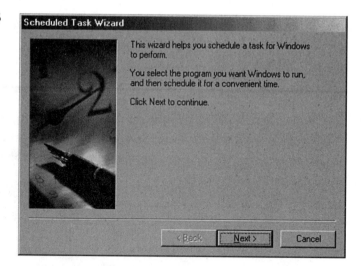

Figure **T.16**

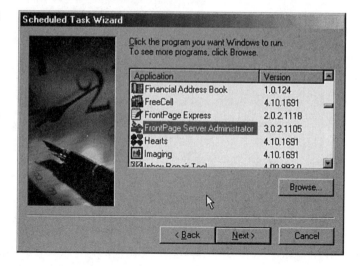

5. Use the screen shown in Figure T.18 to specify the time and day you want the task to start, and click **Next** to continue.

6. The wizard's final screen, shown in Figure T.19, displays the choices you have made. Click the check box if you want to view or modify the **Advanced Properties** screen for this task after you end the wizard process (most applications have different types of advanced properties, so read the prompts carefully for each task).

Figure **T.17**

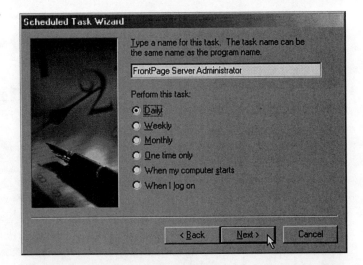

Figure **T.18**

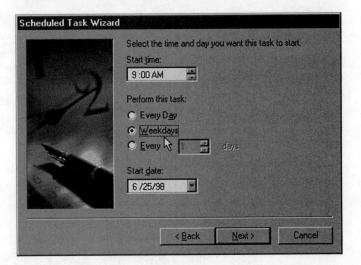

7. Click the **Finish** button to complete the process and return to the **Scheduled Tasks** screen. As shown in Figure T.20, your new task now appears in the window. To run it immediately, right-click the task and choose **Run**.

A
B
C
D
E
F
G
H
I
J
K
L
M
N
O
P
Q
R
S
T
U
V
W
X
Y
Z

Figure **T.19**

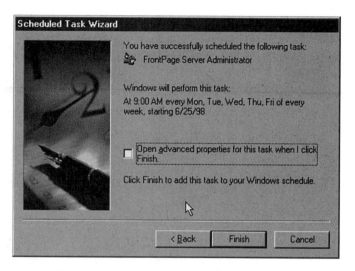

Figure **T.20**

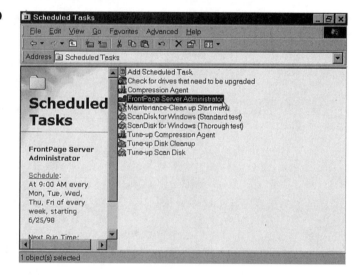

Telephony

Telephony is the process by which the technologies of a PC are coupled with the technologies of the telephone systems. To configure the **Windows 98 Telephony** screens, do the following:

1. Click the **Start** button, choose **Settings**, and then select **Control Panel**, as shown in Figure T.21.

Figure **T.21**

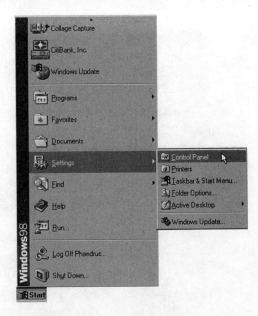

2. Double-click the **Telephony** icon in the **Control Panel** window, shown in Figure T.22.

Figure **T.22**

3. Click the **Telephony Drivers** tab in the **Dialing Properties** dialog to view the screen shown in Figure T.23.

A
B
C
D
E
F
G
H
I
J
K
L
M
N
O
P
Q
R
S
T
U
V
W
X
Y
Z

Figure **T.23**

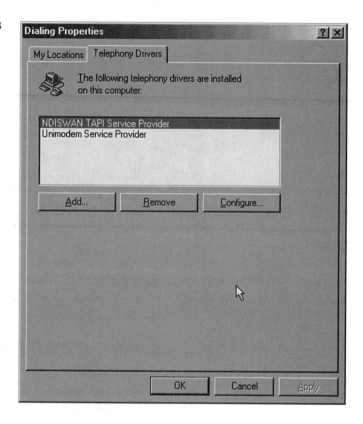

4. To add a new driver, click the **Add** button and follow the prompts.

> **note...** When hardware devices such as ISDN modems and the like are first installed, their drivers automatically show up in this screen. Therefore, it is very unlikely that you will ever use the **Add** button to install new telephony drivers into your Windows 98 system.

5. To remove a driver, click the driver you want to remove and then click the **Remove** button.

6. To configure a particular driver, click that driver to select it, click the **Configure** button, and then follow the prompts.

7. Click on the **OK** button to accept any changes and exit the Dialing Properties dialog.

Toolbar

A toolbar in Windows 98 terminology is nothing more than a starting point for launching applications, programs, and utilities. Four basic types of toolbars are found in the Windows 98 operating system:

- **Address**   You can use this toolbar to type an Internet address or a location on your computer. If you are using the Active Desktop feature, you can use the **Address** toolbar instead of the folder list in the Windows Explorer and **My Computer** toolbar to quickly jump to locations on your hard drive or the Internet.

- **Links**   A **Link** toolbar is like the **Favorites** option off in the **Start** menu. This toolbar provides shortcuts, or *links*, directly to Internet, intranet, or extranet sites (usually Web or HTML-based sites).

- **Desktop**   This toolbar contains all the standard desktop icons (**My Computer**, **Network Neighborhood**, **Recycle Bin**, **Internet Explorer**, and **My Briefcase**), along with any other shortcuts or folders you have added to your desktop.

- **Quick Launch**   This toolbar contains shortcuts that enable you to jump to another program, application, physical disk location, or the Internet without using the standard set of Windows 98 menu options. When Windows 98 is installed, it automatically creates the **Quick Launch** toolbar and places it just to the right of the **Start** button. The following shortcuts appear on the **Quick Launch** toolbar by default:

    - Launch Internet Explorer Browser
    - Launch Outlook Express
    - Show Desktop
    - View Channels

Trial Programs

When you install Windows 98, an additional set of programs known as trial programs is installed. These are just scaled-down versions of various Microsoft applications, including the following:

- Microsoft Money 98
- Microsoft Golf 3.0
- Microsoft Puzzle Collection

A B C D E F G H I J K L M N O P Q R S **T** U V W X Y Z

A

B

C

D

E

F

G

H

I

J

K

L

M

N

O

P

Q

R

S

T

U

V

W

X

Y

Z

- Microsoft Return of the Arcade
- DreamWorks Interactive games (including Dilbert's Desktop Games and Chaos Island: The Lost World)
- My Personal Tutor (learning geared to those in grade school)

The sole purpose of the Microsoft trial programs for Windows 98 is to try to get you interested enough to buy the real full-scale versions of these applications. To use these trial programs, do the following:

1. Click the **Start** button, select **Programs**, choose **Accessories**, click **Entertainment**, and select **Trial Programs**.

2. You are taken to a setup screen where you specify which, if any, of these sample programs you want to install.

U

Upgrading to Windows 98

User Profiles

A
B
C
D
E
F
G
H
I
J
K
L
M
N
O
P
Q
R
S
T
U
V
W
X
Y
Z

A
B
C
D
E
F
G
H
I
J
K
L
M
N
O
P
Q
R
S
T
U
V
W
X
Y
Z

Upgrading to Windows 98

You can install Windows 98 directly over a previous version of Microsoft Windows (either Windows 3.1 or Windows 95), thereby upgrading your system. For more information on the Windows 98 installation process, refer to the section titled "Installing Windows 98."

> **note...** Computers containing Windows versions 3.0, 386, 286, and 1.0 must be upgraded to Windows 3.1 before Windows 98 can be installed. However, it is extremely unlikely (and for the 1.0 and 286 versions, probably technically impossible) that any PCs that were designed to run those earlier versions of Windows could be upgraded enough to support even the most basic installation of Windows 95, much less Windows 98!

User Profiles

User profiles in Windows 98 enable multiple users to operate the same PC, yet each user can have his or her own personalized desktop with specific settings, screen savers, backgrounds, and so forth. To configure your computer to store specific settings, colors, and traits for each person who logs on to it, do the following:

1. Click the **Start** button, choose **Settings**, and then select **Control Panel**, as shown in Figure U.1.

Figure **U.1**

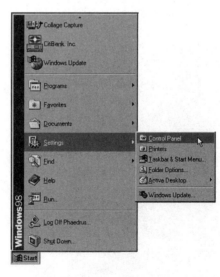

2. Double-click the **Users** icon in the Control Panel window, shown in Figure U.2.

Figure **U.2**

3. The Enable Multi-user Settings Wizard starts (see Figure U.3). Click **Next** to continue.

Figure **U.3**

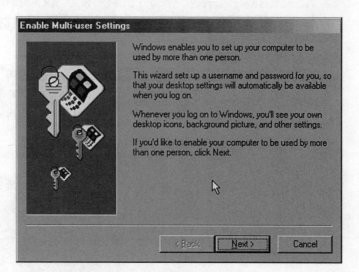

A
B
C
D
E
F
G
H
I
J
K
L
M
N
O
P
Q
R
S
T
U
V
W
X
Y
Z

4. If you are the main user, type your name in the wizard's Add User screen, shown in Figure U.4. If you are not the main user of this computer, type the name of the person who is. Click **Next** to continue.

Figure **U.4**

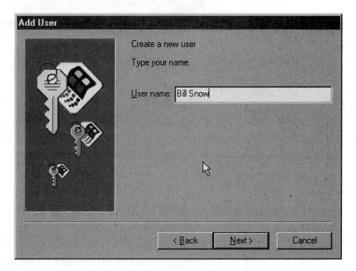

5. If you want to use a password, type it in the Password field of the Enter New Password screen, shown in Figure U.5. Confirm the password by typing it again in the Confirm Password field. Then click **Next** to continue.

Figure **U.5**

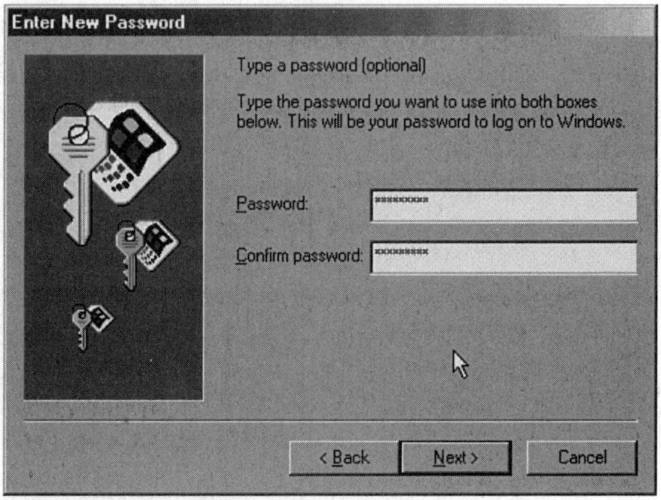

note... Unfortunately, a Windows 98 password does not really protect a PC (pressing the Esc key on the keyboard will bypass the password screen prompt when Windows 98 is first booted). However, it does slow down the person who is attempting to access your data.

note... If you do not want to use a password, you can leave both password boxes blank and continue.

6. In the Personalized Items Settings screen, shown in Figure U.6, click the items you want to personalize, and then specify whether you want to create copies of current items and their content or to create new items to save disk space. It is recommended that you create copies if this is a home PC and that you create new items if this computer is used in a corporate or professional work environment. Click **Next** to continue.

Figure **U.6**

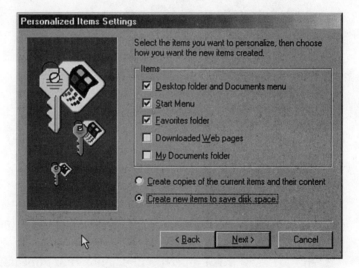

7. Click the **Finish** button in the final screen (see Figure U.7) to complete the wizard. You'll see the message box shown in Figure U.8 while the new user's profile is being created.

8. After the profile is created, you are prompted to restart your computer (see Figure U.9). Click **Yes** to restart the PC so the new user account can be used.

A
B
C
D
E
F
G
H
I
J
K
L
M
N
O
P
Q
R
S
T
U
V
W
X
Y
Z

A
B
C
D
E
F
G
H
I
J
K
L
M
N
O
P
Q
R
S
T
U
V
W
X
Y
Z

Figure **U.7**

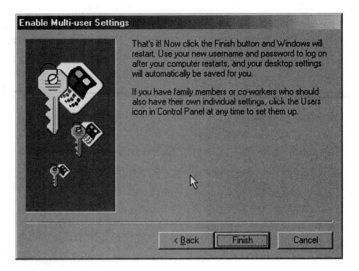

Figure **U.8**

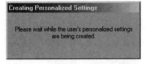

Figure **U.9**

The following steps show an alternative way to configure user profiles:

1. Double-click the **Passwords** icon in the Control Panel window, shown in Figure U.10.

2. In the Passwords Properties dialog box that appears, click the User Profiles tab to see the options shown in Figure U.11.

3. Click the second option button to allow users to customize their preferences and desktop settings. As you can see in Figure U.12, this makes available the User Profile Settings section in the lower half of the tab.

Figure **U.10**

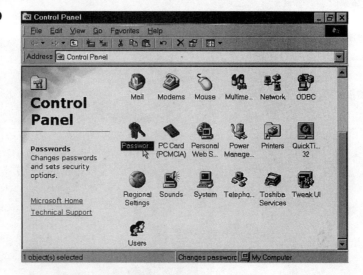

Figure **U.11**

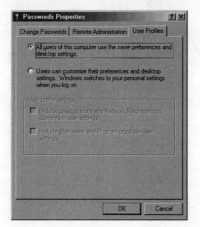

4. If you want a completely customized environment, check the second check box so that the Start menu and program groups are included in the user settings. Otherwise, leave the top box checked so that the desktop icons are set for specific users.

5. Restart the computer to effect these changes.

A
B
C
D
E
F
G
H
I
J
K
L
M
N
O
P
Q
R
S
T
U
V
W
X
Y
Z

A

B

C

D

E

F

G

H

I

J

K

L

M

N

O

P

Q

R

S

T

U

V

W

X

Y

Z

Figure **U.12**

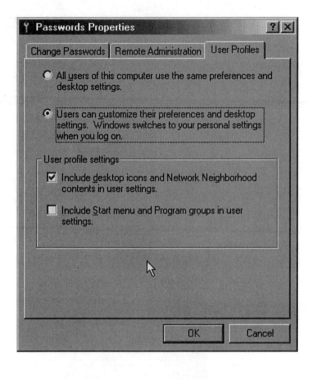

V

A
B
C
D
E
F
G
H
I
J
K
L
M
N
O
P
Q
R
S
T
U
V
W
X
Y
Z

A
B
C
D
E
F
G
H
I
J
K
L
M
N
O
P
Q
R
S
T
U
V
W
X
Y
Z

Video Compression

Video compression within Windows 98 does exactly what it sounds like it would: It compresses video streams to make those videos work better for you. This technology is used in a variety of Windows 98 accessories, such as NetShow Player and Web TV.

Views

In Windows 98, view describes how information appears on your monitor. Numerous Windows 98 applications feature a View menu, which contains a number of choices for changing how that application displays information. This section focuses on configuring the Windows Explorer View menu, but it also provides some insight into how you can continue to personalize your Windows 98 PC so that it feels like it was made just for you.

Follow these steps to customize the View menu in Windows Explorer:

1. Double-click the **My Computer** icon on the Windows 98 desktop (see Figure V.1).

Figure **V.1**

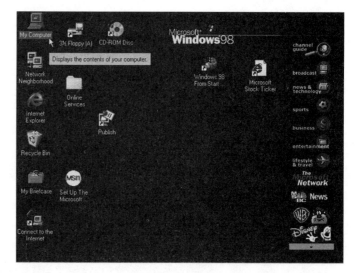

2. The **My Computer Explorer** window appears (see Figure V.2), showing you the drives available on your PC, as well as a few Windows 98-specific system folders.

Figure **V.2**

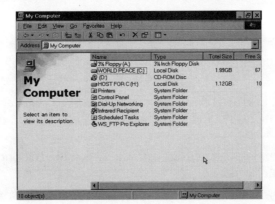

3. Click the **View** menu and choose the menu command you want. Note that every time you select a different option, your screen display changes accordingly.

4. Click the **View** menu and choose **Folder Options**. This opens the Folder Options dialog box. Click the **View** tab to see the screen shown in Figure V.3.

Figure **V.3**

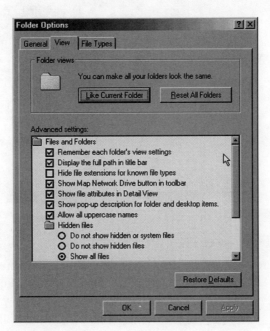

A
B
C
D
E
F
G
H
I
J
K
L
M
N
O
P
Q
R
S
T
U
V
W
X
Y
Z

A
B
C
D
E
F
G
H
I
J
K
L
M
N
O
P
Q
R
S
T
U

note... The Folder Views section at the top of the View tab enables you to specify whether all the folders in your system should be displayed in the
same view as the folder you were in when you opened this dialog box.

note... The Advanced Settings section of the View tab enables you set various
attributes for your files and folders.

5. Make changes as needed, and then click the **OK** button to close the My
Computer window.

6. Click the **View** menu and select **Arrange Icons**, as shown in Figure V.4,
to specify how you want visible files and shortcut links to be arranged on
your screen. For example, if you click the By Type selection, the files and
shortcuts will be sorted according to file type (that is, all .TXT files will be
listed together, all .DOC files will be listed together, and so on).

Figure **V.4**

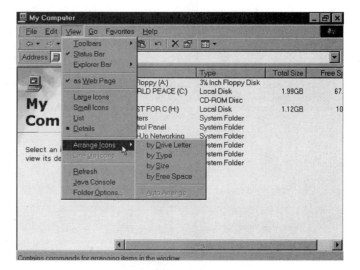

V

Virtual Private Networking

W
X
Y
Z

Virtual Private Networking (VPN) is a networking structure that provides a
secure connection between two sites across either public networks (such as
the Internet) or private networks. VPN relies upon a new networking protocol
known as a *tunneling protocol*; the Windows 98 version of VPN uses PPTP
(Point-to-Point Tunneling Protocol).

PPTP comes in handy when you are trying to connect to your company's computer systems via the public Internet. In such a case, you would probably want to keep your information as private as possible, and the Windows 98 VPN with PPTP allows just that. It gives you your own encrypted "tunnel" directly through the Internet, which automatically prevents others from looking at your information.

To configure a virtual private network connection, you must first ensure that the proper Windows 98 drivers are installed:

1. Click the **Start** button, choose **Settings**, and then select **Control Panel**, as shown in Figure V.5.

Figure **V.5**

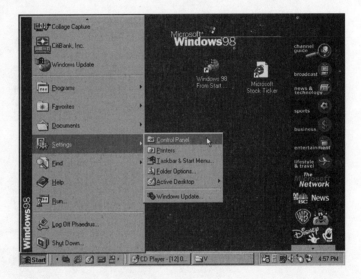

2. Double-click the **Network** icon in the Control Panel window (see Figure V.6).

3. On the Configuration tab of the Network dialog box, shown in Figure V.7, scroll through the components list to determine whether a VPN adapter, such as the Microsoft Virtual Private Network Adapter, is installed.

4. If you do not find an adapter, click **Add** to install one. This opens the Select Network Component Type dialog box. Click the **Adapter** option, and then click **OK**.

Figure **V.6**

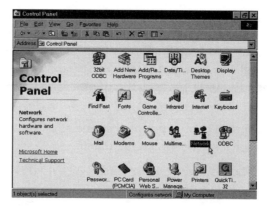

Figure **V.7**

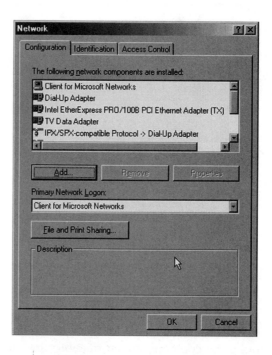

5. The Select Network adapters dialog box, shown in Figure V.8, opens. If you have an installation disk from the manufacturer of your VPN device, click the **Have Disk** button and follow the prompts. Otherwise, select the name of your VPN device's manufacturer (in this example, Microsoft) in the Manufacturers list, and select the name of your VPN device (in this example, Microsoft Virtual Private Networking Adapter) in the Network Adapters list. Click **OK** to continue.

Figure **V.8**

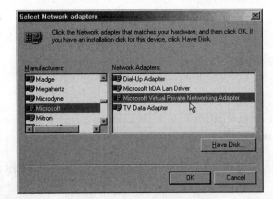

6. You are returned to the Network dialog box, but this time the Microsoft Virtual Private Networking Adapter device appears in the network components list (see Figure V.9). Click **OK** to accept this change, and then follow the prompts for installing the appropriate software drivers for the VPN device.

Figure **V.9**

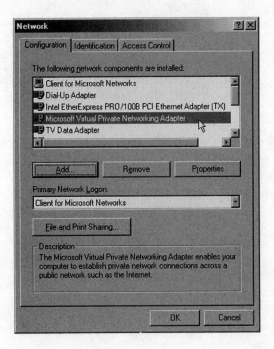

Volume Control

The Volume Control feature of the Windows 98 operating system does exactly what you would expect: It controls the volume settings for your multimedia devices (such as the CD Player, sound card speakers, TV tuner, and so on). To use the volume control, do the following:

1. Click the **Start** button and choose **Programs**, **Accessories**, **Entertainment**, and then **Volume Control** (see Figure V.10).

Figure **V.10**

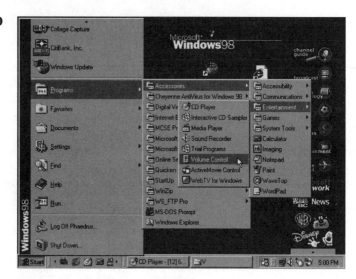

2. The Volume Control screen, shown in Figure V.11, opens. Use the slider bars to control the volume output for each of the devices listed.

Figure **V.11**

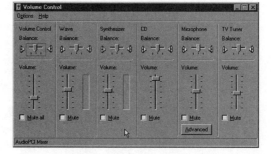

note... Clicking the **Advanced** button in the Microphone Balance section offers a few additional options (not all PCs even have this button).

3. After you make your changes, exit the screen by clicking the × button in the upper-right corner of the screen.

A
B
C
D
E
F
G
H
I
J
K
L
M
N
O
P
Q
R
S
T
U
V
W
X
Y
Z

W

A
B
C
D
E
F
G
H
I
J
K
L
M
N
O
P
Q
R
S
T
U
V
W
X
Y
Z

WaveTop Data Broadcasting

WaveTop Data Broadcasting is a new wireless technology that allows you to acquire the "Best of the Web" content, as well as software downloads, without using either an ISP or a telephone line. WaveTop uses a combination of your local television service and the TV Tuner card that is installed in your PC.

note... If you don't own a TV Tuner card, this service (just like WebTV) isn't for you. Likewise, this technology isn't quite ready for laptop/notebook computer prime time, so don't attempt to use it unless you possess a solid knowledge of your computer's hardware and internal components.

1. To install the WaveTop Data Broadcasting service, click the **Start** button and choose **Settings**, **Control Panel**, as shown in Figure W.1.

Figure **W.1**

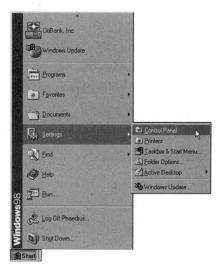

2. Double-click the **Add/Remove Programs** icon in the Control Panel window, as shown in Figure W.2.

3. Click the **Windows Setup** tab in the **Add/Remove Programs Properties** dialog box, and then scroll to the Web TV for Windows selection. Click the **Web TV for Windows** selection box to highlight it, and then click the **Details** button, as shown in Figure W.3.

Figure **W.2**

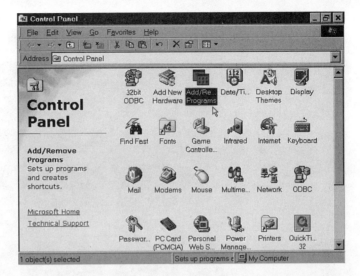

Figure **W.3**

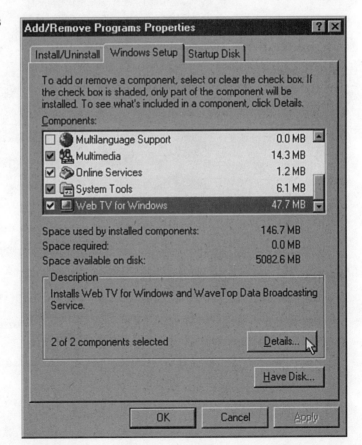

A
B
C
D
E
F
G
H
I
J
K
L
M
N
O
P
Q
R
S
T
U
V
W
X
Y
Z

A
B
C
D
E
F
G
H
I
J
K
L
M
N
O
P
Q
R
S
T
U
V
W
X
Y
Z

4. Click the **WaveTop Data Broadcasting** check box, as shown in Figure W.4, and then click the **OK** button to return to the previous screen.

Figure **W.4**

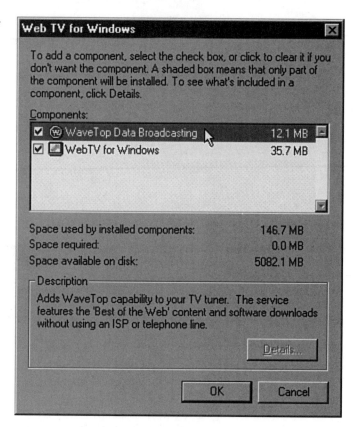

5. Click OK in the Add/Remove Programs Properties dialog box. The software will be installed from the Windows 98 CD-ROM.

Configuring WaveTop Data Broadcasting

To configure the WaveTop Data Broadcasting service, do the following:

1. Click the **Start** button, choose **Programs**, **Accessories**, and then click the **WaveTop** entry, as shown in Figure W.5.

2. The WaveTop Network Initialization window appears, as shown in Figure W.6.

Figure **W.5**

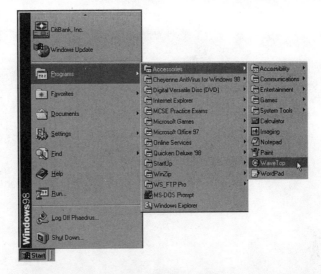

Figure **W.6**

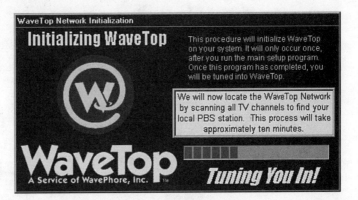

3. The WaveTop software scans all the TV channels in your viewing area in an attempt to find the local PBS station (a public broadcasting station). During this process, the WaveTop Receiver Channel Scan window, shown in Figure W.7, appears. This screen estimates the time remaining for the scanning process.

4. Unfortunately, as shown in Figure W.8, most of the time you'll receive an error message stating that a compatible WaveTop channel could not be found. This shouldn't discourage you from continuing to try to use this service. This idea is way ahead of its time, and as such, will probably take a bit more time for it to work on a regular basis (just like the early days of cellular telephones).

A
B
C
D
E
F
G
H
I
J
K
L
M
N
O
P
Q
R
S
T
U
V
W
X
Y
Z

Figure **W.7**

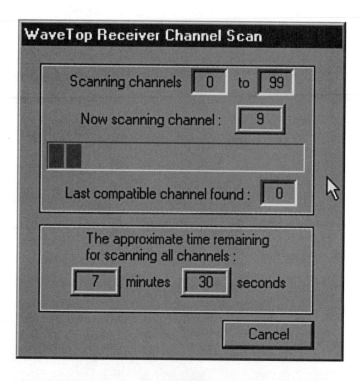

Figure **W.8**

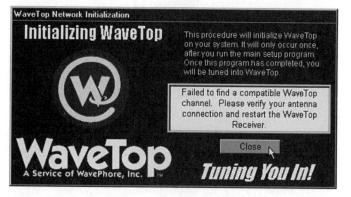

Web-Based Enterprise Management

Web-based Enterprise Management includes the components necessary for system administrators and technical support personnel to provide remote problem tracking and systems administration. This isn't a feature for a home computer, nor is it designed for the non-professionals in the audience.

However, those of you on corporate networks should probably be aware of this feature so that you don't accidentally delete it because you want more hard drive space available for your games.

Web Publishing Wizard

The Windows 98 Web Publishing Wizard provides an easy way to place, or *publish*, your individual Web pages or sites on an Internet or intranet server. To use this utility, do the following:

1. Click the **Start** button, choose **Programs**, **Internet Explorer**, and then click **Web Publishing Wizard**, as shown in Figure W.9.

Figure **W.9**

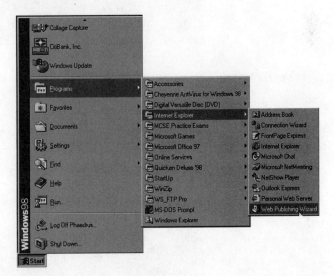

2. The first screen of the Web Publishing Wizard, shown in Figure W.10, provides information about the wizard. Click **Next** to continue.

3. Select the file or folder that you want to publish to the Web in the screen shown in Figure W.11. If you don't know the entire path to the folder or file, click either the **Browse Folders** button or the **Browse Files** button. When the file or folder name is in place, click **Next** to continue.

4. In the screen shown in Figure W.12, type a descriptive name for your Web server, and then click **Next**.

5. Specify your server provider in the screen shown in Figure W.13, and then click **Next** to continue.

Figure **W.10**

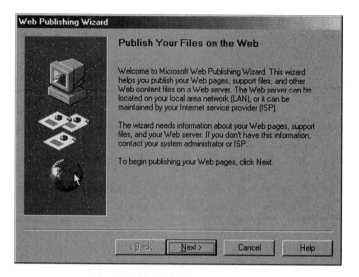

Figure **W.11**

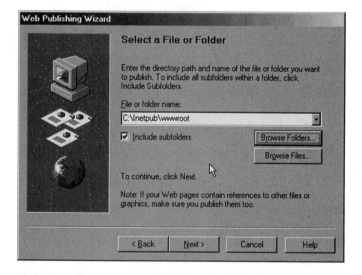

note... It is very important that you select the correct service provider; failure to do so might result in your page being shown incorrectly or not at all. When in doubt, select the **Automatically Select Service Provider** option. This might alleviate some troubles down the road.

6. Specify the URL and directory in the screen shown in Figure W.14, and click **Next** to continue.

Figure **W.12**

Figure **W.13**

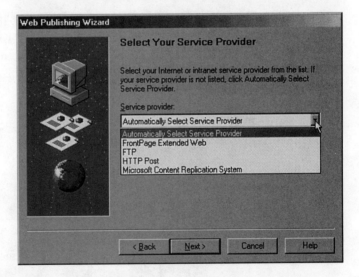

note... The URL is used to locate the Internet or intranet site, whereas the local directory is used to locate files on your hard drive.

A
B
C
D
E
F
G
H
I
J
K
L
M
N
O
P
Q
R
S
T
U
V
W
X
Y
Z

Figure **W.14**

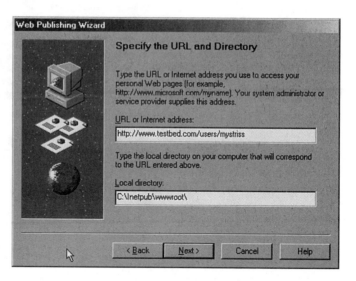

7. If you are publishing a page or site to the Internet, the server name is required. If your service provider is an HTTP post, the posting command will also be required on this screen, as is the case in Figure W.15. (Depending on which service provider you have, this second requirement may vary.) Click the **Next** button to continue.

Figure **W.15**

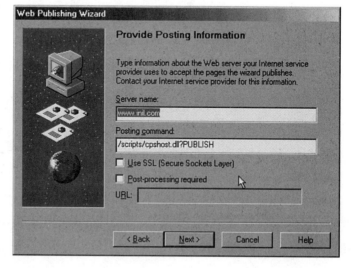

note... All the information required in this screen can be obtained from your network system administrator (if you are posting to your company's intranet site) or your Internet Service Provider (if you are posting to an Internet site).

8. Click the **Finish** button to post the site to the server. You should now be able to view the site online.

WebTV for Windows

WebTV for Windows enables your PC to display both standard and interactive television broadcasts, as well as Internet data broadcasts. You can receive the standard and interactive TV broadcasts only if a TV Tuner card (a hardware device for receiving television broadcasts) is installed on your PC. The Internet data broadcasts, though, will allow you to capture TV broadcast listings and display them in the Windows 98 program guide that is a part of WebTV. To use WebTV for Windows, do the following:

1. Click the **Start** button, choose **Programs**, **Accessories**, **Entertainment**, and then click **WebTV for Windows**, as shown in Figure W.16.

Figure **W.16**

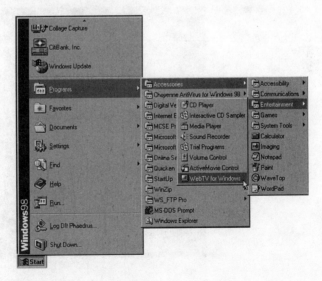

2. The WebTV introductory screen, shown in Figure W.17, appears. Your system will pause here for a few seconds before taking you directly to the

A
B
C
D
E
F
G
H
I
J
K
L
M
N
O
P
Q
R
S
T
U
V
W
X
Y
Z

WebTV Program Guide screen, shown in Figure W.18. Scroll up and down this screen to figure out what television shows are scheduled in your area.

Figure **W.17**

Figure **W.18**

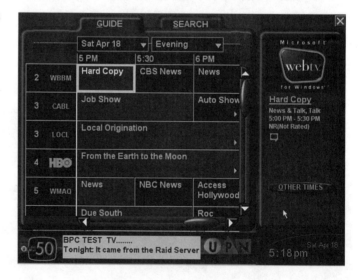

note... As part of the installation process for WebTV, you will be prompted for your zip code. This is how the software knows where you live.

3. Click the **Search** tab to view the screen shown in Figure W.19. Type in the text string that you want to search for, and then click the **Search** button to initiate the search. When you have found the show that you are seeking, click it once to highlight it, and then click the **Watch** button.

Figure **W.19**

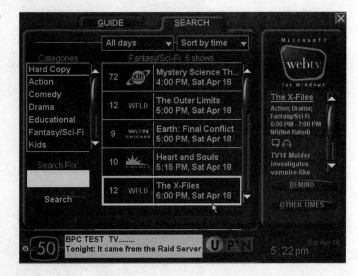

note... The left side of the **Search** tab features a scrollable **Categories** list. WebTV splits the television shows into categories such as Action or Drama. The **Categories** listing enables you to find a TV show that you want to watch, even if you aren't sure of its name.

4. To reconfigure your WebTV settings, you must first return to the channel guide. Click the **Guide** tab to view a screen like the one shown in Figure W.20.

5. Double-click **Channel 96** on the dial. This will take you to a screen like the one shown in Figure W.21.

note... If you want to take the interactive multimedia tour, click the **Next** button at the bottom of the screen, and off you go!

6. To adjust your settings, pull down the menu at the top of the screen (see Figure W.22) and click the **Settings** button.

A
B
C
D
E
F
G
H
I
J
K
L
M
N
O
P
Q
R
S
T
U
V
W
X
Y
Z

A
B
C
D
E
F
G
H
I
J
K
L
M
N
O
P
Q
R
S
T
U
V
W
X
Y
Z

Figure **W.20**

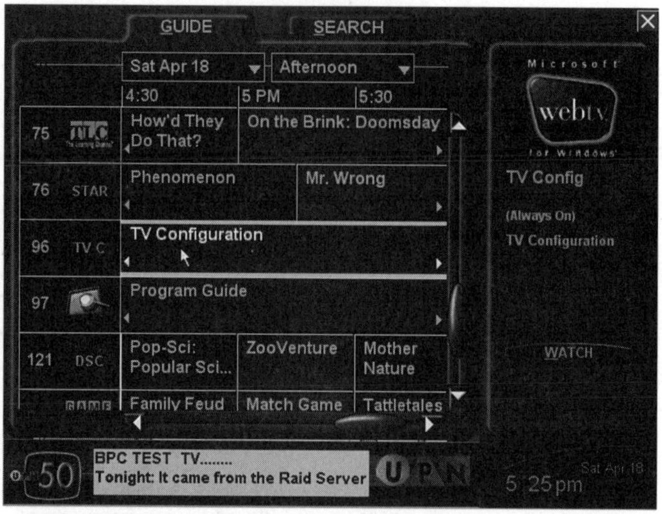

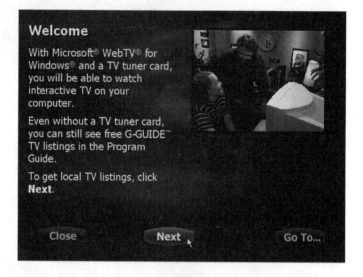

Figure **W.21**

> **note...**   You might want to click the **Help** button for clarification on some of WebTV's more confusing screens and hidden menus (like the Settings menu).

7. A screen like the one shown in Figure W.23 opens. Here you can deselect channels to block them, and you can add closed-captioning to your screen. Click **OK** to return to the previous screen.

Figure **W.22**

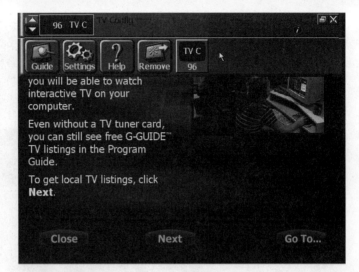

Figure **W.23**

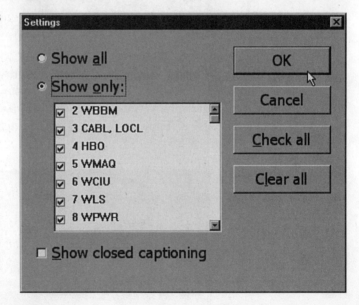

Welcome to Windows

The Windows 98 Welcome to Windows screen will automatically appear the first time you start your computer after installing Windows 98. If you want the screen to continue to appear at boot time, check the check box in the bottom-left corner of the screen. To access this screen at a different time, do the following:

A
B
C
D
E
F
G
H
I
J
K
L
M
N
O
P
Q
R
S
T
U
V
W
X
Y
Z

A
B
C
D
E
F
G
H
I
J
K
L
M
N
O
P
Q
R
S
T
U
V
W
X
Y
Z

1. Click the **Start** button, choose **Programs**, **Accessories**, **System Tools**, **Welcome To Windows**, as shown in Figure W.24.

Figure **W.24**

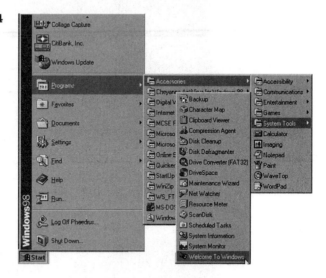

2. The Welcome to Windows 98 screen, shown in Figure W.25, appears. Click any of the options in the Contents menu to jump directly to that online topic. Alternatively, you can hover your mouse pointer over one of these options to view information about it on the right side of the screen, as shown in Figure W.26.

Figure **W.25**

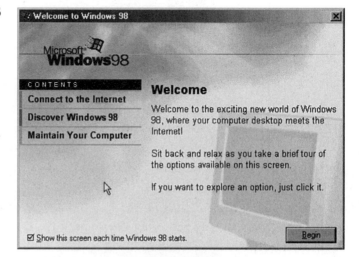

Figure **W.26**

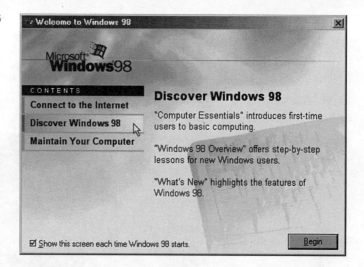

A
B
C
D
E
F
G
H
I
J
K
L
M
N
O
P
Q
R
S
T
U
V
W
X
Y
Z

note... The screen shown in this example varies slightly from the one that will appear immediately after Windows 98 is installed. On the screen shown here, the Register Windows 98 option isn't present because I have already registered my copy of Windows 98. Presumably, you will have registered right away in order to get free product support and updates. For more information, refer to the section titled "Registering Windows 98."

Windows Explorer

Windows Explorer is the most important end-user application in Windows 98. It is everywhere: inside other applications, behind Browse buttons, and inside the Internet Explorer Web browser. It is even the core component of the Windows 98 desktop environment itself.

note... If you've upgraded to Windows 98 from Windows 3.0 or 3.1*x*, consider Windows Explorer the replacement for File Manager.

To use Windows Explorer, do the following:

1. Click the **Start** button and choose **Programs**, **Windows Explorer**, as shown in Figure W.27.

A

B

C

D

E

F

G

H

I

J

K

L

M

N

O

P

Q

R

S

T

U

V

W

X

Y

Z

Figure **W.27**

2. The main Windows Explorer screen, shown in Figure W.28, opens. The contents of this screen represent the contents of your computer. Using the scrollbar, scroll down the left pane until you find the drive letter that represents your CD-ROM/DVD drive (in this case, D:).

Figure **W.28**

3. Click the drive letter; the contents of that drive automatically appear in the right-hand pane (see Figure W.29).

Figure **W.29**

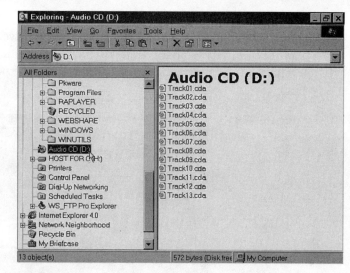

Sharing a Drive

If you are on a network and you want to share a drive or folder, do the following:

1. Start Windows Explorer.
2. Right-click the folder or drive that you want to share (in this case, I've right-clicked the D: drive, as shown in Figure W.30) and select **Sharing** from the shortcut menu.

Figure **W.30**

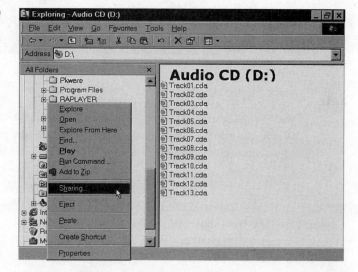

3. The Sharing tab of the drive's (or folder's) Properties dialog box will appear, as shown in Figure W.31. To share the drive, click the **Shared As** option button, type a share name and a description, set the access type, set a password if needed, and click **Apply** to immediately effect the share.

Figure **W.31**

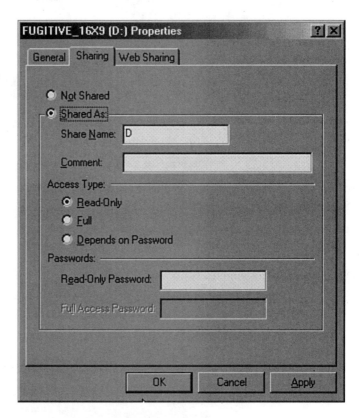

note...   Only 32-bit versions of Windows (Windows 95/98/NT) can see shares with long filenames (containing more than eight characters). The filename you enter in the Share Name field shouldn't contain more than eight characters if those who need this share are using older versions of Windows.

For more information on moving around and accomplishing tasks in Windows Explorer, review the following sections:

- Disk Management
- File Management
- Folders
- Views

Windows 98 Help

Windows 98 contains numerous interactive help screens, demos, quick hints, pop-up messages, and links. To access the primary Windows 98 Help feature, do the following:

1. Click the **Start** button and choose **Help**, as shown in Figure W.32.

Figure **W.32**

2. Click the **Index** tab in the main Windows Help screen that appears to view the screen shown in Figure W.33. Highlight an item, and then click the **Display** button to view information about the topic you selected.

3. Click the **Contents** to view Help information in a table-of-contents-type format.

4. Click the **Search** tab to search for help by entering a keyword.

A
B
C
D
E
F
G
H
I
J
K
L
M
N
O
P
Q
R
S
T
U
V
W
X
Y
Z

A
B
C
D
E
F
G
H
I
J
K
L
M
N
O
P
Q
R
S
T
U
V
W
X
Y
Z

Figure **W.33**

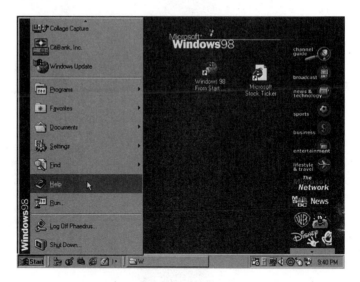

Windows Update

Microsoft is pushing the envelope by presenting Windows Update, an Internet-based software update and delivery system, in a major software application release.

note... You must have Internet access to use this incredible feature.

To use the Windows Update feature, do the following:

1. Establish an Internet connection.

2. Click the **Start** button and choose **Settings**, **Windows Update**, as shown in Figure W.34.

3. Your web browser starts automatically, with the Windows Update web site open by default (see Figure W.35). To start the software-upgrade process, click the **Products Update** option found along the left side of the window or in the middle of the screen (they both take you to the same place.

4. The **Internet Explorer 4.0 Active Setup** message box, shown in Figure W.36, will appear, notifying you that your computer's hard drive will be searched to determine what Microsoft Windows 98-compatible Internet components are already installed on your PC. If this is okay with you, click the **Yes** button (if you click **No**, the Products Update process will not work correctly).

Figure **W.34**

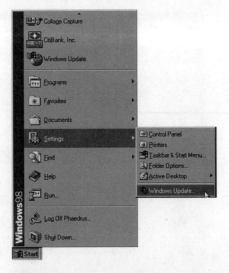

Figure **W.35**

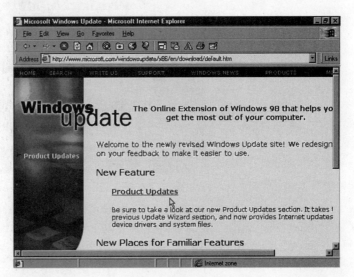

5. When the search is complete, the **Product Updates** web page site, shown in Figure W.37, appears. Scroll down the page, and select the additional Internet components that you want by clicking the check box just to the left of each feature. After you have made your selections, click the **Start Download** button.

A
B
C
D
E
F
G
H
I
J
K
L
M
N
O
P
Q
R
S
T
U
V
W
X
Y
Z

A
B
C
D
E
F
G
H
I
J
K
L
M
N
O
P
Q
R
S
T
U
V
W
X
Y
Z

Figure **W.36**

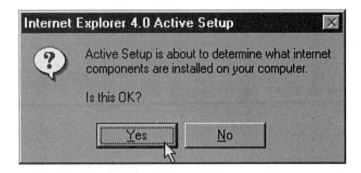

Figure **W.37**

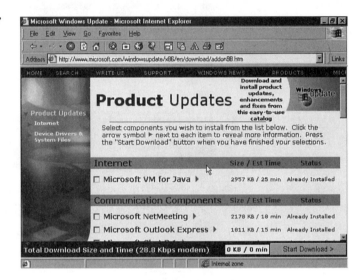

6. The download start screen appears (see Figure W.38). Choose a download site that is the geographically closest to you (this can help to shorten your download time). Because I live in Chicago, the ConXion Corp. site in Chicago is my choice.

7. After you've made your selection, click the **Install Now** button to begin copying files. You see the screen shown in Figure W.39.

8. When the download process has completed, an **Installation Summary** message box like the one shown in Figure W.40 will appear.

Figure **W.38**

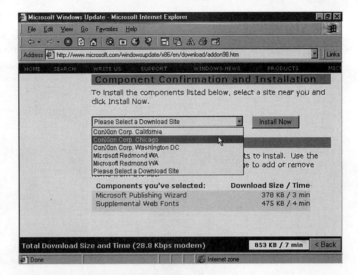

Figure **W.39**

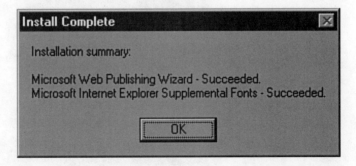

Figure **W.40**

9. Click the **OK** button to return to the **Windows Update** web page, shown in Figure W.41.

A
B
C
D
E
F
G
H
I
J
K
L
M
N
O
P
Q
R
S
T
U
V
W
X
Y
Z

Figure **W.41**

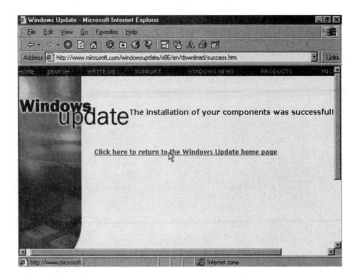

10. Click the **Click Here to Return to the Windows Update Home Page**
    hyperlink to return to the **Windows Update** web page, shown in Figure
    W.42. From here you can click the **Device Drivers and System Files**
    update selection to update those areas of your computer (this installa-
    tion process works just like the **Product Updates** feature).

Figure **W.42**

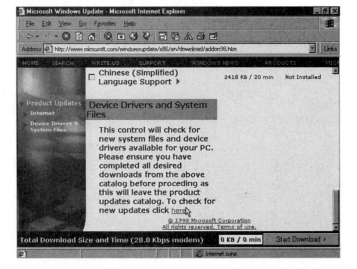

WinPopup

WinPopup provides a great way to send electronic messages between two or more users. To use this utility, do the following:

1. Click the **Start** button and choose **Run**, as shown in Figure W.43.

Figure **W.43**

2. In the Run dialog box, type **winpopup** (as shown in Figure W.44) and then click **OK**.

Figure **W.44**

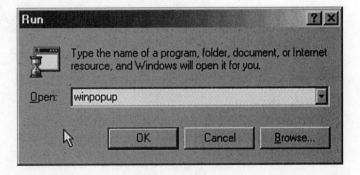

3. Click the envelope icon in the WinPopUp window (see Figure W.45) to initiate a message send.

A
B
C
D
E
F
G
H
I
J
K
L
M
N
O
P
Q
R
S
T
U
V
W
X
Y
Z

Figure **W.45**

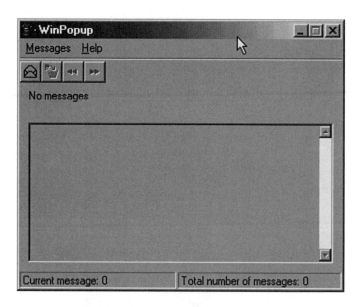

4. Type the name (system logon ID) of the computer, user, or workgroup that you want to receive the message, and then type the message in the box below (see Figure W.46). Click **OK** to transmit the message.

Figure **W.46**

5. You are returned to the main WinPopUp screen. Click the **Options** button to view the dialog box shown in Figure W.47, where you can check any or all of the three options. Click the **OK** button to accept all the changes.

Figure **W.47**

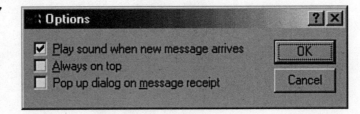

6. You are returned to the main WinPopup screen. When you close WinPopup, the warning shown in Figure W.48 will appear. Click **OK** to end the session.

Figure **W.48**

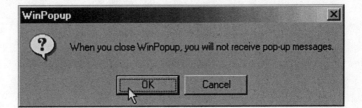

WordPad

WordPad, which is built into Windows 98, enables you to create and edit text. WordPad files can be any size you want, but if they are smaller than 64 KB, consider using Notepad instead. To use WordPad, do the following:

1. Click the **Start** button and choose **Programs**, **Accessories**, **WordPad**, as shown in Figure W.49.

2. The WordPad window, shown in Figure W.50, opens. To begin using the application, just start typing in the white space as soon as the program begins.

3. You can create a new file by clicking the **File** menu option and choosing **New**.

4. To edit an existing file you must first open it by clicking **File** and then **Open**. You'll see a window like the one shown in Figure W.51. Navigate to the file you want to open, click it to select it, and then click **Open**.

A
B
C
D
E
F
G
H
I
J
K
L
M
N
O
P
Q
R
S
T
U
V
W
X
Y
Z

A
B
C
D
E
F
G
H
I
J
K
L
M
N
O
P
Q
R
S
T
U
V
W
X
Y
Z

Figure **W.49**

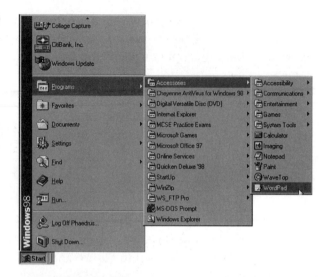

Figure **W.50**

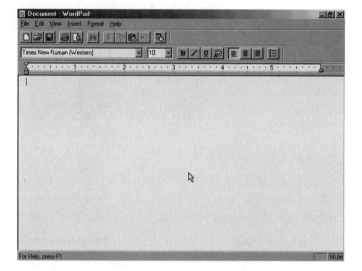

note... The **Files of Type** list box shows which file types are supported by the WordPad application.

5. As shown in Figure W.52, the file you selected opens onto the desktop. Make your changes, and then click the **File** menu option and save, print, or exit the file.

Figure **W.51**

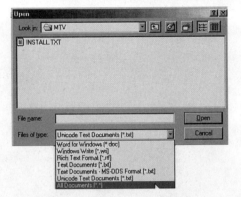

Figure **W.52**

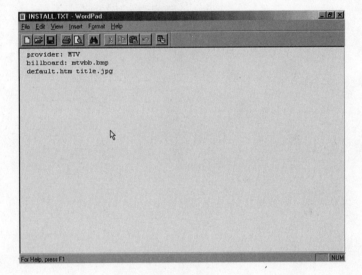

XYZ

A
B
C
D
E
F
G
H
I
J
K
L
M
N
O
P
Q
R
S
T
U
V
W
X
Y
Z

X-Files

Because so few Windows 98 topics start with the letter X, I thought it might be fun to show you how to locate the X-Files web site on the Internet:

1. Initiate a connection to the Internet (refer to the section titled "Dial-Up Networking" for more information about this).

2. Click the Internet Explorer icon on your desktop (see Figure X.1) to start your web browser.

Figure **X.1**

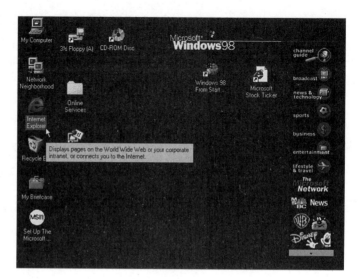

3. Your Internet Explorer start page will appear. Type the URL for Fox TV's *X-Files* web site (**http://www.thex-files.com/**) and press **Enter**. The web site's main page is shown in Figure X.2.

4. Click the **Episode Guide** hyperlink to view the page for accessing information about each of the *X-Files* episodes from various seasons. You'll reach the screen shown in Figure X.3.

5. To view a list of the episodes from a specific season, click the season you want. For example, click **Season 5** to view the screen shown in Figure X.4.

6. Click the title of the episode you want to view, or click another option to move elsewhere in the *X-Files* site. For example, if you click **Unusual Suspects** (the title of the very first show of Season 5), a detailed view of that show's contents appears, as shown in Figure X.5.

Figure **X.2**

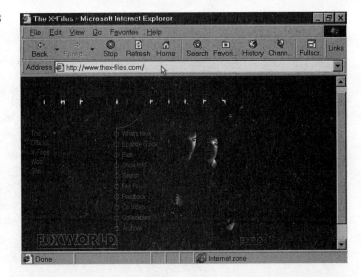

Figure **X.3**

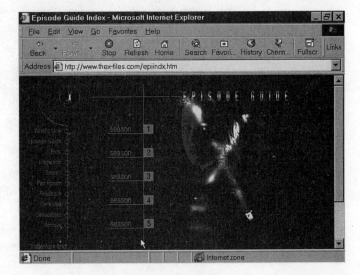

note... If you scroll past the end of the episode's synopsis, you will find the credits for all the show's participants. Underlined names are hyperlinks to additional pages about that character or actor.

A
B
C
D
E
F
G
H
I
J
K
L
M
N
O
P
Q
R
S
T
U
V
W
X
Y
Z

Figure **X.4**

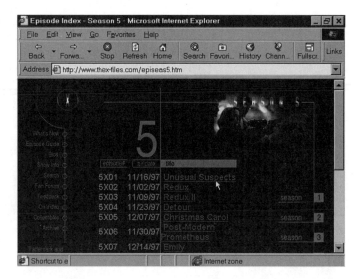

Figure **X.5**

7. Notice the menu bar along the left side of the screen (refer to Figure X.5). This bar contains links to other pages within the web site that relate to this episode. Click the **Print Ad** link to view the advertisement that was used in newspapers, magazines, and so on to promote this episode (see Figure X.6).

Figure **X.6**

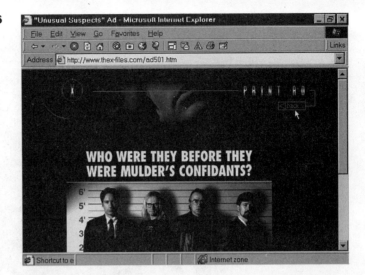

You have mastered the basics for moving around the official Fox Television *X-Files* web site. All you need to do now is wait patiently until the start of next season.

X Windows

X Windows refers to a graphical user interface for a client workstation that either runs on some form of UNIX (an older, multitasking, text-based operating system typically found in academic or scientific communities) or connects to a UNIX file server. X Windows has nothing to do with any form of Microsoft Windows; Microsoft has never even produced any X Windows software.

x86

x86 is a shortened version of the term *80x86*, in which the *x* equals a number that relates directly to the code number for an Intel Corporation central processing unit (CPU). For example, one of the early popular personal computers used an Intel processor known as an 80286 CPU, or *286* for short. Whenever you see the term *x86*, you should recognize that the computer has an Intel processor and runs some version of Microsoft Windows.

A
B
C
D
E
F
G
H
I
J
K
L
M
N
O
P
Q
R
S
T
U
V
W
X
Y
Z

A
B
C
D
E
F
G
H
I
J
K
L
M
N
O
P
Q
R
S
T
U
V
W
X
Y
Z

Yahoo!

Yahoo! was one of the first search engine sites that became a commercial success on the World Wide Web (WWW). If you gain a cursory knowledge of how to use Yahoo!, it will make it that much easier to use other Internet search providers. To use Yahoo!, do the following:

1. Initiate a connection to the Internet (refer to the section titled "Dial-Up Networking" for more information).

2. Click the Internet Explorer icon on your desktop (see Figure Y.1) to start your web browser.

Figure **Y.1**

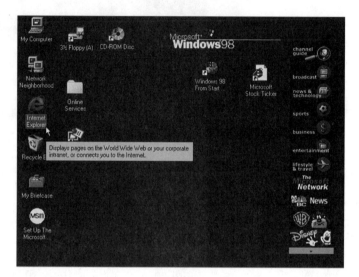

3. Your Internet Explorer start page will appear. Type the URL for Yahoo!'s web site (**http://www.yahoo.com/**) and press **Enter** to view the site shown in Figure Y.2.

4. For the sake of example, let's conduct a search for KPMG, one of the largest public-accounting/systems consulting firms in the world. To start the search, type the basic search criteria (in this case, the name of the company) in the search box, and then click the **Search** button, as shown in Figure Y.3.

5. You are taken to the first Search Results screen, shown in Figure Y.4. This screen lists all sites that match your search criteria.

Figure **Y.2**

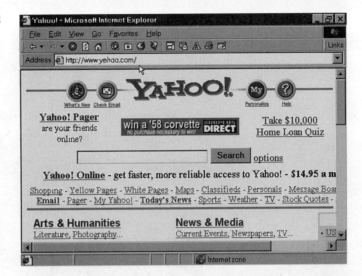

Figure **Y.3**

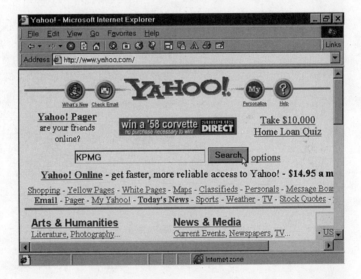

6. Click the entry in either the **Yahoo! Category Matches** list or the **Yahoo! Site Matches** list that you feel best matches your search criteria. For this example, click the entry in the **Yahoo! Category Matches** section; this will open the screen shown in Figure Y.5.

7. Click the hyperlink for the site you desire. In this case, you might click the **KPMG International** link to open its site, shown in Figure Y.6.

A
B
C
D
E
F
G
H
I
J
K
L
M
N
O
P
Q
R
S
T
U
V
W
X
Y
Z

Figure **Y.4**

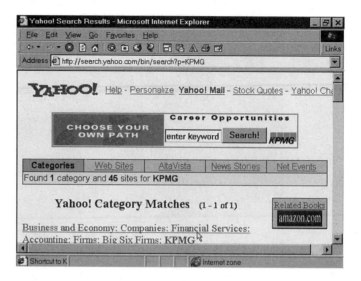

Figure **Y.5**

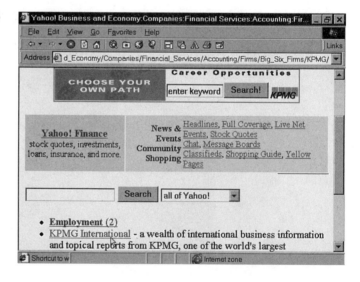

8. If you didn't reach the site you were expecting, you can return to the Search Results screen by clicking the down-arrow button just to the right of the left-arrow toolbar button and then choosing **Yahoo! Search Results** from the menu, as shown in Figure Y.7.

Figure **Y.6**

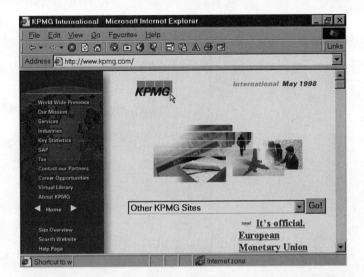

Figure **Y.7**

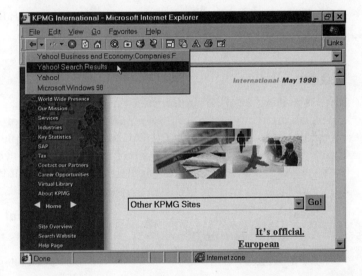

note... If you are not using the Microsoft Internet Explorer web browser, step 8 may not work for you.

9. You are returned to the search results page. Scroll to the bottom of the page, where you will find a Search box containing your original search criteria (see Figure Y.8). Repeat steps 1–7 to find a different site.

A
B
C
D
E
F
G
H
I
J
K
L
M
N
O
P
Q
R
S
T
U
V
W
X
Y
Z

Figure **Y.8**

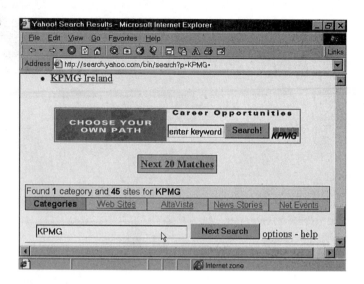

10. When you finish surfing the Internet, close the web browser (click the **File** menu and choose **Exit**).

Zines

Zines is a slang term for an Internet-based electronic magazine, book, or paper, which is typically found as a part of a collection of online web-related magazines (*The Journal of Eclectic Journeys* is an example of a good zine). Countless zines are available (or you can write and post your own). This short list gives you some suggestions of where you might want to look on the Internet:

Site	Content
www.dominis.com/Zines/	E-Zines Database
www.student.com	For college students
www.slip.net/~scmetro/kids.htm	Entertainment for everyone
www.sirius.com/~mcmardon/words/	*The Journal of Eclectic Journeys*
www.webreference.com/magazines/	A comprehensive listing
www.zinebook.com	*The Book of Zines*

Index